Animal Ethics *for* Veterinarians

Edited by
Andrew Linzey
and **Clair Linzey**

COMMON THREADS

An anthology from the
University of Illinois Press

Library of Congress Control Number: 2017949949
ISBN 978-0-252-08319-8 (paperback)
ISBN 978-0-252-05020-6 (e-book)

Printed and bound in Great Britain by
Marston Book Services Ltd, Oxfordshire

Contents

Introduction: Veterinarians and Animal Ethics

ANDREW LINZEY AND CLAIR LINZEY

Few would deny that veterinarians are in the frontline against suffering and abuse. Theirs is an honorable profession, and without their care and expertise, the level of animal suffering in the world would be immeasurably higher. Theirs is also a profession stretching back many years and, in some cases, hundreds of years. A world without veterinarians, that is, professionals directly able to alleviate animal suffering and help cure their diseases, would be unthinkable.

At the same time, our thinking about animals and the rights and wrongs of how we treat them has undergone profound changes in the last forty years. The Royal Society for the Prevention of Cruelty to Animals, the first national animal protection society in the world, was founded in 1824, and the American Society for the Prevention of Cruelty to Animals in 1886, and had as their aims the promotion of kindness and the prevention of cruelty. But many, if not most, people expect much more of these societies than the fulfilment of these simple aims today. They want to know the ethical considerations that lie behind even common practices, and they want to be ethically informed.

Not incidentally, normative questions about animals are being asked in many classrooms and lecture halls in colleges and universities throughout the world. And the reason is simple: Animal ethics is appearing as a topical subject in many curriculums concerned with contemporary moral and social issues, alongside issues such as abortion, capital punishment, torture, and war. Behind these developments has been nothing less than an explosion of academic interest in animals. Way back in 1970, perhaps just one or two books devoted to animal ethics appeared every year. Now that number is at least in the hundreds, so much so that it is difficult for even the most eager student to keep abreast of the intellectual arguments.

And yet these developments have hardly impinged on veterinary education. While it is true that some veterinary curricula include a truncated course on what is now called "animal welfare, science, ethics, and law," these hardly begin to provide the in-depth knowledge that veterinarians require in confronting the complex ethical issues that they and their clients have to deal with. Veterinarians are expected to be in the "know," but their ethical knowledge is often woefully behind keen students of animal ethics.

Hence the importance of this book. In one volume, it places in the hands of veterinarians papers relating to many of the key issues in animal ethics. It provides a useful primer to veterinarians who come new to the subject. The chapters are taken from articles originally published in the *Journal of Animal Ethics* (*JAE*)—the premiere journal in the field. While some veterinarians and some veterinary institutions subscribe to the *JAE*, not all do, which means that many veterinarians may have missed out on the important papers originally published in the *JAE*.

The first section is devoted to a range of professional issues related to veterinary work, not least of all the question of veterinary oaths. To whom should veterinarians be accountable? To the "clients," that is, the keepers of animals—those who bring sick animals to the veterinarians' attention? To the wider society, bearing in mind that infectious diseases can affect both humans as well as animals? To the directives of their own professional body? To the sick or abused animals themselves? The first contribution takes the form of an editorial by Andrew Linzey and Priscilla N. Cohn ("An Ethical Oath for Veterinarians") that engages with the decision of the American Veterinary Medical Association to widen its oath to more definitely include a responsibility to animal welfare. Linzey and Cohn argue that the welfare of the animal subjects should have priority in any ethical oath.

Alongside this, Vanessa Carli Bones and James W. Yeates ("The Emergence of Veterinary Oaths: Social, Historical, and Ethical Considerations") provide a historical account of the way in which veterinary oaths have emerged in many countries. Far from finding convergence, it seems that there are a range of considerations in each country that circumscribe the responsibilities of veterinarians, some of which may be ethical, some decidedly not. It seems that we have a long way to go before an account of veterinarians' professional responsibilities can be articulated in anything like an ethically coherent form, not least of all because the work of animal ethicists has challenged traditional accounts of animals and their moral status.

The following chapter by Judith Benz-Schwarzburg and Andrew Knight ("Cognitive Relatives yet Moral Strangers?") illustrates precisely that problem. There is a mismatch between what we now scientifically know about the cognition and intelligence of animals, and our moral appreciation of their individual worth. Benz-Schwarzburg and Knight assess the evidence for sophisticated cognition in animals and conclude that for some "species such as great apes and dolphins with whom we share major characteristics of personhood welfare considerations alone may not suffice" (p. 45).They argue for "inalienable species-appropriate rights" (p. 45). Veterinarians need to know how the moral debate is changing and how it is fueled by compelling scientific evidence.

More professionally directed Megan Schommer ("Opening the Door: Non-veterinarians and the Practice of Complementary and Alternative Veterinary Medicine") explores the rise of complementary and alternative veterinary medicine and its relationship to traditional veterinary medicine. As the traditional boundary between human and animal intelligence has been questioned, so too has the boundary between the profession of veterinary medicine and alternative forms of treatment. Schommer argues that the veterinary profession should make room for complementary practices, as long as they are professionally regulated to safeguard the welfare of the animals. Veterinarians, it is argued, have been too defensive about alternative forms of care, and Schommer proposes that "the veterinary profession must proactively redefine its definition of the practice of veterinary medicine . . . by looking to human medicine as a model for how to balance conventional and alternative modalities" (p. 78).

The second section concerns understanding cruelty to companion animals and opens with two detailed articles by Eleonora Gullone. Most veterinarians are involved on a daily basis with normative issues concerning the health of companion animals but have also to cope with what seems a growing number of cases of egregious acts of cruelty. How are we to understand them? And what is their social significance? In her first paper ("An Evaluative Review of Theories Related to Animal Cruelty"), Gullone underlines the seriousness of these acts of cruelty and shows their relevance to the larger social context of violence to vulnerable human subjects. By analyzing the major theories relating to animal cruelty, she argues that these acts of animal cruelty are "a marker of development along a more severe trajectory of antisocial and aggressive behaviors" (p. 90).

In her second article ("Risk Factors for the Development of Animal Cruelty"), Gullone expands on her discussion of the link between animal abuse and human violence. Looking at the available research, she asks, "when individuals have been found to be guilty of animal cruelty, what other aggressive behaviors might they be guilty of?" (p. 116). The challenge for veterinarians is how they should respond in the light of this now well-established link between animal abuse and human violence. Gullone argues that veterinarians need to be proactive in identifying warning signs and developing methods of cross referral between professional agencies (see also chapter 21, "A Legal Duty to Report Suspected Animal Abuse—Are Veterinarians Ready?" by Ian Robertson, and chapter 22, "The Role of Veterinarians and Other Animal Welfare Workers in the Reporting of Suspected Child Abuse," by Corey C. Montoya and Catherine A. Miller, both in Linzey, 2009a). She argues that "early detection of such behaviors can provide a valuable opportunity to engage in preventative intervention for young people or for appropriate sanctions to be applied for adults. Such interventions would be beneficial for all, humans and animals alike" (p. 116). In this way, veterinarians should be seen as being on the front line of preventing cruelty not only to animals but also to humans.

Animals that are kept as companions are often considered "cute," and that is one of the principal motivations for keeping them. We have all seen the adorable kitten and the appealing puppy. We feel an affinity with them and respond to their baby features and innocence. But non-cute animals that are similarly sentient are no less worthy of our moral concern—they also have welfare needs and can experience suffering. Mark J. Estren ("The Neoteny Barrier: Seeking Respect for the Non-Cute") argues that there is a "deeply rooted human psychological attraction to and preference for anthropomorphically viewed noetic characteristics" (p. 139), which we need to be aware of if the non-cute are not to be treated in a morally inferior way. Veterinarians can act as vital educators for people who see only cuteness—that is, those who do not also grant deserved respect to non-cute animals. Non-cute animals are often susceptible to abuse.

The following three sections focus on animals in farming, trade, and research—all of which are areas in which veterinarians often have professional obligations, even statutory ones, and where they are frequently employed in a direct supervisory role. Here the conflict of interest—between caring for the individual animals concerned and supporting institutions that may treat animals unjustly—can be acute. Is the role of veterinarians simply to serve these institutions, to ameliorate individual suffering wherever possible, or do they have a deeper obligation to ask critical ethical questions about the nature of these businesses themselves? Many veterinarians have been timid, some would say too timid, in questioning whether these institutions that exploit animals can be justified in the first place. The following three sections seek to illustrate some of the key issues that any thoughtful veterinarian should at least be wrestling with.

First among them is the enormous difference in the way in which farmed animals are treated in comparison with companion animals. Grace Clement ("'Pets or Meat'? Ethics and Domestic Animals") considers this juxtaposition and argues that it "reveals a mistake in our moral thinking" (p. x). Since both kinds of animal are sentient (capable of pleasure and pain) and can be similarly harmed, it follows that "animals used in farming, like companion animals, should be understood within the sphere of care" (p. 146). Likewise, Matthew C. Halteman ("Varieties of Harm to Animals in Industrial Farming"), considers the argument that harms to animals in industrialized farming conditions are only isolated incidents of abuse that are not standard practice and thus do not merit criticism of the industry as a whole. Halteman argues that, even assuming that this is correct, defenders of industrialized farming must also account for the serious harms caused by "procedural harm and institutional oppression" that its animal victims have to endure. He argues that "the procedural and institutional harms create conditions under which abuse is virtually inevitable" (p. 160).Given their access to farmed animals, veterinarians are among the few people in a position to raise fundamental issues, not just about welfare, but also about the systems of exploitation in the first place. The point is reinforced by Drew Leder ("Old McDonald's Had a Farm: The Metaphysics of Factory Farming"), who examines the cultural and philosophical foundations of modern factory farming. He argues that "at the root [of factory farming] is a cultural anthropocentrism that prohibits viewing animals as moral subjects, removing ethical restraints" (p. 172). Factory farming envisions animals as little more than machines within a system.

Another area in which veterinarians are professionally involved is the now almost worldwide trade in animals. They are often called upon to oversee such operations, sometimes required by law to do so. But Simon Coghlan ("Australia and Live Animal Export: Wronging Nonhuman Animals") shows how things can go radically wrong, not least of all when slaughter is unregulated at the place of destination, where few or any legal restrictions prevail. He reviews the controversy that was aroused by the footage of Australian cattle being abused in Indonesian abattoirs and illustrates one of the central problems with the live-export trade, namely, the lack of international agreement on the treatment of animals. While animals may be treated tolerably well in the farms they are raised on in one country, there is no guarantee that they will be treated well either in transit to or upon arrival in another country. At the very least, veterinarians should be at the forefront of calling for consistent animal welfare regulations internationally. It is often their voice, either individually or collectively, that is missing from such debates.

Clifford Warwick ("The Morality of the Reptile 'Pet' Trade") highlights another trade in animals that often goes unnoticed, namely "non-cute" (according to some) reptiles. Warwick considers whether the keeping of reptiles as companion animals can be considered ethical. He specifically focuses on the practical problems "associated with handling, storage, transportation, intensive captive breeding, captivity stress, injury, disease, and high premature mortality" (p. 207) of reptiles along with public health, conservation, and ecological concerns that indicate that reptiles may not be able to be kept in such a way that ensures their welfare. This chapter is relevant to veterinarians who advise on the adequate needs and welfare of reptiles and who may be in a position to discourage the keeping of such animals in the first place.

The final section concerns animals in research. The oversight of veterinarians in animal laboratories is often (notionally at least) a requirement of certain codes of management, if not an actual legal stipulation. This section offers ethical insights into the treatment of those animals in research and considers whether such experiments can be justified. Kay Peggs ("Transgenic Animals, Biomedical Experiments, and 'Progress'") considers the idea of scientific progress in relation to the use of transgenic marmosets in biomedical experiments. She argues that "manipulating the genetics of nonhuman animals to engineer a predisposition to the development of feared human health hazards represents moral deterioration rather than progress" (p. 233). To the extent that veterinarians should be concerned with the health and welfare of the animals in their care, they should be the first to consider the necessity of those experiments and whether they can be understood as morally progressive.

Elisa Galgut ("Raising the Bar in the Justification of Animal Research") provides a case study in how ethical issues are bypassed even, and especially, in animal ethics committees (AECs) that are supposed to address them. Galgut provides a searching moral and practical critique of experiments based on her own experience. She argues that "although AECs do not grant rights to animals, they do accept that animals have moral standing and should not be harmed unnecessarily" (p. 251). Galgut contends that many of the AECs routinely fall short of the justification required and that "taking the moral status of animals seriously . . . should lead to a thorough revision or complete elimination of many of the current practices in animal experimentation" (p. 251). No veterinarian who works in animal laboratories could fail to find her detailed critique other than compelling.

Of course the ethical issues that we have touched upon are only a starter, a primer, in the growing and evolving field of animal ethics. There are so many practical subjects and so many issues that thoughtful veterinarians have to deal with. In this regard, *The Global Guide to Animal Protection* (Linzey, 2013) should be seen as an accompanying handbook to this volume, with its international and practical focus. And the book *Why Animal Suffering Matters: Philosophy, Theology, and Practical Ethics* (Linzey, 2009b) provides a compelling rational basis for extending moral solicitude to animals.

One thing seems certain: As more people become informed of the ethical issues about our treatment of animals, so veterinarians will be increasingly called upon to address them and to make appropriate and informed ethical judgements. We hope that this volume will help serve that end.

References

Linzey, A. (Ed.) (2009a). *The link between animal abuse and human violence*. Brighton, England: Sussex Academic Press.

Linzey, A. (2009b). *Why animal suffering matters: Philosophy, theology, and practical ethics*. Oxford, England: Oxford University Press.

Linzey, A. (Ed.) (2013). *The global guide to animal protection*. Urbana: University of Illinois Press.

1 An Ethical Oath for Veterinarians

ANDREW LINZEY and PRISCILLA N. COHN

As previous contributors have noted (Bones and Yeates, 2012), the nature of the oath that veterinarians, like doctors, should swear upon entering their profession has become increasingly topical.

The American Veterinary Medical Association (AVMA) adopted a revised form of their oath as recently as 2014 which emphasizes animal welfare. Here is the new oath with the additions in italics:

> Being admitted to the profession of veterinary medicine, I solemnly swear to use my scientific knowledge and skills for the benefit of society through the protection of animal health *and welfare, the prevention and* relief of animal suffering, the conservation of animal resources, the promotion of public health, and the advancement of medical knowledge. (AVMA, 2011, emphases in original)

From an animal ethical perspective, these changes are surely to be welcomed. As the AVMA Executive Board Chair John R. Brooks noted, "amending the Veterinarian's Oath was no small proposal . . . But, after extensive debate and deliberation, the board was right to approve the changes because the updated oath reinforces veterinarians' responsibilities to promote animal welfare and is consistent with contemporary veterinary medicine."

Some will be surprised of course that the AVMA was able to exist for so long without a direct commitment to animal welfare (as distinct from animal health). Isn't it the job of veterinarians to seek the welfare of the animals within their care? The question and the implied answer may appear obvious, but it is

Journal of Animal Ethics 5(2): v–vii
© 2014 by the Board of Trustees of the University of Illinois

worth noting that veterinarians generally have supported and defended forms of industrial agriculture and the invasive use of animals in research. The AVMA endorses the use of animals in research,[1] the castration and dehorning of cattle,[2] swine castration,[3] and (albeit as a second preference) the beak "trimming" of poultry.[4] It certainly can't be said that the AVMA policies represent anything like the highest welfare standards for farmed animals in comparison with, say, the standards required by the European Union. In the light of that, we should perhaps be grateful for any movement in a notionally more positive direction, though we have yet to see whether the emphasis on animal welfare will involve any changes in AVMA policies.

At the same time, we should be clear that veterinary bodies generally have a long way to go before they meet the standards of a truly ethical approach to animals. This can be shown by examining the language of the AVMA oath. The overarching motif is that veterinarians should "use [their] scientific knowledge and skills *for the benefit of society . . .*" (our emphases). But the interests of animals and those of society as a whole are not identical, indeed, as phrased, the interests of animals are clearly secondary. Even worse, there is no specific obligation to *individual* sentients as such. That omission flies in the face of an enormous amount of ethical work that has emphasized the weakness of traditional ethics in thinking only of animals as collectivities, breeds, or species, rather than as individuals deserving our moral solicitude. Again, the sub-clause ". . . the conservation of animal resources . . ." reinforces the view that animals are just that: "resources" to be "conserved," rather than individuals whose suffering is to be relieved and prevented. Moreover, the final line "the promotion of public health, and the advancement of medical knowledge" begs many questions, not least of all whether medical knowledge achieved at the expense of the suffering of individual animals should be a moral obligation for veterinarians.

All in all, veterinary bodies, and the AVMA in particular, have a long way to go before they can be seen as serious partners in the establishment of a truly ethical approach to animals. People who visit their veterinarian might be more than a little surprised to find that he or she defends experimentation on animals, accepts the view that animals are "resources," or even supports the mutilation of farmed animals that invariably involves suffering.

And here, it seems to us, is the possibility of real change. As the AVMA Board Chair indicated, the new emphasis on animal welfare among veterinarians was "consistent with contemporary veterinary medicine," by which he might have in mind the increasing emphasis on animal protection over the last

40 years. In fact, many, if not most, people who utilize the expertise of veterinarians are precisely those who have strong convictions about how animals should be treated, not only as companions, but increasingly in research and farming.

If such people decided that they would only seek the services of veterinarians who swore to an ethical oath, then the impetus for change, both practical and financial, could become irresistible.

And what would such an oath look like? We suggest the following:

> I solemnly swear to use my skills and knowledge to care for the individual animals entrusted to my care and the animals referred to me by others. I will not knowingly inflict pain, suffering, distress, fear or trauma on any animal, except when it is essential for an *individual* animal's wellbeing, for example, during a veterinary operation. Also, I will never deliberately kill an individual animal, except when it is in the individual animal's own interest, for example when an animal is suffering incurable and unreliable pain. In addition, I refuse to support practices, such as research involving animals, sport hunting, and intensive farming, that involve the abuse of animals.

This is only a first draft. It can and should be improved. If such an oath were to receive the support of the "animal movement" (for want of a better term), it could transform current veterinary practice and put veterinarians in the forefront of practical animal ethics.

The question is: Will veterinarians and animal protectionists take up the challenge?

Notes

1. "The AVMA recognizes that animals have an important role in research, testing, and education for continued improvement of human and animal health and welfare. The AVMA also recognizes that humane care of animals used in research, testing, and education is an integral part of those activities." What "humane care" might mean in the context of invasive and frequently painful experiments might mean is not spelled out. (AVMA, n.d.d)

2. "The AVMA recognizes that castration and dehorning of cattle are important for human and animal safety when cattle are used for agricultural purposes. Because castration and dehorning cause pain and discomfort, the AVMA recommends the use of procedures and practices that reduce or eliminate these effects." (AVMA, n.d.b)

3. "Castration of swine can help control aggressive behavior and improve the palatability of pork by eliminating most boar taint (an odor found in the meat of some adult male pigs)." (AVMA, n.d.c)

4. "Beak trimming of poultry should be practiced only when necessary to prevent feather pecking and cannibalism. Only trained and monitored personnel should per-

form beak trimming, using proper equipment and procedures that minimize pain, prevent excessive bleeding, promote rapid healing and prevent infection." But since feather pecking and cannibalism arise principally in the intensive farming of poultry, this statement must be seen as an implicit acceptance of this kind of "farming." (AVMA, n.d.a)

References

American Veterinary Medical Association (AVMA). (n.d.a). Beak trimming of poultry. Retrieved from: https://www.avma.org/KB/Policies/Pages/Beak-Trimming.aspx

American Veterinary Medical Association (AVMA). (n.d.b). Castration and dehorning of cattle. Retrieved from: https://www.avma.org/KB/Policies/Pages/Castration-and-Dehorning-of-Cattle.aspx

American Veterinary Medical Association (AVMA). (n.d.c). Swine castration. Retrieved from: https://www.avma.org/KB/Policies/Pages/Swine-Castration.aspx

American Veterinary Medical Association (AVMA). (n.d.d). Use of animals in research, testing, and education. Retrieved from: https://www.avma.org/KB/Policies/Pages/Use-of-Animals-in-Research-Testing-and-Education.aspx

American Veterinary Medical Association (AVMA). (2011). Veterinarian's Oath revised to emphasize animal welfare commitment. Retrieved from: https://www.avma.org/News/JAVMANews/Pages/x110101a.aspx

Bones, V. C., and Yeates, J. W. (2012). The emergence of veterinary oaths: Social, historical, and ethical considerations. *Journal of Animal Ethics* 2(1), 20–42.

2 The Emergence of Veterinary Oaths: Social, Historical, and Ethical Considerations

VANESSA CARLI BONES and JAMES W. YEATES

Veterinary oaths are public declarations sworn by veterinarians, usually when they enter the profession. As such, they may reflect professional and social concerns. Analysis of contemporary veterinary oaths may therefore reveal their ethical foundations.

The objective of this article is to contextualize the ethical content of contemporary oaths, in terms of the origin and development of veterinary medicine and wider societal changes such as the intensification of farming and the rise of animal welfare. This informs a comparison of oaths from the United States, Canada, the United Kingdom, and Brazil.

This analysis suggests some ways in which the oaths might be developed to better reflect contemporary societal values.

KEY WORDS: animal ethics, ethics, oaths, animal welfare, veterinary ethics

INTRODUCTION

Oaths may be sworn by large numbers of veterinarians in many countries, and analyzing the sociohistorical context and normative content of different oaths can provide a valuable insight into contemporary veterinary roles, responsibilities, and motivations. Yet there has been little analysis of veterinary oaths to date.

Oaths are social structures, and each country's oath is situated within the historical context of the veterinary profession in that society. But the contemporary responsibilities of the veterinary profession may be different from its historical role, and it may be more appropriate for present-day oaths to be based on the contemporary roles of the modern profession. This article therefore also considers the contemporary social contexts of four examples of contemporary veterinary oaths in the United States, Canada, the United Kingdom, and Brazil.

Journal of Animal Ethics 2 (1): 20–42

This analysis will provide a foundation for future work on how veterinary oaths should be improved.

THE ROOTS OF VETERINARY MEDICINE: AN OVERVIEW

The development of veterinary medicine was not a single, spontaneous event. The practice developed through a gradual process of cultural and technological advance, which both mirrored and influenced changes in society.

The very earliest record of human-animal relations is Upper Paleolithic cave art in the Franco-Cantabrian region. These are estimated to be 10,000–40,000 years old, and they present one of the richest, most complex records of the cultural adaptations of prehistoric hominids in the world (Straus, 1995). Many of the prehistoric paintings are of animals, and even these early artworks depict "veterinary" issues, with animal pathologies represented, for instance, by pictures showing wounded animals (Dunlop & Williams, 1996). Many different animals are represented in these prehistoric paintings, especially horses and ruminants such as cattle, bison, deer, and ibex, with whom hunters personally and deliberately interact. However, the paintings may represent more than food sources. A side chamber contains images of more dangerous animals such as bear, large felids, and rhinoceroses, suggesting that the artistic intent may have been motivated not completely or only by animals' instrumental value but perhaps also by a respect for animals and nature.

Later development in human-animal relations within civilizations can be considered as one of continued—if not increasing—instrumentalization. Predation and competition progressed to domestication (Swabe, 1999) and deliberate population control. Animals increasingly provided people with food, energy, protection, transport, entertainment, wealth, and other resources. This instrumental usefulness made it beneficial to protect animals' health. Early civilizations in Africa, Asia, and Europe started to contribute ideas on medicine and animal health and care. Egyptian and Ancient Greek theories laid the foundations for scientific and medical thought. These were extended and systematized through the Roman and Byzantine cultures, translated by Arab scholars, and revived in the Italian Renaissance. Here they inspired the nascence of modern disciplines such as comparative anatomy and surgery, followed by anesthesiology, immunology, epidemiology, chemotherapy, pathology, microbiology, and parasitology (Karasszon, 1988; Swabe, 1999). Progress was practical as well as theoretical. Novel methods were developed through praxis, folklore, and trial and error and dispersed through oral communication and imitation (paralleling the early development of human medicine).

The greatest motivation for care in the post-Enlightenment period was centered on horses (Karasszon, 1988; Stafford, 2006). There was a growing need for fit and healthy horses both for power and transport of products and passengers and for war. This led to the establishment of positions such as the horse marshals and trades such as blacksmiths, grooms, and horse doctors. In addition to shoeing, farriers developed skills in a number of procedures such as firing, bleeding, castrating, and tail docking. Many of them also developed their own herbal dressings, ointments, and powders, and by the 18th century, these were routinely applied to cattle, sheep, and pigs (Hunter, 2004).

The care of animals used in farming also gained in importance. European farmers came under increasing pressure to raise productivity to support the population growths between 1700 and 1850. As the productivity and financial value of "livestock" increased, owners became anxious about protecting their animals against diseases. Outbreaks of disease resulted in huge losses of resources and money (Radford, 2001) and threatened human health, creating an important role for veterinarians.

It was in this context that the first veterinary schools were set up. The first college was established at Lyon, in France, by Claude Bourgelat, director of the local Academy of Equitation, in response to recent cattle plagues (Jones, 2008; Wilkinson, 1992). Most of the bibliographic sources locate the foundation of the first school in 1762, although some authors argue that it happened in 1761 (hence the 2011 anniversary celebrations of World Veterinary Year) or even 1760 ("Claude Bourgelat," 2011). Over the next 20 years, Bourgelat's example was followed by others at Alford in France, Turin in Italy, Copenhagen in Denmark, Vienna in Austria, Dresden and Gottingen in Germany, Budapest in Hungary (Hunter, 2004), Hannover in Germany, Padua in Italy, and Skara in Sweden (Karasszon, 1988). The first U.K. veterinary college opened in London in 1792, led by Charles Vial de Sainbel (Dunlop & Williams, 1996). Most students were recruited from their positions as stud grooms, drivers, smiths, surgeons, and pharmacists and their apprentices (Karasszon, 1988).

Despite the new veterinary schools, quackery developed to capitalize on the burgeoning demand for veterinary care of horses and other animals (Dunlop & Williams, 1996; Hunter, 2004). This was partly due to the lack of scientific knowledge and official regulation and to the limited regulation of educational entrance requirements and standards.

This prompted efforts by veterinarians to gain formal recognition, in order to avoid charlatanism and to ensure professional standards and legal regulation (Hall, 1994; Porter, 1994). In the United Kingdom in 1844, two years after a major foot-and-mouth disease outbreak, a royal charter established the

Royal College of Veterinary Surgeons (RCVS). This created an official register of veterinarians, which assisted control of the professionals who were legally working in the country. A second royal charter, in 1876, allowed veterinarians to be removed from the register for misconduct. In 1881, this royal charter was rendered into law by the Veterinary Surgeons Act, which made it an offense to falsely claim to be a veterinarian without being on the register (RCVS, 2010). In the same year, the nonregulatory British Veterinary Association (BVA) was created (Boden, 2010).

Other countries established equivalent bodies for similar purposes. The American Veterinary Medical Association (AVMA) was founded in 1863. Rather later, the Canadian Veterinary Medical Association (CVMA) was founded in 1949, and the Brazilian Conselho Federal de Medicina Veterinária (CFMV), or Federal Council of Veterinary Medicine, was established by law in 1968 to regulate admissions to the veterinary profession (Brasil, 1968). Formal recognition allowed tighter standards, including higher requirements on the education of graduates.

The better-educated profession needed better information, which was provided by increasing scientific and technological developments. In the United Kingdom, for instance, the 18th century had seen significant advances in agriculture and industry on one side and, on the other side, in the medical disciplines of physiology, histology, and pathology. Veterinary medicine began to catch up, and the discovery of anesthesia and germ theory in the 19th century made possible tremendous advances in surgery and disease control.

This information was disseminated through increasing numbers of veterinary schools, such as the second U.K. school, which was established in Edinburgh by William Dick in 1823 with the specific aim of improving the "rudimentary" training provided at the London school. By 1904, there were six U.K. schools: two in Edinburgh and one each in Glasgow, Dublin, London (Jones, 2008), and Liverpool (Hunter, 2004). These universities, against the social background of the Enlightenment, helped to create a scientific mentality among practitioners. Graduates could share similar education, scientific outlook, communication, and coordination.

In comparison, institutionalized veterinary medicine in the Americas developed relatively late (Derbyshire, 2004; Silveira Prado & Etxaniz Makazaga, 2007). Until the last third of the 19th century, the practice of veterinary medicine was restricted to small numbers of European immigrants and large numbers of unqualified farriers. There was a lack of initial training and machinery to give the profession cohesion and few means for the profession to control its own affairs (Mitchell, 1938). Only in 1862 did British graduates found the Ontario Veterinary College in Toronto, with the Montreal Veterinary College following four years later. Soon afterward, in 1868, the first veterinary course was created at the University of Cornell in Ithaca, and in 1879, the first public veterinary school was established in Iowa.

In Latin America, the first veterinary college was opened in 1883 in the Instituto Superior de Agronomía y Veterinaria de Santa Catalina, which later constituted the Universidad Provincial (Provincial University), followed by the Facultad de Ciencias Veterinarias de la Universidad de La Plata in Buenos Aires (Silveira Prado & Etxaniz Makazaga, 2007). The first public school, the Escola Superior de Agronomia e Medicina Veterinária in Rio de Janeiro, was established in 1913, followed a year later by the Escola Superior de Agricultura e Veterinária do Mosteiro de São Bento in Olinda and the Escola Veterinária do Exército in Rio de Janeiro (Hatschbach 2006).

The early 20th century saw a further number of scientific and social developments. A "golden age" of veterinary medicine, mirroring that of human medicine, came with the discovery of antibiotics, fluid therapy, analgesia, and the disciplines of immunology, epidemiology, chemotherapy, molecular biology, and genetics (Hunter, 2004).

These developments began largely in Europe and the United States but spread to South America with the immigration of European citizens, stimulating more intensive breeding methods, agricultural mechanization, and the building of large-scale slaughterhouses and dairies. This intensification had several effects on the veterinary profession. It contributed favorably to the development of agronomic and veterinary education (Hatschbach, 2006), and it brought greater credibility to the veterinary profession's role in herd health.

But the intensification of farming also shifted the emphasis of veterinary practice. As stock numbers increased and traction became mechanized, farm profitability became more dependent on population-level than individual-level husbandry (Rollin, 1981). This made the veterinary care of individual animals less financially worthwhile for farmers.

THE DEVELOPMENT OF THE CONTEMPORARY ROLE OF THE VETERINARY PROFESSION

This intensification of farming had another effect on the veterinary profession. The 18th century had seen an increasing formal appreciation of animals' interests, through the rise of utilitarianism, the postulation of a common ancestry suggesting the possibility of similar feelings (Sandøe, Christiansen, & Forkman, 2006), and the recognition of links between human and animal abuse (Linzey, 2009a). These had led to animal protection laws, such as the United Kingdom's Martin's Act in 1810 and Pease's Act in 1829, which prohibited cruelly beating, abusing, or ill-treating horses, sheep, or cattle. To enforce these laws, the Society for the Prevention of Cruelty to Animals was created; it received its royal charter in 1840 (Royal Society for the Prevention of Cruelty to Animals, 2008), four years before the RCVS. Thus, animals' welfare was increasingly important to society but was not necessarily considered a veterinary matter.

The introduction of systemic welfare problems through more intensive breeding and husbandry systems meant that poor animal welfare was no longer usually caused by deliberate cruelty or thoughtless neglect. The latter half of the 20th century saw a number of critiques of widespread husbandry practices (e.g., Harrison, 1964; Singer, 1974; Rollin, 1981) and increasing concern for animal welfare, an idea that reflects the increasing societal emphasis on avoiding suffering and offering animals a good life. This led to the creation of animal welfare science as a discipline (Fraser, 2007), notably with the launch of the Brambell Report (Brambell, 1965) and the establishment of the U.K. Farm Animal Welfare Council (FAWC) in 1979 (FAWC, 2009). Animal welfare was distinguished from animal health since animals may have their basic physiological needs met while potentially suffering significant welfare compromises (Webster, 1994; Nordenfelt, 2006; Broom, 2008). Thus, the concepts of animal health, which relates to animals' physical condition, and animal cruelty, which relates to the infliction of unreasonably unnecessary suffering, were complemented by a societal concern to avoid suffering.

The veterinary profession had two involvements in this issue. First, it had been instrumental in the intensification of farming, especially by prescribing pharmaceuticals (e.g., antimicrobials) and operations (e.g., castration and debeaking), and the profession continued to contribute to the feasibility and profitability of such enterprises. Second, veterinarians could provide valuable insights into animal welfare issues (Rushen, 2003), and newer veterinary schools such as Cambridge and Bristol became centers for animal welfare science. These two involvements created an ethical conflict for veterinarians between helping animal's guardians and helping the animals themselves (Arkow, 1998; Tannenbaum, 1993; Rollin, 2006a).

At the same time, there was a drift in the profession's workload from predominantly farm and equine work to an increasing proportion of companion animal work (MacKay, 1993; Brown & Silverman, 1999). This reflected societal changes, with increases in the number and status of companion animals (Fudge, 2009). Many companion animals' guardians became happy to fund treatment far beyond their animal's financial value (Albert & Bulcroft, 1987) and entrepreneurial veterinarians re-identified themselves to cater to this market. By dissociating treatment costs from animals' financial value, such clinicians could capitalize on the opportunity to develop diagnostic and therapeutic advances more closely related to evidence-based human medicine than to large-animal praxis.

The focus on companion animals paralleled social developments in animal ethics. Deontological and animal rights–based theories were developed (Regan, 1983; Rollin, 1981; Pluhar, 1995), and although few veterinarians focus on animal rights (de Graaf, 2005), there is a recent recognition that they have a responsibility not to exploit their patients for wider utilitarian gains (Yeates, 2009). Care-based animal ethics also developed (e.g., Bernstein, 2004; Engster, 2006), and the latter 20th century also saw an increasing number of females in the profession (Aitken, 1994; Herzog, Betchart, & Pittman, 1991; Miller, 1998), who may be more open to care-based approaches (Adams, 1994; Adams & Donovan, 1995).

The 21st century also saw an increasing recognition of global issues such as global warming and food security, in which veterinarians may have several roles. First, animals, both free-living and domesticated, may be affected by environmental changes, raising concerns about disease control. Second, domesticated animals contribute to the problems through taking up resources and producing greenhouse gases (Ilea, 2009; Gjerris, Gamborg, Olesen, & Wolf, 2009). Third, uses of domesticated animals can contribute to the solutions—for instance, through farming methods such as the pig tower (ArchiNed, 2001), carbon sequestering in cattle pasture (Knight, 2010), or use of their tissue for development of "vegetarian meat" (Hopkins & Dacey, 2008). Thus, veterinarians may be increasingly required by society to be concerned with global issues (Brown, Thompson, Vroegindeweyg, & Pappaioanou, 2006), such as ecological issues, public health, food safety, and disease control (Murray, Sischo, & Hueston, 2006; Willis et al., 2007).

Veterinarians' responsibilities now are different from those of their predecessors when the professions were being formed. The profession has increasingly moved from solely serving the economic or military aims of animals' owners and users to holding increasing concern for the animal patients and their guardians and for wider issues such as broader animal welfare, public health, and environmental concerns. This historical and social contextualization of the veterinary profession can inform an analysis of veterinary oaths currently employed.

CONTEMPORARY VETERINARY OATHS

Oaths are solemn affirmations of a belief or a pledge to adhere to certain standards of behavior ("Oath," 2003; "Oath," 2007). They are intended to allow oath-takers to understand and publically declare their role in society and to guide their daily practices and help other members of society to understand how they can rely on them. They may also help to encourage a self-identification with virtues and qualities. Many countries, including the United States, Canada, and the United Kingdom, have oaths of citizenship (Office of Public Sector Information, 1981; U.S. Citizenship and Immigration Services, 2009; Minister of Public Works and Government Services Canada, 2005). The medical profession uses variants of the Hippocratic oath to espouse the judicious use of knowledge and to help patients understand doctors' responsibilities and basic principles, such as the promise *primum non nocere* ("above all, do no harm") (Miles, 2004).

Several countries have veterinary oaths (Morgan, 2006). These are usually sworn by graduates on entering the profession, are used to frame discussions within the profession, and are accessed by other members of society. Countries differ in how oaths are used, and a comparison of veterinary oaths from four countries—the United States, Canada, the United Kingdom, and Brazil—can help to highlight these differences.

Oaths are used in the United Kingdom and Brazil as a mandatory condition of entering the veterinary profession. In contrast, the American and Canadian oaths are voluntary. These differences in whether a professional body's oath is mandatory may reflect the role of the veterinary body in that country. For example, the CVMA provides representation to the Canadian government, but it is not run by it directly (CVMA, 2010). Similarly, the AVMA has some relations with the government—for instance, as the U.S. Department of Education–designated accrediting body for veterinary schools—but is not a governmental body (AVMA, 2011). In contrast, the United Kingdom's RCVS is defined by a specific regulation (Veterinary Surgeons Act, 1966) and is answerable to the Privy Council; a similar situation is seen in Brazil (Brasil, 1968). Thus, there appears to be some contingent connection between the degree to which the body has a regulatory function and whether the oath is mandatory.

There are also differences in veterinary oaths' content between countries (Table 1), and these are worthy of further analysis. From the preceding

TABLE 1: Elements Included and Excluded by the Veterinary Oath in Different Countries

Country	Elements included	Elements excluded	Virtues	Oath-taking
United States	Scientific knowledge for the benefit of society Protection of animal health Animal welfare Prevention and relief of animal suffering Conservation of animal resources Promotion of public health Advancement of medical knowledge Clinical compliance with ethical standards	Other aspects of animal welfare Environment	Dignity	Voluntary
Canada	Scientific knowledge for the benefit of society Promotion of animal health and welfare Release of animal suffering Protection of public health and environment Advance of comparative medical knowledge		Clinical compliance with consciousness, dignity, and ethical standards Continuousness in improving professional knowledge and competence Highest professional and ethical standards for self and profession	Voluntary
United Kingdom	Animal welfare	Environment Public good	Uprightness of conduct Obedience and loyalty to the RCVS (to observe the professional ethics principles) Care	Mandatory
Brazil	Performance of legal and normative requirements Combination of science and art; application of knowledge to scientific and technological development Benefit of health and welfare of animals Improvement of the quality of animal products Prevention of zoonoses Promotion of sustainable development Protection of biodiversity Improvement of life quality Progress of human society		Respect for professional ethics code, public order, and good customs	Mandatory

sociohistorical accounts, several elements can be identified that one may expect to be represented in contemporary oaths. One is some responsibility toward coordinating a profession-wide ethic—for example, by declaring a duty to the interests of the profession, a promise to obey codes of conduct, or an oath to develop and use scientific knowledge, perhaps complemented with a recognition of the importance of more practical skills. Another element is some duty to benefit stakeholders. These might include humans, for whom animals are instrumentally important as economic units or health threats, or society more generally. They might also include animals, in terms of both animal health and animal welfare. One might also expect elements relating to global issues such as human and animal public health and environmental concerns. With these possibilities in mind, it is useful to consider the oaths of the United States, Canada, the United Kingdom, and Brazil in more detail.

The United States

The veterinary oath that was created by the American Veterinary Medical Association in 1954, amended in 1969, 1999, and most recently, 2010, reads as follows:

> Being admitted to the profession of veterinary medicine, I solemnly swear to use my scientific knowledge and skills for the benefit of society through the protection of animal health and welfare, the prevention and relief of animal suffering, the conservation of animal resources, the promotion of public health, and the advancement of medical knowledge.
>
> I will practice my profession conscientiously, with dignity, and in keeping with the principles of veterinary medical ethics.
>
> I accept as a lifelong obligation the continual improvement of my professional knowledge and competence. (AVMA, 2011)

This recently updated version contains many of the elements one might expect: the use of science and skills, benefit to society, concern for animal health, and animal welfare (Table 1). Before its revision in 2010, there was no general reference to animal welfare; only the narrower elements of animal health and relief of suffering were addressed. This may be taken as an improvement. The aims of "the protection of animal health and welfare" and "the prevention and relief of animal suffering" are not presented as primary or paramount roles. They still appear to be subordinated to anthropocentric interests, since the oath appears to consider them to be means *through which* the veterinarian may use his or her scientific knowledge and skills for the benefit of society. This is an important distinction when the U.S. oath is compared to those of other countries. Furthermore, the term "animal resources" implies a view that animals can be legitimately used as means to an end (Reyes-Illg, 2006).

This lack of welfare concern may reflect the situation in the United States in general, as also evinced by the relative lack of federal animal welfare legislation (Rollin, 2006b). The United States, the largest national user of animals in laboratories, excludes mice, rats, birds, fish, reptiles, and amphibians under the Animal Welfare Act (1985) (USDA, 2005), even though these species make up well over 90% of animals used in scientific procedures (Taylor et al., 2008); and the new Farm Security and Rural Investment Act (2002) still excludes birds bred for research and rats and mice (Silverman, Suckow, & Murthy, 2007).

In addition to considering animals as instrumentally beneficial to society, the U.S. oath also focuses on their possible threat, in the form of public health. The link between veterinary medicine and public health in the United States is fundamental (Olsen & Remington, 2008; Pappaioanou, 2006). This is reflected in the U.S. oath, which considers the public good a priority, unlike the oaths from the United Kingdom and Brazil. In comparison, the environment itself is not included, perhaps reflecting a more general U.S. outlook, which has been criticized for its failure to sufficiently consider environmental issues. For instance, the country refused to ratify the Kyoto Protocol in 1997, a document that was signed by many developed countries and that has served as a keystone in international climate change policy (Cosgrove, 2009).

But despite the weakness of the U.S. veterinary oath's concern for animal welfare and the fact that the discussed update was achieved only in 2010, it does represent a significant advance on the previous version. The goal of coordinating the profession provides an overarching reason for individuals to overcome any personal resistance to the new emphasis on animal welfare in the oath. Part of being a professional involves engaging with the profession's societal role and accepting that social changes may mean that previously common or acceptable practices cease to be acceptable. Another part of professionalism, and one that we have shown is intrinsic to the use of an oath, is to coordinate the profession—and for that coordination to be publically apparent.

Canada

In Canada, students do not have to swear an oath in order to enter the veterinary profession (Hewson, 2006). There is an oath cited by the CVMA (2004), which is employed by some universities. This states,

> As a member of the veterinary medical profession, I solemnly swear that I will use my scientific knowledge and skills for the benefit of society.

I will strive to promote animal health and welfare, relieve animal suffering, protect the health of the public and environment, and advance comparative medical knowledge.

I will practise my profession conscientiously, with dignity, and in keeping with the principles of veterinary medical ethics.

I will strive continuously to improve my professional knowledge and competence and to maintain the highest professional and ethical standards for myself and the profession.

The Canadian oath shares much of its content with its American equivalent (Table 1). This similarity reflects the relationship between the veterinary educational and professional structures of the United States and Canada. However, the Canadian oath does have some differences, perhaps partly because of dissatisfaction with the U.S. oath and partly because of differences between the American and Canadian societies in which the professions function.

One such difference is that the Canadian oath includes more duties to the environment, which might reflect a greater concern in Canada or simply the relative recency of the Canadian oath. Another difference is the inclusion of a promise to maintain "the highest professional and ethical standards for myself and the profession," which is more aspirational than the American promise to adhere to specific ethical principles.

A third difference is that the Canadian concern for animal welfare is more forceful and wide-reaching. The duty toward animal health is described as a "promotion" rather than "protection." "Promotion" requires active steps to improve animal welfare, not just guarding against possible threats. The Canadian oath also specifies welfare as a general concern, as well as more constrained concerns of health and suffering. The Canadian oath separates the promises to benefit society and to promote animal welfare into different sentences. The description of animals as resources also has not been adopted. This means that it is possible to read the oath as expressing concern for animals' own good, and not necessarily subordinating animal welfare to human concerns. These differences reflect the CVMA's mission of serving and representing the veterinarians of Canada and being committed to professional excellence and to the well-being of animals (CVMA, 2010).

The United Kingdom

In the United Kingdom, practicing veterinarians must be members of the RCVS (RCVS, 2010). To enter the RCVS, graduates must swear the following:

Inasmuch as the privilege of membership of the Royal College of Veterinary Surgeons is about to be conferred upon me

I PROMISE AND SOLEMNLY DECLARE

That I will abide in all due loyalty to the Royal College of Veterinary Surgeons and will do all in my power to maintain and promote its interests

I PROMISE ABOVE ALL

That I will pursue the work of my profession with uprightness of conduct and that my constant endeavour will be to ensure the welfare of animals committed to my care.

The U.K. oath does not refer to generic "professional medical ethics," as do the American and Canadian oaths. Rather, it specifies that the oath-taker "abide in all due loyalty to the RCVS," the regulatory body. This loyalty might be taken to include a duty to observe the provisions of the professional ethics principles that are laid out in significant detail in the *Guide to Professional Conduct,* or GPC (RCVS, 2010). However, this implication is not specified in the oath's current format, which appears to imply that loyalty to the RCVS would be a duty even if the GPC were abolished or completely rewritten.

This highlights a general danger in swearing an unconditional oath to one's professional body. Even if the current GPC were perfect, the function of the RCVS could change over time; indeed, plans for the restructuring of its council and a possible new Veterinary Surgeons Act are underway. No organization can be guaranteed to always and flawlessly uphold the best clinical or ethical standards. So a promise to an institution could require loyalty to a body that has come to uphold ethical or clinical standards very different from those it held at the time the relevant oath was first formulated, with no guarantee that all such changes are necessarily positive. Similarly, if the RCVS were *not* to alter its approach, despite changes in circumstances (such as new disease threats, changes in societal values, or progress in animal welfare science, ethics, and law), then unthinking allegiance might be inappropriate in such later circumstances. In addition, the RCVS—and any organization—inevitably includes bureaucratic or political elements that have nothing to do with ethical standards: It seems inappropriate for veterinarians to swear unconditional loyalty to those elements.

The U.K. oath also specifies that the oath-taker's "constant endeavor will be to ensure the welfare of animals committed to [his or her] care." This appears at first glance to be subordinated to respecting the RCVS. However, this impression is misleading for several reasons. First, the RCVS's role is to "safeguard the health and welfare of animals committed to veterinary care through the regulation of the educational, ethical and clinical standards of the veterinary profession" and "act as an impartial source of informed opinion on animal health and welfare issues and their interaction with human health" (RCVS, 2005). Thus, a commitment to the RCVS is, at least currently, an indirect commitment to "safeguard the health and welfare of animals committed to veterinary care." Second, the duties to the RCVS and to animal welfare are separate, unconnected sentences. The duties to animal welfare are not subordinated to the duties to the RCVS.

Furthermore, the concern for animal welfare is communicated in much stronger tones than in the U.S. or Canadian oaths. This may leave limited scope for other concerns. The U.K. oath lacks any duty regarding environmental or public health concerns. Such concerns are perhaps included in the duty to promote the interests of the RCVS. The RCVS role "to safeguard the health and welfare of animals" is linked to "*thereby* protecting the interests of those dependent on animals and assuring public health," suggesting that these ends are part of the RCVS's goal. The GPC also describes many principles focused on clients and humans (RCVS, 2010).

This focus on patients' welfare may reflect the perception of animal welfare in the United Kingdom, and perhaps the European Union more widely. The United Kingdom can claim to have instigated much of the concern for animal welfare. The utilitarian ethicists Jeremy Bentham and John Stuart Mill were both British. The first animal protection society, the Royal Society for the Prevention of Cruelty to Animals (RSPCA), was English (RSPCA, 2008). The 1965 Brambell Report, which preceded the 1966 Veterinary Surgeons Act (RCVS, 2010) that invested the powers of the RCVS, was a U.K. governmental report. The United Kingdom has also recently introduced a progressive law that places a wide-ranging duty of care on all veterinarians (and other people responsible for animals) to ensure the welfare of animals for whom they are responsible (Animal Welfare Act, 2006). Some of the stances of the U.K. veterinary profession also appear more progressive than those of their U.S. equivalents. For example, mutilations aimed at human benefits that are practiced in the United States, such as declawing cats (to avoid furniture damage) and debarking dogs (to avoid unwanted noise), are not permitted by the United Kingdom's RCVS. Thus, the concern for animal welfare in the oath should be of no surprise.

Brazil

In Brazil, the CFMV published a resolution in 2002 containing the "Código de Ética Profissional do Médico Veterinário" (Veterinary Medical Professional Ethics Code). This includes an official veterinary oath that should be used by all universities, which (translated by the authors) reads,

> Under God's protection, I promise that, in the practice of veterinary medicine, I will fulfill the legal and normative requirements, with special respect

for the Professional Ethics Code, always aiming to combine science and art and to apply my knowledge to scientific and technological development for the benefit of the health and welfare of animals, the quality of their products and the prevention of zoonoses, having as compromises the promotion of sustainable development, the protection of biodiversity, the improvement of quality of life and the fair and balanced progress of human society. I promise to do all of this, with the maximum respect for public order and for good customs. So I promise.

The national and unified oath includes many, if not all, of the provisions contained in other countries' oaths, which could be explained by its relatively recent creation and Brazil's history of importing ideas from Europe and North America.

The health and welfare of the animals appear to be prioritized. Other concerns, such as human interests, sustainability, and environmental concerns, are listed as compromises to be made with the duties toward animal welfare. (Note, however, that some universities have their own "unofficial" oaths, several of which prioritize public good above animal welfare.) The concern for animal welfare, not seen in the U.S. oath, may be due to the fact that for a long time Brazilian farmers were not under the same pressure as the American agricultural industry to raise productivity. But it may also reflect the rapidly increasing concern for animal welfare in Brazil. There are many legislative instruments in the early stages of consideration by the government (as "projects of law") or only recently approved (Brasil, 2008; Brasil, 2009; CFMV, 2008). Brazilian animal welfare law may still have a long way to go, but the oath reflects a public declaration of the veterinary profession's role in these changes.

The inclusion of the environment in the oath may again reflect the Brazilian oath's recentness, but it may also reflect the importance of environmental issues in this tropical country. Brazil has a long history of concern for its natural resources (Hatschbach, 2006) and has played a major role in the history of the world environmentalist movement (Hochstetler & Keck, 2007; Viola, 2009).

One element of the Brazilian veterinary oath that does not appear in any of the other countries' oaths is the reference to God. This refers to a claim to "God's protection," rather than any explicit responsibility to follow God's ordinances (which may be considered to be supportive or opposed to various other ethical principles). Nevertheless, it highlights the historical links between religion and government and the importance of Catholic influences on the morality of a large proportion of the Brazilian population, which may extend to veterinarians' professional lives.

One final inclusion is important. As well as considering the importance of science, as in the oaths of the United States and Canada, the Brazilian oath specifically recognizes that veterinary practice should be "always aiming to combine science and art." This reflects the early, pre-scientific origins of veterinary practice. Although modern biological and clinical disciplines are providing increasing amounts of scientific evidence, many aspects of contemporary practice still largely remain "arts," including alternative medicines, inpatient care, many "established clinical practices," communication skills, and ethics.

IMPROVING VETERINARY OATHS

Consideration of the oaths of the United States, Canada, the United Kingdom, and Brazil in their sociohistorical contexts reveals aspects of the veterinary profession's moral role in these countries. Similarities in what is included suggest concerns that are common to the histories of several countries, such as concern for the profession's status, animal and public health, the use of science, and professional coordination. Differences in oaths reveal variations in how the professions function in each nation, influenced by the nation's specific historical and societal contexts. Such analysis of the oaths' social and historical contexts is vital to understanding how contemporary oaths have been formulated. The differences identified by the comparisons between countries may highlight candidate areas for improvements (Table 1).

There remains an additional question of how future oaths should be developed, how influential each oath's historical context should be, or whether new oaths should be based on contemporary, more progressive thinking. If so, how should the oath be used? And what elements should be included? Although this is intended as a descriptive rather than prescriptive article, its sociohistorical analysis can provide some prescriptive suggestions for how these questions might be answered.

The descriptive analysis here has mentioned that the sociohistorical context of the profession has changed, and these changes have brought about the contemporary veterinary oaths. Such changes have included developments in the opinions of people in society and in the profession and progressive ethical principles recognized by policymakers and professional bodies. This observation suggests two corresponding models for how the veterinary oaths of the four countries might be improved.

The first model would be for contemporary oaths to be informed by the opinions of society and practitioners. This would have several implications. On this model, different countries might legitimately have different oaths, insofar as they reflect the opinions of different societies. It would similarly imply that different times may legitimately result in different oaths. This means that earlier oaths may have been suitable for earlier stages in the development of the profession but not for modern times. As the societal demands change, veterinary oaths should change with them. Steps to change contemporary oaths therefore do not represent an admission that the previous oaths were inappropriate but merely represent a recognition that society has inevitably changed. Indeed, what would be inappropriate would be to fail to make necessary changes as society progresses in its views. This model would suggest that oaths should reflect *contemporary* societal concerns.

An alternative model would be for oaths to be based on fundamental ethical principles, rather than reflecting contingent societal opinions. There may be debate over what fundamental ethical principles should be included, but this is no more problematic for the issue of veterinary oaths than for other normative questions. The implications of this approach for the question of globalizing oaths depend on whether one takes a universalist stance that the same ethical principles should apply to veterinarians in all countries, which would imply that all veterinary oaths should be the same, or a more relativist stance, which might allow for different ethical principles to apply in different countries. Nevertheless, each country might usefully consider the content of the other countries' oaths as a baseline for reconsideration of their own. With this possibility in mind, the comparisons provided in this article can suggest some general proposals for what might be included.

More progressive and proactive thinking is required in the formulation of veterinary oaths for the next generation of veterinary practitioners. The professional bodies of the various countries might usefully engage in sociological studies to discern what society and practitioners would wish veterinary oaths to include, in ethical discussions to consider how oaths might best reflect and implement the requisite moral values, and in discussions between the bodies of the different countries to assist one another. But only by such work can professional bodies hope to have oaths that are appropriate to the role of the 20th-century veterinary profession in the contemporary society.

WHITHER THE VETERINARY OATH?

These considerations do suggest some possible improvements to veterinary oaths and some questions that should be answered. These include the procedural elements of how veterinary oaths are used, as well as what they include and exclude.

Procedural Elements of Veterinary Oaths

The question of whether oaths should be voluntary or obligatory could be informed by an analysis of the relative effectiveness of oaths in countries where swearing is voluntary versus where it is mandatory. There may well be advantages to each (Hewson, 2006). Voluntary oaths may engender more "ownership" and personal pride in the oaths' content, which may improve their personal ethical standards in practice. They can also provide a "mantra" to aid decision-making (e.g., U.K. veterinarians frequently cite that their primary obligation is to their patients as a foundational principle for their ethical reasoning). However, this advantage may be weakened if the voluntary oaths are less demanding than the compulsory ones or if voluntary oaths are adopted only by individuals who already endorse the elements included.

More detailed empirical evidence is needed to assess how individuals are motivated by each, and this could begin, for instance, with research comparing the professional ethical standards in the United States and Canada versus those in the United Kingdom and Brazil. If animal welfare is to be the main priority for the profession and the main rationale for the oath, then this empirical work could be aimed at seeing whether different oaths lead to better welfare outcomes. Other parameters may also be worth studying, such as public perceptions or veterinarians' motivations. Inevitably, such research would face methodological challenges, such as the large number of sociological differences that are likely to contribute to varying standards, and these challenges would be difficult to eliminate or control entirely.

A related question is whether veterinary oaths should be personal, institutional, national, or international. The function of the oaths in coordinating the profession may suggest that oaths should be coordinated as widely as possible. It may be especially important for oaths to be coordinated internationally, given that the veterinary profession is expected to become global. Conversely, the function of encouraging self-identification with the elements in the oath would suggest that oaths might be tailored to individuals or institutions. Again, the reported differences in this article suggest ways to empirically answer this question. For example, comparative international studies could analyze the effects of similar oaths (e.g., those of the United States and Canada) compared to different oaths (e.g., those of the United States and United Kingdom). Similarly, studies could evaluate the effects of having institutional oaths, as used in

Brazil, to see if there are advantages to oaths being closely connected with the curriculum in each institution.

Another question concerns the time at which an oath should be sworn. Bearing in mind that oaths are intended to allow oath-takers to understand their role in society, it might be useful for oaths to be sworn not only by veterinarians entering the profession but also by students on entering their studentship so that it colors their learning and prepares them for their future work. It may also be beneficial for practicing veterinarians to reaffirm their earlier path, in order to be reminded of their earlier promises.

What Should Be Included in Veterinary Oaths

Without intending to provide a definitive prescription as to the content oaths should include (the topic for another article), the models for development advocated by this article seem to strongly suggest that one value that should be represented in all veterinary oaths is a concern for animal welfare. This is suggested by both the contemporary societal concerns model and the fundamental ethical principles model.

The contemporary societal concerns model might suggest that all veterinary oaths should reflect increasing societal concern for animal welfare or environmental protection, insofar as these appear to be increasingly widespread societal values. Similarly, oaths might better reflect the increase of companion animal work and the profession's engagement with animal welfare concerns raised by intensive farming systems by not subordinating animal welfare to the economic value of animals. These obvious claims about societal values are as much as we can state here. More detailed suggestions might be obtained by in-depth sociological studies of contemporary attitudes to animals and the veterinary profession—not the reflections of a minority of the profession's elite.

The fundamental ethical principles model would also suggest that animal welfare should be deserving of respect. Veterinary oaths should include a provision that patients' welfare, care, and relief of suffering are to be assured in order to encourage veterinarians to take responsibility for their patients' welfare. Expanding on this position would require a longer article in which a full argument is described, but the position can be sketched here.

This responsibility to animal welfare should be a direct responsibility. Animals do have extrinsic, instrumental value for humans, so it is legitimate to aim to improve society through helping animals. But this is not the only—or the main—reason to help animals. Modern writings, such as those by Francione, Linzey, Regan, Rollin, and Singer, have contained detailed and convincing work on the interests of animals. Scientific evidence increasingly suggests (if it cannot prove) the complexity of animals' lives and the value they place on their own goals. Whatever country they are in, animals are moral subjects and should be respected and well treated. Respect for animals is a laudable value among humans—and one that goes back to the early Upper Paleolithic cave art in the Franco-Cantabrian region. Avoidance of preventable animal suffering is an important ethical principle, and animals' protection is morally important (Linzey, 2009b). Put simply, there are moral reasons to protect animals other than for human benefit. Concern for animal welfare within veterinary oaths should be a direct value, as it is in the Brazilian, Canadian, and U.K. oaths, and not be subordinated to concern for human interests—veterinarians should not protect animal health and welfare "for the benefit of society" but because doing so is fundamentally and directly valuable.

This raises the question of what specific welfare-based duties oaths should endorse. Some are very basic duties that every human agent has, whether the person is a veterinarian or a lay person. For example, all people have an agent-neutral responsibility to avoid causing unnecessary harm to an animal. Perhaps it might at first seem inappropriate to express concern for these agent-neutral duties in the veterinary oath, for several reasons. First, everyone has these duties, not just veterinary practitioners, so one might demand a reason that veterinarians should be asked to promise this and not, say, doctors or all citizens. Second, it is perhaps too obvious an obligation to warrant inclusion (the oath also does not contain elements against murder or rape). Third, we cannot take for granted that veterinarians do not harm animals. This could damage public confidence, leading to less presentation of animals for veterinary surgeries (as is currently the case for some people who fear that if they take their animal companion in for veterinary surgery, the animal will be euthanized), leading to greater animal welfare problems.

On the other hand, one might argue that these duties are still ones that veterinarians should endorse in an oath. First, it could be argued that even if everyone should have these duties, veterinarians do already swear an oath. Other citizens of many countries do not. In fact, it would be valid to argue that everyone should publicly promise not to harm animals, at least where there is a system in place for such promises (thus, one might even argue that it should be included in medical and citizenship oaths). Second, it could be argued that the responsibility not to harm animals is one that applies to vet-erinarians over and above the obligation placed on lay persons. Veterinarians may be more able to avoid harming animals or be able to harm animals less.

For example, if they run over a cat, an ability to provide first aid and analgesia may minimize the harm done. Veterinarians may also have less defense when they do harm to animals since they should have greater knowledge about animals' interests. Third, veterinarians have an especially potent ability to harm animals. They have clinical knowledge and legal privileges that allow them, and not lay persons, to prescribe medication and perform operations. Such interventions can cause direct, iatrogenic harms inflicted by the clinician in the course of veterinary treatment, such as nontherapeutic mutilations or perpetuating the lives of terminally suffering animals. Veterinary interventions may also engender other harms, such as the intensification of the farming of animals facilitated by the routine use of antibiotics and growth promoters. Some harms may be unavoidable or necessary to avoid greater harms, for example in order to treat an underlying disease. But others may be unnecessary. Making vets swear not to harm their *patients* may help them to avoid causing such harms.

Some arguments could go further and argue that concern for patients' welfare is a particular obligation that veterinarians hold and should be willing to promise to fulfill. It could be argued that caring for animals is a core part of the veterinary profession's role (Mullan & Main, 2001; Rollin, 2006a). In addition to the obligation not to harm their patients, veterinarians have other additional responsibilities that are specific to their relationship with their patients (Yeates, 2009). Practitioners have patients under their care, and they may have a care-based ethic or positive obligation to care for those animals. This obligation can be strengthened by a duty to clients, a duty not to breach the trust of the patients' guardians, who place their trust in their veterinarian when they place their companion animal in his or her care.

In addition, oaths perhaps ought to widen veterinarians' responsibilities to include wider issues. For example, practitioners could be encouraged to be more progressive and proactive, through commenting on animal welfare issues, taking greater steps to promote welfare in their communities, and providing data on animal welfare issues. This would fit with some suggestions from particular interest groups. For example, the Association of Veterinarians for Animal Rights in the United States (now the Humane Society Veterinary Medical Association) suggested an alternative oath in which veterinarians should promise "to protect the health and well-being of all nonhuman animals, to relieve pain and suffering in nonhuman animals, [and] to strengthen the understanding of the inherent needs and interests of all nonhuman animals" (Crowell-Davis, 2008).

What Should Be Excluded from Veterinary Oaths

The sociohistorical consideration of the function of oaths also suggests things that should not be included in oaths. We would suggest that veterinary oaths should not include a responsibility to the client. Although clients' interests are important, these duties can instead be ensured through legal promises. Furthermore, the veterinarian-client relationship, though important for veterinarians, is substantively no different from the relationship between clients and car mechanics, who are not expected to promise to promote the interests of car owners (unless, as previously noted, everyone were expected to make such a promise). Indeed, if there is a difference between veterinarians and car mechanics, it is that the veterinary profession is trusted to be concerned with the interests of the third party, the animal under their care.

A similar argument applies to principles that are derived from medical ethics and the Hippocratic oath. Medical ethical concerns are therefore not directly applicable to veterinary work. For example, the doctrine of informed consent that is "translated" from medical ethics to veterinary ethics may be problematic, and the professional ethics to which veterinary oaths often refer should reflect these differences. These issues are due to several differences between medical and veterinary practice. The three-party nature of veterinary work makes it very different from medical practice. In most medical practice the clinician's patients are also the clients. In some (e.g., pediatrics and mental health practice), other proxies may give consent or advice, but the patient remains the primary responsibility. Veterinary practice is more like these roles, but pediatricians' patients are not "owned" by the proxy, and so veterinary work requires a different degree of interaction with the client. This role of interacting with both patient and client may lead to a greater range of ethical concerns.

Thus, unthinking translation of ethical principles from medical to veterinary ethics and policy is unwarranted. Either the transfer of concepts from human to nonhuman context would need to be justified and defended, or the question of practitioners' responsibilities to their patients must be considered directly as an independent question. Either way, the issue must be addressed at a more fundamental and theoretical level before veterinary bioethics can draw on medical bioethics, and it is important for the veterinary profession to develop its own ethical frameworks and oaths. These may parallel elements of medical ethics, such as a direct responsibility to one's patients, but this is for separate, if similar, fundamental reasons.

We would also suggest that although oaths might stipulate a responsibility to one's professional peers, it is inappropriate for an oath to prescribe an absolute loyalty to a professional body itself. First, this is an unnecessary duplication where the professional body controls the legal ability to perform acts of veterinary surgery in most countries, and so adherence to the professional codes of conduct is already required by practicing veterinary surgeons. Second, even if the professional body may represent laudable ethical principles at one time, the composition, purpose, or ethos of that body may change over time. So an unthinking and unconditional loyalty may be misguided. Third, such loyalty may have deleterious effects, such as defensiveness, where fear of protecting the profession's reputation hamstrings veterinary surgeons into compliance with clients, or where fear of disciplinary action reduces transparency. Rather, the veterinary oath should encourage a self-identification with virtues and qualities of the veterinarian as an individual, which the professional body should then reflect.

CONCLUSION

This article has analyzed a number of differences between the veterinary oaths of the United States, Canada, the United Kingdom, and Brazil. It is important that each country continue to revise its oath, as the United States has recently done, and this paper also has suggested a number of ways in which the professional bodies of these countries might aim to improve the content and use of their veterinary oaths. It might be added that the development of these oaths should be based not on what the profession—or the profession's elite—*want* to promise, but on what they *should* promise, given the place of the profession within its contemporary society and moral duties to animal in general and patients in particular. It is hoped that these considerations will prompt further improvement of the oaths, including further progressive changes to the recently altered U.S. oath, in order to give greater weight to the fundamental ethical duties of the veterinary professions and to achieve greater effectiveness in improving the welfare of animals committed to veterinary care.

Acknowledgments

The authors would like to thank the editor and three anonymous referees for many helpful comments on the paper.

References

Adams, C. J. (1994). *Neither man nor beast: Feminism and the defence of animals.* New York, NY: Continuum.

Adams, C. J., & Donovan, J. (Eds.). (1995). *Animals and women: Feminist theoretical explorations.* Durham, NC: Duke University Press.

Aitken, M. M. (1994). Women in the veterinary profession. *The Veterinary Record, 134,* 546–551.

Albert, A., & Bulcroft, K. (1987). Pets and urban life. *Anthrozoos, 1*(1), 9–25.

American Veterinary Medical Association (AVMA). (2011). *About the AVMA: Who we are.* Retrieved from http://www.avma.org/about_avma/whoweare/oath.asp

Animal Welfare Act. (2006). Retrieved from http://www.legislation.gov.uk/ukpga /2006/45/contents

ArchiNed discussion: Pig city. (2001). *ArchiNed.* Retrieved from http://www.classic .archined.nl/news/pigcity/pigcity_eng.html

Arkow, P. (1998). Application of ethics to animal welfare. *Applied Animal Behaviour Science, 59*(1–3), 193–200.

Bernstein, M. (2004). *Without a tear: Our tragic relationship with animals.* Urbana: University of Illinois Press.

Boden, E. (2010). *Practice and politics: The British Veterinary Association 1881–1919.* Retrieved from http://www.bva.co.uk/public/documents/BVA_history_1881-1919.pdf

Brambell, F. W. R. (1965). Report of the Technical Committee to enquire into the welfare of animals kept under intensive livestock husbandry systems. Cmnd. 2836, December 3, 1965. London, England: Her Majesty's Stationery Office.

Brasil. (1968). *Lei federal n° 5.517, de 23 de outubro de 1968.* Retrieved from http://www .planalto.gov.br/ccivil_03/Leis/L5517.htm

Brasil. (2008). *Lei n° 11.794, de 8 de outubro de 2008.* Retrieved from https://www .in.gov.br/imprensa/visualiza/index.jsp?jornal=1&pagina=1&data=09/10/2008

Brasil. (2009). *Decreto n° 6.899, de 15 the julho de 2009.* Retrieved from http://www.planalto .gov.br/ccivil_03/_Ato2007–2010/2009/Decreto/D6899.htm

Broom, D. M. (2008). Welfare assessment and relevant ethical decisions: Key concepts. *ARBS Annual Review of Biomedical Sciences, 10,* T79–T90.

Brown, C., Thompson, S., Vroegindeweyg, G., & Pappaioanou, M. (2006). The global veterinarian: The why? The what? The how? *Journal of Veterinary Medical Education, 33*(3), 411–415.

Brown, J. P., & Silverman, J. P. (1999). The current and future market for veterinarians and veterinary services in the United States. *Journal of the American Veterinary Medical Association, 215,* 161–183.

Canadian Veterinary Medical Association (CVMA). (2004). *Canadian Veterinary Oath.* Retrieved from http://canadianveterinarians.net/about-oath.aspx

Canadian Veterinary Medical Association (CVMA). (2010). About us. Retrieved from http://canadianveterinarians.net/index.aspx

Claude Bourgelat. (2011). In *Wikipedia.* Retrieved from http://en.wikipedia.org /wiki/Claude_Bourgelat

Conselho Federal de Medicina Veterinária (CFMV). (2002). *Resolução n° 722, de 16 de agosto de 2002.* Retrieved from http://www.cfmv.org.br/portal/legislacao /resolucoes/resolucao_722.pdf

Conselho Federal de Medicina Veterinária [CFMV]. (2008). *Resolução nº 879, de 15 de fevereiro de 2008.* Retrieved from http://www.cfmv.org.br/portal/legislacao /resolucoes/resolucao_879.pdf

Cosgrove, S. (2009). The United Nations framework convention on climate change: 15th conference of the parties—the Copenhagen protocol. Presented at the Asia-Pacific Model United Nations Conference (AMUNC), St. Lucia.

Crowell-Davis, S. L. (2008). Animal behaviour and animal welfare. Retrieved from http://www.vetlearn.com/Portals/0/Media/PublicationsArticle/PV_30_07_372.pdf

De Graaf, G. (2005). Veterinarians' discourses on animals and clients. *Journal of Agricultural and Environmental Ethics, 18,* 557–578.

Derbyshire, J. B. (2004). Contributions by British graduates to the early development of veterinary medicine in Canada. *Veterinary History, 12*(3), 282.

Dunlop, R. H., & Williams D. J. (1996). *Veterinary medicine: An illustrated history.* St. Louis, MO: Mosby-Year Book.

Engster, D. (2006). Care ethics and animal welfare. *Journal of Social Philosophy, 37*(4), 521–536.

Farm Animal Welfare Council (FAWC). (2009). *Farm animal welfare in Great Britain: Past, present and future.* London, England: Author.

Fraser, D. (2007). *Understanding animal welfare: Science in its cultural context.* London, England: UFAW/Wiley-Blackwell.

Fudge, E. (2009). *Pets.* Stocksfield, England: Acumen.

Gjerris, M., Gamborg, C., Olesen, J. E., & Wolf, J. (Eds.). (2009). *Earth on fire: Climate change from a philosophical and ethical perspective.* Copenhagen, Denmark: Narayana Press.

Hall, S. A. (1994). The struggle for the charter of the Royal College of Veterinary Surgeons. *Vet Record, 134,* 536–540.

Harrison, R. (1964). *Animal machines.* London, England: Vincent Stuart.

Hatschbach, P. I. (2006). *História da veterinária.* Retrieved from http://www.crmvgo .org.br/index.php?comando=historicoVeterinaria

Herzog, H. A., Betchart, N. S., & Pittman, R. B. (1991). Gender, sex role orientation and attitudes towards animals. *Anthrozöos, 4,* 184–191.

Hewson, C. J. (2006). Veterinarians who swear: Animal welfare and the veterinary oath. *Canadian Veterinary Journal, 47,* 807–811.

Hochstetler, K., & Keck, M. E. (2007). *Greening Brazil: Environmental activism in state and society.* Durham, NC: Duke University Press.

Hopkins, P. D., & Dacey, A. (2008). Vegetarian meat: Could technology save animals and satisfy meat eaters? *Journal of Agricultural and Environmental Ethics, 21,* 579–596. doi:10.1007/s10806-008-9110-0

Hunter, P. (2004). *Veterinary medicine: A guide to historical sources.* Aldershot, England: Ashgate.

Ilea, R. C. (2009). Intensive livestock farming: Global trends, increased environmental concerns, and ethical solutions. *Journal of Agricultural and Environmental Ethics, 22,* 153–167.

Jones, B. V. (2008). Editorial: The rocky road from Odiham. *Veterinary History*, *14*(3), 201–204.

Karasszon, D. (1988). *A concise history of veterinary medicine*. Budapest, Hungary: Akadémiai Kiadó és Nyomda Vállalat.

Knight, A. (2010). Climate change: The animal connection. *Veterinary Practice*, *42*(2), 52–53.

Linzey, A. (Ed.). (2009a). *The link between animal abuse and human violence*. Eastbourne, England: Sussex Academic Press.

Linzey, A. (2009b). *Why animal suffering matters: Philosophy, theology, and practical ethics*. New York, NY: Oxford University Press.

Mackay, C. A. (1993). Veterinary practitioners' role in pet overpopulation. *Journal of the American Veterinary Medical Association*, *202*(6), 918–921.

Miles, S. H. (2004). *The Hippocratic oath and the ethics of medicine*. New York, NY: Oxford University Press.

Miller, G. Y. (1998). Earnings, feminisation and consequences for the future of the veterinary profession. *Journal of the American Veterinary Medical Association*, *213*(4), 340–344.

Minister of Public Works and Government Services Canada. (2005). *A look at Canada*. Retrieved from http://www.cic.gc.ca/english/pdf/pub/look.pdf

Mitchell, C. A. (1938). A note on the early history of veterinary science in Canada. *Canadian Journal of Comparative Medicine*, *2*(4), 91–95.

Morgan, C. (2006). Session 1. The veterinarian's oath: A critical review [Abstract of the AVMA convention, July 15, Honolulu, Hawaii]. *Newsletter of the Society for Veterinary Medical Ethics*, *12*(2).

Mullan, S., and Main, D. C. J. (2001). Principles of ethical decision-making in veterinary practice. *In Practice*, *23*, 394–401.

Murray, A. L., Sischo, W. M., & Hueston, W. D. (2006). Perspectives in professional education: Evaluation of veterinary public practice education programs. *Journal of the American Veterinary Medical Association*, *228*(4), 529–536.

Nordenfelt, L. (2006). *Animal and human health and welfare: A comparative philosophical analysis*. Wallingford, England: CABI.

Oath. (2003). In Collins *English Dictionary* (p. 1872). Glasgow, Scotland: HarperCollins.

Oath. (2007). In *The New Encyclopaedia Britannica* (Vol. 8, p. 1044). Chicago, IL: Encyclopedia Britannica.

Office of Public Sector Information. (1981). *Citizenship oath and pledge.* Retrieved from http://www.legislation.gov.uk/RevisedStatutes/Acts/ukpga/1981/cukpga _19810061_en_13

Olsen, C. W., & Remington, P. L. (2008). The dual DVM/MPH degree at the University of Wisconsin-Madison: A uniquely interdisciplinary collaboration. *Journal of Veterinary Medical Education*, *35*(2), 177–181.

Pappaioanou, M. (2006). Veterinarians in public health: Assuring conditions in which people can be healthy. *Leadership in Public Heath*, *7*(2), 27–33.

Pluhar, E. B. (1995). *Beyond prejudice*. Durham, NC: Duke University Press.

Porter, A. (1994). Veterinary charters and veterinary statutes. *Vet Record, 134,* 541–543.

Radford, M. (2001). *Animal welfare law in Britain*. Oxford, England: Oxford University Press.

Regan, T. (1983). *The case for animal rights*. Berkeley: University of California Press.

Reyes-Illg, G. (2006). Animals in veterinary medical education: Increasing coherence between principles and practice. *Newsletter of the Society for Veterinary Medical Ethics, 12*(2).

Rollin, B. E. (1981). *Animal rights and human morality*. Buffalo, NY: Prometheus Books.

Rollin, B. E. (2006a). *An introduction to veterinary medical ethics*. Iowa City, IA: Blackwell.

Rollin, B. E. (2006b). The regulation of animal research and the emergence of animal ethics: A conceptual history. *Theoretical Medicine and Bioethics, 27*(4), 285–304.

Royal College of Veterinary Surgeons (RCVS). (2005). *Guide for new members*. Retrieved from http://www.rcvs.org.uk/shared_asp_files/uploadedfiles/293E9C3D-BD71-4D6D-BFDB-59CFF5ECF8AF_members_guide05.pdf

Royal College of Veterinary Surgeons (RCVS). (2010). *About RCVS*. Retrieved from http://www.rcvs.org.uk/Templates/Internal.asp?NodeID=89678

Royal Society for the Prevention of Cruelty to Animals [RSPCA]. (2008). *About RSPCA: History*. Retrieved from http://www.rspca.org.uk/servlet/Satellite?pagename=RSPCA/RSPCARedirect&pg=about_the_rspca&marker=1&articleId=996827934749

Rushen, J. (2003). Changing concepts of farm animal welfare: Bridging the gap between applied and basic research. *Applied Animal Behaviour Science, 81,* 199–214.

Sandøe, P., Christiansen, S. B., & Forkman, B. (2006). Animal welfare: What is the role of science? In J. Turner & J. D'Silva (Eds.), *Animals, ethics and trade: The challenge of animal sentience* (pp. 41–52). London, England: Earthscan.

Silveira Prado, E. A., & Etxaniz Makazaga, J.-M. (2007). Las primeras escuelas de Veterinaria en América. *REDVET. Revista electrónica de Veterinaria, 8*(9), 1–11.

Silverman, J., Suckow, M. A., & Murthy, S. (2007). *The IACUC handbook* (2nd ed.). Boca Raton, FL: CRC Press.

Singer, P. (1974). *Animal liberation*. Wellingborough, England: Thorsons.

Stafford, K. J. (2006). *The welfare of dogs*. Dordrecht, the Netherlands: Springer.

Straus, L. G. (1995). The upper Paleolithic of Europe: An overview. *Evolutionary anthropology: Issues, news, and reviews, 4*(1), 4–16.

Swabe, J. (1999). *Animals, disease and human society: Human-animal relations and the rise of veterinary medicine*. Routledge Studies in Science, Technology and Society. London, England: Routledge.

Tannenbaum, J. (1993). Veterinary medical ethics: A focus of conflicting interests. *Journal of Social Issues, 49*(1), 143–156.

Taylor, K., et al. (2008). Estimates for worldwide laboratory animal use in 2005. *Alternatives to Laboratory Animals, 36,* 327–342.

U.S. Citizenship and Immigration Services. (2009). *Oath of allegiance for naturalized citizens.* Retrieved from http://www.uscis.gov/portal/site/uscis/menuitem .5af9bb95919f35e66f614176543f6d1a/?vgnextoid=931696981298do10VgnVCM 10000048f3d6a1RCRD&vgnextchannel=d6f4194d3e88do10VgnVCM10000048 f3d6a1RCRD

USDA, Animal and Plant Health Inspection Service, Animal Care. (2005). *FY 2005 AWA inspections.* Retrieved from http://www.aphis.usda.gov/animal_welfare/downloads/ awreports/awreport2005.pdf

Viola, E. J. (2009). The ecologist movement in Brazil (1974–1986): From environmentalism to ecopolitics. *International Journal of Urban and Regional Research, 12*(2), 211–228.

Webster, A. J. F. (1994). *Animal welfare: A cool eye towards Eden.* Oxford, England: Blackwell.

Wilkinson, L. (1992). *Animals and disease.* Cambridge, England: Cambridge University Press.

Willis, N. G, Monroe, F. A., Potworowski, J. A., Halbert, G., Evans, B. R., Smith, J. E., . . . Bradbrook, A. (2007). Envisioning the future of veterinary medical education: The Association of American Veterinary Medical Colleges foresight project, final report. *Journal of Veterinary Medical Education, 34*(1), 1–41.

Yeates, J. (2009). Response and responsibility: An analysis of veterinary ethical conflicts. *The Veterinary Journal, 182*(1), 3–6.

3 Cognitive Relatives yet Moral Strangers?

JUDITH BENZ-SCHWARZBURG and ANDREW KNIGHT

This article provides an empirically based, interdisciplinary approach to the following two questions: Do animals possess behavioral and cognitive characteristics such as culture, language, and a theory of mind? And if so, what are the implications, when long-standing criteria used to justify differences in moral consideration between humans and animals are no longer considered indisputable? One basic implication is that the psychological needs of captive animals should be adequately catered for. However, for species such as great apes and dolphins with whom we share major characteristics of personhood, welfare considerations alone may not suffice, and consideration of basic rights may be morally warranted—as for humans. Although characteristics supporting the status of personhood are present to differing degrees among the diverse array of animal species, this is a barrier to moral consideration only if anthropocentric, exclusive, and monolithic viewpoints about the necessary prerequisites for personhood are applied. We examine the flaws inherent within such positions and argue for inalienable species-appropriate rights.

KEY WORDS: cognition, culture, language, theory of mind, great apes, dolphins, animal welfare, enrichment, personhood, inalienable rights, human rights

INTRODUCTION

The comparison of the cognitive abilities[1] of adults with those of children and of humans with those of nonhuman animals (hereafter "animals") have long been topics of significant philosophical interest.[2] Considered sources of "pure natural behavior," children and animals have provided valuable insights into human nature, which have supported the proposition that the human adult is

Journal of Animal Ethics 1(1): 9–36

what the child is not yet able to be and what the animal will never be (Gigon, 2002, pp. 63–64).

Clearly, humans are endowed with exceptional social, cognitive, and other psychological capacities. We form cultures, use languages, and interact with one another, cooperatively, competitively, and in other ways. The purported human-uniqueness of such abilities has long been considered adequate justification for attributing to humans a moral status markedly superior to that granted to animals and for justifying very different standards of treatment.

However, empirical studies from different scientific fields provide increasing evidence that certain animals demonstrate at least some aspects of these phenomena. Accordingly, a review of the moral status and treatment of such animals is warranted. In this article we review such evidence, focusing on animals' cultural, linguistic, and psychological capacities. We examine the implications in two important cases: the welfare of captive animals and the case for granting basic rights to animals, similar in some respects to fundamental human rights.

ANIMAL CULTURES

Van Schaik and colleagues (2003) provided a broad definition of culture as "a system of socially transmitted behavior" (p. 102). Whiten (2005) further specified that the culture of a community consists of a unique array of traditions (p. 52). These traditions must demonstrate a certain level of complexity, they must be transmitted to new individuals through specific learning mechanisms, and any spread to new communities must not be attributable to ecologic or genetic causes.[3]

Culture in Chimpanzees

Some chimpanzee traditions appear to meet these conditions. At least 39 traditional behavior patterns have been identified among seven African chimpanzee study sites (Whiten et al., 1999). Results are assembled within the Behaviour Definition and Distribution Database,[4] which collates available information about these traditions, including the use of "leaf-sponges" to collect water and the so-called hand-clasp, a special handholding position during grooming, which was the first documented social tradition in chimpanzees (McGrew & Tutin, 1978). The best-known chimpanzee cultural traditions are probably nut-cracking (Boesch & Boesch, 1983) and termite-fishing (Goodall, 1964).

Chimpanzee traditions are very complex. Chimpanzees use different tool sets for different tasks, including different two-part sets when confronted with different types of insects and their mounds or nests (Sanz, Call, & Morgan, 2009; Sanz, Morgan, & Gulick, 2004; Sanz, Schöning, & Morgan, 2009). They manipulate and modify potential tools, for example, by removing parts, shortening them to appropriate lengths, or abrading the materials. They use tools for very different purposes, and their traditions show both technological and sociological aspects.

An interesting example recently reported by Hernandez-Aguilar, Moore, and Pickering (2007) was the use of tools by savanna chimpanzees in Ugalla, Tanzania, for harvesting the underground storage organs of plants such as root vegetables. This behavior is considered to have played a key role in the initial hominin colonization of savanna habitats, in the development of the skull and tooth morphology of the genus *Australopithecus*, and in the evolution of the genus *Homo*—the underground storage organs of plants served as "fallback foods" in times when food was scarce (Hernandez-Aguilar et al., 2007, p. 19210).

The underlying learning mechanism of culture transmission in chimpanzees has been described as utilizing a "master-apprenticeship" relationship (Matsuzawa et al., 2001). Although direct assistance or active teaching by the skilled master is absent, such masters nevertheless interact socially with their naive apprentices. They show unusually high levels of tolerance and allow long-term repetitive observation, with access to tools.[5] Captive chimpanzee mothers have been observed to offer tools to their infants (Hirata, 2006, pp. 202, 209–211). In addition, infants selectively use the same tools chosen by adults, which indicates that tool selectivity is transmitted (p. 211). Other experimental data on captive chimpanzees similarly shows evidence of the transmission of traditions (Whiten, Horner, & de Waal, 2005).

As with human infants, learning by young free-living chimpanzees occurs at certain sensitive ages, within very strong mother–infant interactions (Lonsdorf, 2006). However, human children appear more strongly reliant on imitation, choosing to imitate actions demonstrated, even when it becomes obvious that such actions will no longer achieve desired goals. In contrast, apes change from imitative to *emulative* behaviors—that is, flexible behaviors more likely to achieve such goals (Horner & Whiten, 2005).[6]

Culture in Other Great Apes

Cultural traditions have also been described in other great apes. Van Schaik and colleagues reported at least 19 highly complex behavioral patterns in orangutans in Borneo, serving a wide range of purposes relating to the achievement of subsistence, comfort, or social communication (van Schaik et al., 2003; van Schaik, van Noordwijk, & Wich, 2006). Tool use in free-living gorillas in northern Congo has been similarly described. Examples include the use of sticks, branches, and trunks for different purposes, including as walking sticks and as poles to determine water depth (Breuer, Ndoundou-Hockemba, & Fishlock, 2005).

Culture in Other Animals

Tool use is certainly not limited to great apes. Australian bottlenose dolphins, for example, use marine sponges as foraging tools. Genetic analysis has indicated that transmission of this behavior occurs matrilinearly[7] (Krützen, 2005).

New Caledonian crows are also skilled tool users, as was exemplified in a 2002 report from British scientists (Weir, Chappell, & Kacelnik, 2002). A young female was observed using a wire to extract a small bucket containing food from a tube. When at first she was unsuccessful using a straight piece of wire, she bent the wire into a hook, with which she successfully extracted the bucket—despite no prior experience with the material or situation. Hunt and Gray similarly reported that New Caledonian crows modify pandanus tools,[8] from straight ones to a variety of stepped tools, ranging from single- to multistep tools with greater efficiency (Hunt & Gray, 2003, pp. 867, 872–873). This could indicate diversification and evolution of tool designs, although to date supporting examples have been described only in New Caledonian crows and chimpanzees (Whiten, 2005, p. 53).

In some respects, tool use in New Caledonian crows seems to represent innate behavior. However, social input nevertheless plays an important role in the transmission and evolution of specific techniques and tool designs. Young crows in captivity, for example, prefer to use objects that they have observed a human using (Kenward, Rutz, Weir, & Kacelnik, 2006, p. 1340; Kenward, Weir, Rutz, & Kacelnik, 2005).

Recently, even meta-tool use[9] has been observed in New Caledonian crows. Taylor, Hunt, Holzhaider, and Gray (2007) observed crows mastering recursive tasks, including the use of a short stick to extract a longer stick, which was used in turn to extract food from a box.

Culture in Animals and Humans

Certain animal behaviors appear to meet reasonable definitions of culture, at least in the case of the highly complex and socially transmitted traditions among chimpanzees and orangutans. Tool use in cetaceans and corvidae, for example, also seems to possess cultural aspects.

Obviously, many (although not all) human cultural activities demonstrate great depth and complexity, as evidenced by achievements such as elaborate artistic performances or creations and advanced technological constructions. Yet such complexity is not necessary for the manifestation of culture (Sommer, 2007). If it were, the cultures of many contemporary human and early hominin communities could not be acknowledged as such.

In fact, human cultures are socially acquired, usually between birth and adulthood. Children pass through all stages, from non-cultural newborns to encultured children and teenagers, during which time they become progressively more aware of the traditions of their societies (e.g., Rogoff, 2003). On the other hand, culture also represents behavioral patterns that have evolved over many generations. For example, early hominin culture included ivory sculptures produced during the middle and late Pleistocene, more than 30,000 years ago (e.g., Conard, 2007), and Oldowan stone tools,[10] which are about 2.5 million years old (e.g., Semaw, 2000). Such cultural achievements have since evolved into those of modern art and technology. Acknowledging the evolutionary and developmental progression of human culture overcomes the common misperception that our culture is necessarily divorced from the natural world.[11]

ANIMAL LANGUAGE

The characteristic most prominently used to argue for a moral distinction between humans and animals has been our purportedly unique ability to speak.[12] However, considerable research has investigated the communicative abilities of animals.

Language in Chimpanzees

In 2007, one of the most famous contributors to chimpanzee linguistic studies passed away. By the time of her death, Washoe the chimpanzee had successfully mastered around 250 distinctive American Sign Language (ASL) signs, some of which she had taught to her adopted son Loulis and two other chimpanzees. This was claimed to be the first animal-to-animal transfer of a human language. These chimpanzees routinely used—and continue to use—ASL, vocalizations, and gestures in their interactions with humans and each other.

Widespread initial excitement about Washoe's reported language abilities (Gardner & Gardner, 1975) was followed by several criticisms, including claims that Washoe's apparent linguistic skills actually may have been more reflective of the techniques used to teach her than of her innate abilities (Seidenberg &

Petitto, 1979). For some, however, Washoe's various reputed abilities stimulated a fundamental reexamination of chimpanzee psychology (Fouts, 2000).

Other apes also have communicated with humans using sign languages or symbols (via boards or computers). Such apes have demonstrated their ability to use language creatively by inventing new combinations of words (e.g., combining labels for "white" and "tiger" to describe a zebra and combining labels for "listening" and "drinking" when confronted with a fizzy tablet in water), and they have generalized to new contexts words learned within a specific context.[13]

Language in Monkeys

Animals' communicative abilities are also demonstrated by their natural means of communication. Perhaps the most complex examples of "proto-syntax" in animal communication discovered to date have been described recently in Campbell's monkeys (Ouattara, Lemasson, & Zuberbühler, 2009). These monkeys vocalize six different types of alert calls, which are combined within long sequences in highly context-specific ways. Stereotyped sequences convey information about group cohesion and travel, falling trees, neighboring groups, non-predatory animals, nonspecific predatory threat, and specific predator classes. Callers follow relatively sophisticated principles when concatenating sequences, including nonrandom transitions between call types, incorporation of specific calls within existing sequences to form new ones, and recombination of two sequences to form a third. Ouattara and colleagues concluded that these primates have overcome some of the constraints of limited vocal control through combinatorial organization.

Seyfarth and Cheney (1993) similarly described the use of different alarm calls for different predators in vervet monkeys. It has been postulated that these alarm calls also fulfill the function of words with semantic content.

Language in Dolphins

One of the most interesting acoustic and non-acoustic communication systems with language-like features is dolphins' use of whistles, echolocation clicks, and certain postures and behaviors. Although related research remains in its infancy, it is already known, for example, that dolphins use signature whistles for each individual, equivalent to names, which aptly demonstrates their awareness of the individuality of other dolphins and themselves (Janik, Sayigh, & Wells, 2006; White, 2007, pp. 56–57, 96–116, 141–146). Dolphins are also able to understand instructions given to them in artificial languages, consisting of acoustic, computer-generated whistles or hand gestures. They seem to understand these arbitrary symbols and the rules used to combine them because they follow instructions perfectly when a sentence is semantically reversed. For example, to both humans and dolphins, the English sentence "Go to the hoop at the surface and take it to the basket at the bottom" means something quite different when "hoop" and "basket" are exchanged (White, 2007, pp. 96–116, especially p. 100, with reference to Hermann, Richards, & Wolz, 1984).

Language in Parrots

Language comprehension studies in parrots are especially interesting because of their ability to pronounce many human words. Irene Pepperberg worked with her African Grey parrot Alex for more than two decades, until his death in 2007 (Pepperberg, 2002, 2008).[14] She described her use of the so-called Modal-Rival Training System to introduce new words, which appears particularly effective: One person acted as a trainer, and a second person acted as a model for Alex, as well as being a rival for the attention of the trainer. When the model and rival engaged in a conversation about a new item, Alex intruded, naming the item, apparently motivated by curiosity, jealousy, and a desire to regain the attention of the trainer.

A flexible learning situation was created. The roles of the questioner and the respondent were reversed among the humans, occasionally including the bird in interactions. Alex did not simply hear stepwise vocal duets, "but rather observed a communicative process that involves reciprocity." He learned that communicating with the labels was an interplay—"a two way street in that one person is not always the questioner and the other always the respondent"—and a process that "can be used to effect environment change" (Pepperberg, 2002, pp. 26–29, esp. 26). He acquired, for example, names of different objects, colors, materials, and numbers. Even short sentences (e.g., "wanna go" requests), as well as interrogative pronouns, were part of his vocabulary. Additionally, he knew the words "color," "same," and "different."

When shown different toys, Alex demonstrated several skills related to object classification (Figure 1). He was able to tell whether a toy fell within a certain category. If shown a red key and a yellow wooden cube, for example, and asked, "What toy red?" he would answer, "Key!" But Alex could also classify objects with respect to different categories. When shown the yellow wooden cube and asked, "What color?" he would answer, "Yellow." If asked, "What matter?" his answer was "wood." Especially impressive was his ability to classify objects as similar or different with respect to different categories. When confronted with a yellow wooden cube and a yellow key and asked, "What's

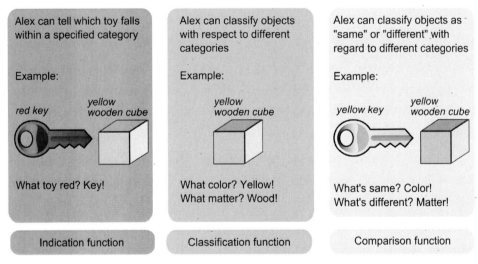

FIGURE 1: Alex, an African Grey parrot, demonstrated several skills related to object classification. According to Bartels (2005), the parrot's concepts can be described via functional roles.

same?" his answer was "color"—even if he had never seen this color before. When asked, "What's different?" he answered, "Matter" (Bartels, 2005, pp. 156–186, especially 175–181; Pepperberg, 2002).

In over 80% of cases, Alex answered correctly when asked three different questions about the same visible item.[15] If he did not understand, he would have been expected to provide the same response in all three cases or to give responses determined by chance. Alex thereby demonstrated the ability to modify his response according to auditory stimuli from different questions, while the visual stimuli remained constant (hence demonstrating independence from these visual stimuli).

The existence of concepts is closely linked to the existence of "meta-concepts." For example, a speaker who is aware that she or he has made a mistake must be able to have a thought now considered to be correct, about a former belief now considered to be false (Tietz & Wild, 2006, p. 18). In a strict sense Alex could not *correct* his reaction after receiving additional information, but he was able to *modify* it (Bartels, 2005, p. 178). Furthermore, his concepts were clearly organized in small networks, including main categories such as color and subcategories such as yellow, red, and green (Pepperberg, 2002, p. 184). According to Andreas Bartels, who refers to Donald Davidson,[16] these last two characteristics meet the two most important criteria for the possession of concepts (Bartels, 2005, p. 178). Alex clearly had an understanding of perception-based concepts, which, though different from human concepts, can nevertheless be functionally interpreted and described (Bartels, 2005, pp. 11, 185–187; see similar in Newen & Bartels, 2007). Alex's concept for yellow, for example, had three functional roles: to indicate, classify, and compare (see Figure 1 and Bartels, 2005, p. 184).

Based on this philosophical interpretation of concepts, Alex possessed perception-based concepts, or conceptual representations, which are organized within small networks and can be described functionally. Although these are not nearly as complex as the concepts underlying human language, they can nevertheless be regarded as another important example of preliminary linguistic ability in an animal.[17] Without concepts there can be no language or linguistic capacity.

ANIMAL THEORY OF MIND

Theory of mind is also a consciousness-based core capacity of human beings, and there is some evidence of it in animals. The term *theory of mind* (ToM) describes a commonsense psychology (Bartsch & Wellmann, 1995, p. 4). Those who have a ToM impute mental or psychological states to themselves and others. Such states include beliefs and desires, as well as perceptual states such as seeing (Bischof-Köhler, 2000, p. 9; Premack & Woodruff, 1978, p. 515).[18] The assumption that everybody holds such mental states serves to explain and predict social behavior and interaction (Bartsch & Wellmann, 1995, p. 5).

Theory of Mind in Chimpanzees

In crucial experiments investigating chimpanzee knowledge of perceptual states, groups of two individuals competed for hidden food items (Hare, Call, Agnetta, & Tomasello, 2000; Hare, Call, & Tomasello, 2001). In one of the tests, the subordinate chimpanzees could see the hiding process and could also see whether the dominant chimpanzees had seen the hiding process, based on their doors being opened or closed. The subordinates then avoided food that the dominants had observed being hidden but retrieved food that they had not (Hare et al., 2001; Tomasello, Call, & Hare, 2003a, p. 154).[19] This indicated that the subordinate chimpanzees knew the dominant chimpanzees had seen something at an earlier time, knew that the dominant chimpanzees were likely to remain aware of this at a later time, and knew that this awareness was likely to determine the dominant chimpanzees' behavior.

The significance of these results remains under discussion. Whether they clearly indicate that chimpanzees have a ToM is controversial (Povinelli & Vonk, 2003), but they do add to a weight of accumulating evidence (Call & Tomasello, 2008; Tomasello et al., 2003a, p. 156; Tomasello, Call, & Hare, 2003b). Combined evidence from multiple studies suggests that chimpanzees understand the intentions, goals, visual (and sometimes auditory) perception, and knowledge of other chimpanzees. Even if there is no evidence (yet) of understanding false beliefs,[20] they seem to understand others within a perception–goal psychology (Call & Tomasello, 2008; Kaminski, Call, & Tomasello, 2008; Krachun, Carpenter, Call, & Tomasello, 2009).

Tomasello and colleagues (2003a) concluded that "chimpanzees—and perhaps other animal species—possess a social-cognitive schema" (p. 156) that helps them understand something about the intentional structure of behavior and about how perception influences it. This social-cognitive schema is clearly not a "full-blown" or "human-like" ToM. On the other hand, Tomasello and colleagues concluded that it was "simply too sweeping" to understand ToM as something monolithic[21] that exclusively incorporates human cognitive characteristics, while completely excluding those of other species. They suggested that further research should focus on determining which of the many different kinds of psychological states chimpanzees are able to comprehend and on describing the extent to which they are able (p. 156).

The Incremental Progression of Cognitive, Social, and Psychological Capacities

As with culture and language, ToM consists of many different sociocognitive processes and abilities, constituting a "toolkit" with different components or building blocks. False-belief understanding may be a core capacity, but there are other core capacities such as understanding perceptual states that are included within the classical definition of ToM provided by Premack and Woodruff in 1978.

Reducing, for example, ToM to false-belief comprehension, culture to advanced technical specialization, or language to grammar competence ignores the bundled character of cognitive, social, and psychological abilities. Claiming that an individual possesses culture, language, or ToM only when showing the full spectrum of subsumed capacities denies the incremental evolutionary and ontogenetic development of these abilities within and between species.[22] Animals and humans who lack the full spectrum of capacities yet, or who no longer possess them, are by definition excluded. Asserting that the full spectrum must be congruent with the abilities of a healthy human adult is even more exclusive than anthropocentrism—which discriminates in favor of all humans generally, rather than privileged subsets. The failure of such claims is linked to their premises and unsatisfying definitions of cognitive, social, and psychological abilities, rather than the application of cognition theory to animals.

The limitations of monolithic and exclusive conceptualizations of ToM, for example, are exemplified by examining ToM in children. The classical ToM test for children is called the Maxi Test,[23] which reveals children's level of understanding of false beliefs. The test utilizes the following story: Maxi stores his chocolate in the green kitchen cupboard, but while he is playing in the garden, his mother removes it to the blue one. Children are then asked where Maxi will search for the chocolate when he returns to the kitchen. Three-year-olds mostly answer, "In the blue cupboard," whereas almost 50% of 4-year-olds and more than 80% of 5-year-olds answer, "In the green cupboard." Thus, based on this classical test designed by Wimmer and Perner (1983), most 3-year-olds are unable to distinguish between their own knowledge and that of Maxi. Even when alerted to the fact that Maxi did not witness his mother moving the chocolate, they still expect him to search the blue cupboard. They have not yet perceived that knowledge states depend on information received and that different people may therefore possess different knowledge states and subsequently might harbor false beliefs if their knowledge is incomplete or incorrect (for a brief discussion of the Maxi Test, see Kasten, 2005, pp. 134–137).

Results from false-belief tests indicate that children younger than 4 to 5 do not understand false beliefs (Bischof-Köhler, 2000, p. 11; Kasten, 2005, p. 135). But does this mean that children younger than 4 years old do not possess a ToM? Is it instead possible that available tests may simply fail to show the ToM abilities of children between 2 and 4 years of age?

There are obviously problems connected with false-belief tests such as the Maxi Test. Such tests presuppose significant additional cognitive abilities (such as linguistic abilities, given that the tests are normally language-based). They result only in a pass or fail and cannot provide quantitative measures of ability. This correlates with monolithic conceptualizations of ToM as a characteristic entirely present or entirely absent, which fails to detect or acknowledge its progressive development. As Workman and Reader (2004) put it, "since the test[24] is all-or-none . . . it has the effect of making what might be a gradual developmental profile look like a sudden stage-like shift" (p. 128). Finally, although such tests examine the relatively sophisticated understanding of false beliefs, and although such understanding may constitute a cornerstone of ToM, it is far from being the only important characteristic. The limitations of false-belief tests are increasingly acknowledged, with researchers expressing their disaffection with existing paradigms in general and specifically. Gopnik and colleagues aptly expressed such sentiments: "There is an unfortunate syndrome loose in developmental psychology: call it 'neurotic task fixation'" (Gopnik, Slaughter, & Meltzoff, 1994, cited by Hülsken, 2001, p. 7).

At least two lines of argument support approaching the ToM of children via other methods and applying new theoretical frameworks. First, results from non-language-based false-belief tests indicate that 15-month-old infants already "possess (at least in a rudimentary and implicit form) a representational ToM: they realize that others act on the basis of their beliefs and that these beliefs are representations that may or may not mirror reality" (Onishi & Baillargeon, 2005, p. 257). Similarly, Buttlemann, Carpenter, and Tomasello (2009) presented positive results from an active helping paradigm, involving false-belief understanding in 18-month-old infants.

Second, children younger than 4 are known to use mental verbs (e.g., "know," "think," and "believe") and other terms of mental reference in a meaningful way, in their everyday child language. Researching the way children talk about the mind is made possible through linguistic databases such as the Child Language Data Exchange System (CHILDES),[25] which contains transcribed conversations. Above all, analyses of the data demonstrate that very young children use so-called contrastives: utterances that mark different mental states within one sentence or a very small context. As defined by Bartsch and Wellmann (1995),

> Contrastive utterances, which distinguish a person's thoughts and beliefs from other states of affairs, potentially come in several overlapping varieties: Those contrasting belief with reality, fiction with belief, one's own mental state at one time with a later changed state, one's own mental state with another's, the contrasting mental states of two other people, and so on.[26] (p. 44)

Such contrastive utterances might be of the form "I didn't know X, but now I know X" or "You think X, but I think Y." According to Bartsch and Wellmann (1995), contrastives emerge in child language well before the fourth birthday, at a mean age of 3 years. The children they studied were between 2 years 8 months and 3 years 8 months when such utterances were first used (and they might have used them even earlier, when no tape recorder was present; p. 47).

An analysis of the CHILDES data about two German girls named Caroline and Simone supports these findings for the German child language:

contrastives were used by Caroline at the age of 2 years and 1 month and by Simone at the age of 2 years and 7 months (Benz, 2004, pp. 50–59, 75–89, 106–108). Caroline was 2 years and 5 months old when she participated in the following conversation with her mother:

TABLE 1: Contrastive Use by Caroline (age 2 years 5 months) in Conversation With Her Mother

	German dialogue		Translation by J. Benz-Schwarzburg
Mother:	*Die Aysche sagt das finde ich aber kein gutes Spiel.*	Mother:	Aysche says that's not a nice game.
Child:	*Ich aber find lustig wenn Aysche runter hoppala.*	Child:	But I think it's funny, when Aysche falls down.
Mother:	*Findest du lustig wenn die Aysche runterfällt?*	Mother:	You think it's funny, when she falls to the ground?
Child:	*Ja und au.*	Child:	Yes and ouch.

Note. The data has been modified marginally to improve readability, without changing the semantic content of the utterances.

Caroline very clearly points out that she, in contrast to her mother, likes the idea of Aysche falling to the ground. She even confirms her statement and indicates what she considers to be so funny: the fact that Aysche hurts herself (Benz, 2004, p. 82).

The importance of this conversation becomes apparent when considering that most developmental psychologists recently believed, or indeed still believe, that children younger than 3 1/2 to 4 lack a ToM. Bischof-Köhler (2000) states,

> Children under the age of three and a half years are naïve realists. . . . That is, they don't understand yet that their beliefs about facts are just beliefs that may represent those circumstances appropriately as well as inappropriately. They also take it for granted as a matter of course that other persons live in the same reality and that they percept and know exactly the same things they do. They don't apprehend yet that other persons can hold different opinions on the same fact. . . . This changes when a theory of mind appears at about the age four. (p. 11, see similar p. 34, translation J. Benz-Schwarzburg)

This viewpoint is clearly rendered incorrect by Caroline's narrative and similar data.

Research on ToM in animals as well as infants has demonstrated that this complex phenomenon cannot correctly be considered an all-or-nothing trait. This is similarly true for other higher cognitive abilities (DeGrazia, 2006, p. 42). Moreover, the human ToM does not suddenly appear but emerges gradually during ontogeny.[27] Children already possess some of its components before the age of 4, as shown by nonlinguistic tasks and contrastive utterances (Bartsch & Wellmann, 1995, p. 47; Benz, 2004, pp. 106–108; Buttlemann et al., 2009; Onishi & Baillargeon, 2005). It therefore seems appropriate to reject monolithic concepts of ToM, at least when considering the evolution and ontogeny of social cognition (Tomasello et al., 2003b, p. 240).

Disregarding these arguments leads to an unsatisfying simplification of the phenomenon of ToM and inhibits comparative research between species or between different age or ability groups (such as healthy vs. otherwise) within species. However, accepting the conceptual and methodological challenges of defining and testing cognitive abilities yields important implications for future research: we need nonlinguistic false-belief tests for children and animals (Onishi & Baillargeon, 2005, p. 257) and species-appropriate tests in general. We should abandon all-or-nothing test designs that correlate with monolithic conceptualizations of cognitive abilities and should instead focus on their incrementally progressive character.

ETHICAL IMPLICATIONS OF ANIMAL ABILITIES

The moral consideration afforded to animals is markedly less than that afforded to most humans (exceptions may include, for example, victims of major human rights violations). The main justifications for such profound differences in moral consideration and treatment depend on major purported differences in cognitive and related psycho-sociological capacities, such as culture, language, and ToM.[28] However, studies increasingly suggest the existence of such characteristics—or at least of important aspects of these and other cognitive abilities—in some animal species. Additionally, as pointed out by Rogers and Kaplan (2004), we must consider that "only a handful of species have been researched and current findings would suggest that many more species might be found to have exceptional cognitive abilities, if we only looked" (p. 193).

To what extent has such changing awareness altered the human–animal relationship? Unfortunately, to date the answer remains "very little." Although the cognitive relationship of some animals to humans is far closer than previously believed, on the whole we continue to treat such cognitive relatives as moral strangers, denying them moral consideration to an extent very rarely applied to our fellow human beings.

Acknowledging this changing awareness of animal abilities yields a range of implications, from the basic to the profound. One basic implication is that the psychological needs of captive animals should be adequately met. However, this presupposes that keeping animals in captivity is ethically defensible, as long as welfare standards are upheld.

A more profound implication is that welfare considerations alone may not suffice and that consideration of basic rights may be morally warranted for species such as great apes and dolphins with whom we share major characteristics of personhood. The granting of such rights might, for example, disallow the involuntary confinement of such animals in captivity. Each of these implications is examined in the following sections.

Environmental Enrichment for Captive Animals

Although it has long been understood that involuntary confinement may fail to meet the *physiological* needs of captive animals, it is increasingly understood that the advanced cognitive, other psychological, and social characteristics of some species may make it very difficult to cater adequately to their *psychological* needs in captivity. The great apes—our closest nonhuman relations—provide obvious examples.[29] As Rogers and Kaplan (2004) have asserted, "the ultimate aim must surely be that we do not just want animals to survive but want them to have a quality of life commensurate with their needs and dignity: physical, psychological, social, and cultural" (p. 196).

Zoos are increasingly aware of such psychological, social, and cultural needs of captive animals, and increasing numbers of modern zoos have accordingly attempted to enrich their lives by providing them with additional stimuli (see Jantschke, 1997, p. 406). Common examples include the introduction of novel items to enclosures, or the provision of visual and olfactory cues. Such interventions are directed at stimulating curiosity-driven or investigative behavior, which results in mental and physical activity or exercise and decreases stereotypical and undesirable behavior indicative of chronic stress (see Hutchins, Kleiman, Geist, & McDade, 2003, pp. 203–204). Since 2009, Great apes at the Leipzig Zoo in Germany, for example, have been provided with so-called shaking-boxes, rotary discs, and food-knots.[30] Unfortunately, however, environmental enrichment efforts remain poor or absent in many institutions internationally. And the ethical case for enrichment has scarcely been addressed by philosophers to date.[31]

An exception is David DeGrazia (1996, pp. 258–297, especially pp. 294–297). His arguments are grounded in the basic principle of nonmaleficence, which exhorts us "not to cause extensive unnecessary harm to others without their consent." This principle is further elaborated within 15 rules, 2 of which directly address the keeping of animals in zoos: Rule 3 is "don't cause significant suffering for the sake of your or others' enjoyment," and rule 14 is "provide for the basic physical and psychological needs of the zoo animal, and ensure that she has a comparably good life to what she would likely have if in the wild" (pp. 258–281).[32] This last rule clearly asserts psychological needs and the necessity of providing comparable life conditions. DeGrazia's ethical evaluation of zoos according to these principles provides the conclusion that in most cases they can adequately provide for their animals' needs, even if too few presently do (pp. 290, 296).

However, adequately catering for certain animals is rendered particularly difficult by their advanced cognitive, psychological, and social characteristics. According to DeGrazia (1996), keeping great apes in zoos is ethically defensible only if zoos can guarantee family preservation, considerable space, and highly enriched environments, containing ample opportunities for climbing, exploring, problem-solving, and playing (p. 297).[33] In such cases psychological needs arising from cognitive abilities are central to assessments of welfare, demonstrating the necessity of species-specific welfare assessments and species-appropriate environmental enrichment. Again, underlying all such considerations, however, is the assumption that keeping animals in captivity is ethically defensible, as long as welfare standards are upheld.

Rights and Responsibilities Implied by Cognitive, Psychological, and Social Abilities

Do we, however, owe animals more than best-practice welfare standards? After all, animals such as great apes possess to varying degrees cognitive, psychological, communicative, and social attributes once considered uniquely human, characteristics that have previously served to support the establishment of human rights. The following question therefore arises: Is it ethically justifiable at all to subject such animals to involuntary confinement within zoos or elsewhere?

Interestingly, DeGrazia (1996) rejects keeping dolphins in zoos because of the practical impossibility of providing them with surroundings in aquatic exhibits sufficiently comparable to those of their natural habitats (p. 297). In doing so he establishes a moral line, beyond which even compliance with the best welfare standards cannot be considered adequate to justify the involuntary confinement of certain species.

Thomas White (2007) describes his view of this moral line by noting that our expectations of certain treatment standards from other people stem from our self-identification as "self-conscious, unique individuals who are vulnerable to a wide range of physical and emotional pain and harm, and who have the power to reflect upon and choose our actions." Because we value these traits so deeply, we rarely consider it acceptable for other people to hurt, coerce, threaten, or manipulate us.

> We object to such actions so strongly that we label them not just "inconvenient" or "unpleasant," but as "wrong." Ethics—our labeling actions as "right" or "wrong"—is grounded in the idea that the type of consciousness that we have gives us special capacities and vulnerabilities. When we label something as "wrong," then, we're saying that it crosses the line with regard to not respecting some fundamental feature that makes us human. (White, 2007, p. 155)

Immanuel Kant described certain human core characteristics as providing sufficient justification for the granting of *inalienable* human rights. He asserted that the human being is an end in itself (German: *Selbstzweck*) and has dignity (German: *Würde*). Kant (1785/2008) deduced that there are conditions and expressions of (well-)being and personhood that a person should never be deprived of (p. 65; see also Hilpert, 1998, p. 675, and footnote 41).[34]

Similarly, the advanced cognitive, psychological, and social abilities of animals such as dolphins and great apes confer special capacities and vulnerabilities on them, including a profound ability to suffer when deprived of fundamental psychological or social requirements. Increasing numbers of ethicists and biologists argue that these animals share with us fundamental characteristics of personhood, such as consciousness and self-consciousness, a wide range of cognitive abilities (including those giving rise to culture, language, ToM, and other abilities such as episodic memory), and the capacity to experience a wide range of emotional states (including, for example, happiness, fear, and empathy).[35] It is therefore arguably more accurate to consider such animals as nonhuman persons,[36] who should be granted at least basic rights concordant with those granted to humans. One implication is that the moral boundary that ethical actors are obliged to respect is violated when these animals are subjected to a range of contemporary human purposes, such as confinement within zoos and involuntary participation within biomedical research.[37]

The Great Ape Project, founded by Peter Singer and Paola Cavalieri, similarly argues for an extension of the "community of equals" to include all great apes. It calls for equivalence of basic rights among all members, including the right to life, the protection of individual liberty, and the prohibition of torture. The project was primarily founded in recognition of the moral significance of the cognitive abilities of great apes.[38] It relies on the proximity of specifically their cognitive characteristics to those of humans, rather than phylogenetic characteristics generally—thereby implying that the community of moral consideration is potentially open to species beyond those evolutionarily close to humans, such as elephants, cetaceans, or corvidae (Cavalieri & Singer, 1994, pp. 8–9, 463–476; similarly White, 2007, p. 11).

Despite morally important similarities, such species obviously differ from human persons (as they do from each other). Nevertheless, they could be included within such a community of moral consideration. After all, so-called marginal human persons, such as the very young, old, injured, or ill, who lack the full range of psychological and social characteristics and abilities exhibited by healthy human adults, are nevertheless valued as persons. They are valued as partially conscious, partially self-conscious, or partially autonomous beings, with unique personalities, and are accordingly granted human rights.

It appears logically consistent to assign similar moral significance to comparable grades or stages of mental complexity in animals who possess them.

This need not necessarily imply that such nonhuman persons should be granted rights and responsibilities equivalent to those of normal human adults. The same is true of children or the mentally ill, for example. Although we may grant such people rights to life, liberty, and freedom from serious abuses such as torture, we do not necessarily stress their right or responsibility to work or their equality before the law. On the contrary, we grant them exemptions from certain social responsibilities, such as protection from child labor, and exemptions from, or mitigations of, judicial punishment. The United Nations Declaration of the Rights of the Child asserts such child-specific needs and rights. A Declaration of the Rights of Great Apes could similarly assert their specific needs and inalienable rights.

CONCLUSIONS

The Kantian foundation for human rights stems from the ideal of the rational person and the principle that every person is equally rational, self-conscious, and autonomous.[39] However, the case for the equal application of human rights transcends this core idea. No matter how equal all humans *actually are,* all are *considered equal* in *dignity and rights.* Modern civilized societies aim to extend such moral equivalence to all human beings, no matter where they live, the color of their skin, their gender, their culture, or their cognitive capacities. Almost every country has now ratified the Charter of the United Nations, which recognizes the existence of human rights and calls for their respect and practical implementation. Most have also incorporated basic human rights within their national laws.

Such moral and social progress has been hard-won and reached only after millennia of social injustice. We should value and defend the gains we have made and seek further progress where warranted. In many countries grave human rights violations continue on a daily basis, demonstrating the need for further progress. Additionally, as ethical actors we may consciously choose whether to grant moral consideration and personhood status to beings who do not yet possess, who have possessed and lost, or who may never possess the full suite of relevant psychological and social attributes displayed by healthy human adults.

Existing evidence supports the inclusion within the moral community of persons of those animals who share with us major characteristics of personhood. What about animals whose personalities or cognitive capacities are more different from our own, however? The diversity of animals' cognitive, psychological, and social capacities yields a dilemma: such characteristics are clearly morally relevant in justifying inalienable—and hence indivisible—rights, consistent with the granting of such rights to humans; yet those same characteristics are distributed throughout the animal kingdom, where the differences of degree are frequently small. By assigning such inalienable and indivisible rights to some species but denying them completely to others, we would impose a profound all-or-nothing division on a large and diverse array of living creatures, who may differ only incrementally in the extent to which they exhibit the necessary characteristics.

Thus, frameworks such as the Great Ape Project should be considered only the beginning of a more fundamental process of reconsideration: If basic human rights such as the rights to life, liberty, and freedom from torture are relevant when morally significant cognitive, psychological, and social abilities are present in other species, then it follows logically that this should lead to corresponding inalienable rights. However, not all rights will hold the same importance for all species. Interspecies variation of morally relevant characteristics justifies the establishment of species-appropriate subgroups of rights. Some rights are more broadly applicable than others. The prohibition of torture, for example, is morally warranted for all species able to experience significant suffering or other adverse effects accruing from such abuse—whether or not they possess the psychological criteria for personhood.

Classical concepts of personhood rely on the possession of human-like psychological characteristics. On the one hand, the identification of such characteristics within animals, and those animals' subsequent inclusion within the community of moral consideration, facilitates their protection from a range of human abuses. On the other hand, focusing solely on human-like characteristics is intrinsically anthropocentric. We should also consider the possibility that some species might satisfy less anthropocentric definitions of personhood. White (2007) prefers to conceptualize dolphins as "alien beings" (pp. 12, 155–184)[40]: Their perception of the marine world, communication, and social interactions are very different from our own. Yet these characteristics are not necessarily of lesser importance when determining moral standing. Where reasonable doubt remains about the existence of morally relevant animal characteristics, as ethical actors we should afford such animals the benefit of that doubt.

Acknowledgments

We thank Prof. Dr. Eve-Marie Engels (Chair of Ethics in the Life Sciences, University of Tübingen) and Dr. Miriam Haidle (The Role of Culture in Early Expansions of Humans research project, Heidelberg Academy of Sciences and University of Tübingen) as well as five anonymous reviewers for their helpful comments on our manuscript. We thank Prof. Dr. Hanno Würbel (University of Giessen), Prof. Dr. Albert Newen (University of Bochum), and Dr. Juliane Kaminski and Dr. Daniel Haun (both MPI EVAN, Leipzig) for their helpful discussions and the Research Training Group "Bioethics" at the International Centre for Ethics in the Sciences and Humanities, University of Tübingen, for providing a stimulating academic environment in which many of our ideas were initially developed. We thank the German Research Foundation (DFG) for partially funding this research. Any remaining flaws are solely our own responsibility.

Notes

1. The term "cognition" is used in many different ways. Fundamentally, it refers to "mental processes that are presumed to occur within the animal, but which cannot be observed directly" (McFarland, 2006, p. 32). However, this is a very broad definition—"cognitive" then becomes very similar to "psychological." To define the term more precisely, McFarland's *Oxford Dictionary of Animal Behavior* identifies both strict and more general meanings: "In its stricter sense, cognition refers to a particular kind of knowledge: namely 'knowing that' rather than 'knowing how.' Cognition is the manipulation of explicit knowledge. In its more general sense, cognition refers to any kind of mental abstraction of which an animal seems to be capable. . . . In the study of navigation, problem solving, social interactions, deceit, language, and thinking in animals, scientists have found it necessary to postulate cognitive processes" (p. 32). To emphasize the mental abstraction underlying phenomena such as culture, language, and theory of mind, we generally intend the latter, more general definition when referring to cognition.

2. The systematic study of animal cognition first evolved during the late 1970s, when Donald Griffin (1976) established cognitive ethology as a biological subdiscipline. Increasing numbers of philosophers engaged in the topic in the 1970s and

1980s (see Perler & Wild, 2005). The publication of key texts by philosophers such as Peter Singer and Tom Regan helped develop the related field of animal ethics.

3. Traditions are defined as behavior patterns that are customary or habitual in at least one site, but absent elsewhere (Whiten, 2005, p. 52, Figure 1). They are shared by two or more individuals within a social unit, they persist over time, and new practitioners acquire them in part through socially aided learning (Whiten, 2005, p. 53, with reference to Fragaszy & Perry, 2003).

4. See the homepage of the Behaviour Definition and Distribution Database (http://culture.st-and.ac.uk/chimp/) and Whiten (2005), p. 53.

5. According to Matsuzawa and his colleagues (2001), the master–apprentice relationship includes long-term repetitive exposure to a problem, which stimulates a strong motivation within the apprentice to imitate the behavior of the master. High levels of tolerance by the master are also apparent. They believe this combination to be very educationally effective. They note that some human educational traditions, such as teaching the Japanese art of sushi making, include these elements—deliberately excluding verbal explanation, written instruction, or other assistance. The sushi apprentice, for example, is traditionally forbidden to touch utensils, rice, fish, or other ingredients for years during the initial training. The apprentice just carefully observes the master, "until one day the master suddenly gives him permission to attempt making his first sushi. It is no exaggeration to say that the apprentice produces exquisite sushi from the start" (p. 573). Matsuzawa and colleagues also note that the word "educate" originates from "educe" (Latin: *educere*), which means "to extract." "Education" thus refers to "the drawing forth of one's potential abilities." Although active teaching is regarded to be the most advanced form of education in many societies, it may be neither the only means of educating nor necessarily the best in every circumstance. Matsuzawa and colleagues consider that such active teaching may not stimulate student motivation as effectively as the master–apprentice relationship described (pp. 572–573).

6. Horner and Whiten (2005) explored the tendency of both young chimpanzees from an African sanctuary and 3- to 4-year-old children to use emulation or imitation to solve a problem using tools, and examined whether their tendency to choose either strategy was determined by the availability of causal information. Both groups observed a human demonstrator use a tool to retrieve a reward from a puzzle box: "The demonstration involved both causally relevant and irrelevant actions, and the box was presented in each of two conditions: opaque and clear. In the opaque condition, causal information about the effect of the tool inside the box was not available, and hence it was impossible to differentiate between the relevant and irrelevant parts of the demonstration. However, in the clear condition causal information was available, and subjects could potentially determine which actions were necessary. When chimpanzees were presented with the opaque box, they reproduced both the relevant and irrelevant actions, thus imitating the overall structure of the task. When the box was presented in the clear condition they instead ignored the irrelevant actions in favor of a more efficient, emulative technique. These results suggest that emulation

is the favored strategy of chimpanzees when sufficient causal information is available. However, if such information is not available, chimpanzees are prone to employ a more comprehensive copy of an observed action. In contrast to the chimpanzees, children employed imitation to solve the task in both conditions, at the expense of efficiency. We suggest that the difference in performance of chimpanzees and children may be due to a greater susceptibility of children to cultural conventions, perhaps combined with a differential focus on the results, actions and goals of the demonstrator" (p. 164).

7. Through the maternal line.

8. Little "spears" made of thorny leaves that are used to extract insects from holes in trunks.

9. The application of one tool to another.

10. Oldowan stone tools were first discovered at the Olduvai Gorge in Tanzania. They were used by prehistoric hominins of the Lower Paleolithic era and are the oldest manufactured tools discovered to date.

11. The word "nature" is derived from the Latin word *natura,* which implies "essential qualities or innate disposition" or, more literally, "birth" (Latin: *nasci*). The word "culture" (Latin: *cultura*) stems from *colere* and means "to cultivate" (Hoad, 1991, pp. 108, 309). Throughout the history of philosophy and anthropology, nature and culture have been described as occupying separate spheres. Human cultures have been considered divorced from nature or from animal societies and behaviors (Grant, 1996, pp. 206–207). However, if culture is part of nature in the sense that "natural beings" (animals, as well as early hominins) also display or displayed cultural behavior, then definitions of culture as behavioral patterns present solely in modern humans, and absent in nature and other animals, become invalid.

12. Aristotle defined the human being as *zoon logon echon*—the being who is endowed with reason and speech (the Greek term *logos* refers to both). This characterization has proven very persistent throughout the history of philosophy and science. Hoffmann (2007) states that the possession of language and speech (or of central characteristics thereof) have "almost always" been claimed to be uniquely human (p. 21). Very often, language is linked to thinking in general and is used as *differentia specifica* to differentiate humans from other animals (Hoffmann cites examples provided by the Stoic philosophers, Descartes, Herder, Humboldt, Popper, and Eccles). Some scientists claim that language acquisition and linguistic abilities are connected to special sociocultural traits, which are more or less exclusive to human cultures and societies. Hoffman analyzes this position in regard to Herder and Humboldt but also mentions the theories of Wygotski, Wittgenstein, Tomasello, Lieberman, and others.

13. For a summary of primate language-training experiments, see Klann-Delius (1999), pp. 81–85. For reviews of animal linguistic abilities describing word invention and generalization, see Gould and Gould (1999), pp. 170–191, and Hauser (2001), pp. 215–259.

14. Pepperberg also worked successfully and still works with other African Grey parrots.

15. For Alex's ability to categorize with respect to color and shape, see Pepperberg (2002), p. 58. For his discrimination between same and different, including his transfer abilities with respect to new items, see p. 73. For his understanding of the labels, and of relative concepts, see pp. 125–167.

16. Donald Davidson (1982) writes in his essay "Rational Animals" that whether a dog can believe that an object is a tree depends on whether she or he has certain general beliefs about trees (that they need soil and water, have leaves or needles, are growing, etc.). According to Davidson, beliefs are located within a dense network of related beliefs such as this (pp. 320–321). Davidson further argues that in order to have a belief, it is necessary to have the concept of belief, which includes beliefs about beliefs (p. 324). He explains, "Much of the point of the concept of belief is that it is the concept of a state of an organism which can be true or false, correct or incorrect. To have the concept of belief is therefore to have the concept of objective truth" (p. 326). Davidson himself rejects the idea that any animal has concepts. Interestingly, Bartels (2005) and Newen and Bartels (2007) describe how some of his ideas can nevertheless be used to describe Alex's abilities.

17. It is very difficult to compare language-like or concept-like abilities in animals because very different aspects have been researched in a very diverse range of species, and interpretational frameworks that might facilitate comparison are lacking. Given that concepts or sentence-based concepts are cognitive information processes, distinctions between animals could be made by referring to different classes of informational processes (see Newen & Bartels, 2007). Quite complex behavioral routines may result from noncognitive information processes, which do not necessarily imply concepts. These are typically stimulated by a consistent physical stimulus and trigger a consistent behavioral response (reflexes are a subcategory). No stable representation is formed that may be transferred to other contexts (Newen & Bartels, 2007, p. 294). Cognitive information processes, however, entail nonconceptual, conceptual, and sentence-based or propositional representations. Nonconceptual representations are, for example, involved in the homing behavior of ants: "The spatial orientation of the ant is based on registering the position of the sun and registering the movements of its own legs. . . . If you transfer the ant to a new location at the moment it finds some food, it will start to run in the direction that would have been the right one given its previous location. The representation of the location relative to its nest that is built in one context is also used in a new context. . . . This indicates that the ant has built a stable representation of its spatial relation to the nest" (Newen & Bartels, 2007, pp. 294–295). Newen and Bartels (2007) conclude that "although the homing behavior is rather flexible . . . it is nevertheless essentially dependent on key stimuli and is not based on the capacity of object identification. The lack of object representations is the main reason to claim that, in the case of the ant, the underlying representation is only a nonconceptual one" (p. 295). Real conceptual information systems (see our discussion on Alex) can identify and re-identify objects and properties and show a relative stimulus independence and a certain level of abstraction. Classification here is more than stimulus generalization; it involves

class formation and the existence of minimal semantic nets (see Newen & Bartels, 2007, p. 295).

An even more sophisticated category of representations is that of sentence-based or propositional concepts. Newen and Bartels (2007) state that these concepts can so far only be ascribed to humans and the bonobo Kanzi, who is trained to formulate sentences via symbol combination. Kanzi can describe events that occurred when the listener was absent and can express desires (e.g., to walk through a forest via a specific route). They note, "Assuming . . . that the description of Kanzi's capabilities is essentially correct, Kanzi is a paradigmatic case of an animal that has propositional representations because he has conceptual representations . . . and he produces compositional representations for describing events or for expressing his desires. Moreover, there is evidence that his symbolic system forms a basic natural language, partly because he can understand human natural language to a remarkable degree" (pp. 300–301).

18. "In saying that an individual has a theory of mind, we mean that the individual imputes mental states to himself and to others. . . . A system of inferences of this kind is properly viewed as a theory, first, because such states are not directly observable, and second, because the system can be used to make predictions, specifically about the behavior of other organisms" (Premack & Woodruff, 1978, p. 515).

19. Moreover, they adjusted their behavior accordingly when such a dominant individual was replaced with another one who had not witnessed the baiting procedure, thereby demonstrating their ability to keep track of precisely who has witnessed what. Similarly, ravens and scrub jays, for example, seem to possess cognitive representations of what they believe observing conspecifics to know. They accordingly adjust their own caching strategies, to minimize potential pilfering (see, e.g., Bugnyar & Heinrich, 2005; Emery & Clayton, 2001).

20. Someone who understands that beliefs may be false grasps the special relation between mental state and reality: mental states are not direct reflections of reality, but representations, which may or may not be accurate. Thus, understanding false beliefs is considered a "cornerstone of social competence" (Onishi & Baillargeon, 2005, p. 255). It clearly represents the developmental change from a nonrepresentational to a representational ToM.

21. By "monolithic" we mean, with reference to Tomasello et al. (2003a), intrinsically indivisible.

22. Charles Darwin (1879/2004) stated in chapter 6 of *The Descent of Man* that "the mental faculties of man and the lower animals do not differ in kind, although immensely in degree." He concluded that "a difference in degree, however great, does not justify us in placing man in a distinct kingdom" (p. 173). He rejected the idea of a linear *scala naturae*, proceeding from "lower animals" to humans as the "pride of creation." Darwin clearly applied ideas of continuity and gradualism to animal abilities and characteristics and overthrew the dogma of separate creation. Yet although he denied fundamental differences in kind, Darwin's theory of evolution nevertheless allows the possibility that many gradual steps can eventually lead to profound differ-

ences, including with respect to mental capacities (for a good discussion of Darwin and his theories, see Engels, 2007, especially pp. 66–68, 74–76, 146–158, 166, and 197–204). However, according to the theory of evolution, species are ideally matched to their biological niches, and additional development would frequently constitute a biologically unjustified expenditure of energy. Describing animals as "higher" or "lower" in a normative way fails to adequately reflect this reality. Additionally, Darwin's theory allows the possibility of convergent evolution, resulting, for example, in complex mental faculties in animals, such as birds, to whom we are only distantly related.

23. This test is also known as the Location-Change Task. It was developed by Wimmer and Perner (1983) and modified by Baron-Cohen, Leslie, and Frith (1985), who named it the Sally-Anne Test. Other false-belief tests are the Deceptive-Box Test and the Appearance-Reality Test (see Call & Tomasello, 1999, p. 381).

24. This refers to the false-belief test in its several versions.

25. See http://childes.psy.cmu.edu

26. For the different types of contrastives, see Bartsch & Wellmann (1995), p. 32, and Shatz, Wellmann, and Silber (1983), p. 309.

27. Growth and development.

28. Throughout the history of philosophy and anthropology, the human being has always been characterized by the formula "the human is an animal plus X" (Wild, 2008, p. 26). According to this formula, humans have, for example, been characterized as the rational animal, the animal endowed with language and hands, or the animal who forms communities (Aristotle) and as the animal who has a soul (Descartes); has the ability to reason, including moral reasoning (Kant); has knowledge about death (Hölderlin); or has extraordinary adaptive abilities (Dostojewskij). Humans have been described as the animal who is not fixed (Nietzsche), who has an eccentric position (Plessner), or who has a world (Heidegger; see Wild, 2008, p. 26). Several books provide an overview or discussion of these and other classical characterizations that rely on purported cognitive, social, and psychological differences between humans and animals. Matthew Calarco's (2008) book *Zoographies*, for example, challenges the anthropocentrism of the Continental philosophical tradition and calls for the abolition of classical versions of the human–animal distinction. Schütt (1990) presents the main classical writings on animals' (supposedly absent) rationality, from Plato to Schopenhauer. Perler and Wild (2005) and Lurz (2009) concentrate on publications from the 20th and 21st centuries (e.g., addressing language, beliefs, representation, behavior, communication, mind-reading, and consciousness in animals). Kalof and Fitzgerald's *The Animals Reader: The Essential Classic and Contemporary Writings* (2007) presents a variety of perspectives on animals and humans, ranging from Aristotle to postmodern philosophers and from orangutans to cyborgs. It also contains contributions from a large range of cultural historians, ecological writers, and contemporary animal rights activists. An even more detailed approach to the human–animal relationship is given by the six volumes of the *Cultural History of Animals*, covering 4,500 years of human–animal interaction, from Antiquity to the

Modern Age. Each volume also explores philosophical beliefs of the time (Kalof & Resl, 2007).

29. Because of length constraints, we restricted this discussion mainly to the example of great apes. Furthermore, animal cognition research has clearly been primatocentric (Rogers & Kaplan, 2004, p. 195), and ethical discussions often mirror this bias. We acknowledge, however, that many of the arguments presented here could similarly be applied to a range of other captive species.

30. See http://wkprc.eva.mpg.de/english/files/enrichment.htm

31. Additionally, not all problems associated with confining wild animals within zoos can be solved by environmental enrichment or other welfare improvements. Fundamental problems remain with zoos and the arguments used to legitimize them, some of which are explored in the following section. Another example is the purported conservation role of zoos, as promulgated by the World Association of Zoos and Aquariums and others. However, critics note that many zoos in late modernity are undergoing crucial changes, which are contrary to this conservation vision, and are very ethically problematic. It has been claimed that a "Disneyization" of zoos is observable, in which the major foci are entertainment and commercialization (see Beardsworth & Bryman, 2001).

32. DeGrazia derives his rules from his first principle—the principle of nonmaleficence, which asserts that we should not cause "extensive unnecessary harm" to others. Rule 3 prohibits causing significant suffering for the sake of enjoyment. Hence, enjoyment is considered by DeGrazia to be a potential reason for causing harm that lacks sufficient necessity. This is highly relevant to the range of harms that zoos cause to their animals, given that a major purpose of zoos remains human entertainment.

33. However, DeGrazia's list was not exhaustive. Opportunities for foraging behavior, for example, should also be provided.

34. We believe that beings with sufficient characteristics should qualify for the status of personhood. We agree with Kant and others that such persons should posses certain *inalienable* rights, which are theoretically unable to be repudiated, surrendered, annulled, or transferred—that is, *alienated,* in any way. Nevertheless, we also recognize that scenarios existing in the real world (or even other theoretical worlds) may conflict with such theoretical ideals. For example, individuals may deliberately violate the rights of others for personal gain. We do not consider such actions to be morally excusable. Individuals may also violate the rights of others as a result of unconscious reflexes—for example, in self-defense—or as a result of deliberate, rational choices, such as to achieve utilitarian objectives (when defending the *equivalent rights* of a greater number of others). In cases such as these, we consider such violations of otherwise inalienable rights to be morally excusable.

35. For evidence of emotional abilities in animals, see Bekoff (2007). It is possible that the ability to experience emotional states such as empathy may be a prerequisite for understanding and adhering to moral codes of behavior. For evidence of fairness in animals, see Bekoff (2007), pp. 85–109. For evidence of altruistic helping in chimpanzees, see Warneken and Tomasello (2006).

36. White (2007) uses the term "non-human persons," as does the Great Ape Project. DeGrazia (2006) prefers the term "borderline persons." Along with White and the Great Ape Project (Cavalieri & Singer, 1994), others such as Wise (2000) and Diamond (2006) have questioned contemporary perceptions of the moral status of animals or their legal status as human property (e.g., Francione, 1995).

37. Such experiments are mostly intended to benefit humans. However, large-scale systematic reviews have consistently demonstrated that their human benefits are usually minimal (Knight, 2007, 2008a, 2008c; Lindl, Völkel, & Kolar, 2005), and a growing range of non-animal alternative research methodologies exist or are being developed (Knight, 2008b).

38. See Cavalieri and Singer (1994), especially pp. 8 and 12, as well as http://en.wikipedia.org/wiki/Great_Ape_Project

39. There are different traditions underlying the concept of human dignity, including religious ones (asserting that human dignity derives from the creation of humans in the image of god); secular, philosophical ones (relying mainly on reasoning capacity or "natural law" to justify special moral status); and more empirical and historical ones (deducing the idea of human rights *ex negativo* from seeking to prevent recurrences of injustice); see Bayertz (1999). Similarly, traditions of human rights are diverse, ranging, for example, from liberal to naturalistic or ontological ones, and referring to ideas such as those deriving from transcendental philosophy or discourse theory (see Hilpert, 1998, pp. 674–675). However, despite traditional variety, modern secular foundations of human rights adhere closely to the philosophy of enlightenment and mainly to Kantian ideas (see, e.g., Hilpert, 1998, p. 675; similarly Bayertz, 1999, p. 824; Ganslandt, 1995, p. 847; Klenner, 1990, p. 367). Additionally, modern and postmodern philosophy linked the idea of human dignity and rights to the status of the *person*. Here again, influences came, for example, from Boethius, Rawls, and mainly Locke, but the most fundamental and eminent refinement goes back to Kant, who first conceptualized a direct connection between personhood and human rights within the Second Maxim (German: *Selbstzweckformel*) of his categorical imperative (see Sturma, 2002).

40. White refers to Diana Reiss (1990), who described dolphins as "an alien intelligence" (Reiss, 1990, p. 32).

References

Baron-Cohen, S., Leslie, A. M., & Frith, U. (1985). Does the autistic child have a "theory of mind"? *Cognition, 21*, 37–46.

Bartels, A. (2005). Kognitive Ethologie: Repräsentationale Theorien des Verhaltens. In *Strukturale Repräsentation* (pp. 156–186). Paderborn, Germany: Mentis.

Bartsch, K., & Wellmann, H. M. (1995). *Children talk about the mind.* Oxford, England: Oxford University Press.

Bayertz, K. (1999). Menschenwürde. In H. J. Sandkühler, D. Pätzold, A. Regenbogen, & P. Stekeler-Weithofer (Eds.), *Enzyklopädie Philosophie* (Vol. 1, pp. 824–826). Hamburg, Germany: Meiner.

Beardsworth, A., & Bryman, A. E. (2001). The wild animal in late modernity: The case of the disneyization of zoos. *Tourist Studies, 1,* 83–104.

Bekoff, M. (2007). *The emotional lives of animals: A leading scientist explores animal joy, sorrow, and empathy—and why they matter.* Novato, CA: New World Press.

Benz, J. (2004). Epistemische Ausdrücke in der Kindersprache. Eine linguistische Korpusuntersuchung zum Erstspracherwerb mit quantitativer und qualitativer Auswertung. Unpublished master's (state exam) thesis, University of Tübingen, Tübingen, Germany.

Bischof-Köhler, D. (2000). *Kinder auf Zeitreise: Theory of Mind, Zeitverständnis und Handlungsorganisation.* Bern, Switzerland: Huber.

Boesch, C., & Boesch, H. (1983). Optimization of nut-cracking with natural hammers by wild chimpanzees. *Behaviour, 83,* 265–286.

Breuer, T., Ndoundou-Hockemba, M., & Fishlock, V. (2005, November). First observation of tool use in wild gorillas. *PloS Biology, 3*(11), e380.

Bugnyar, T., & Heinrich, B. (2005). Ravens, *Corvus corax,* differentiate between knowledgeable and ignorant competitors. *Proc Biol Sci, 272,* 1641–1646.

Buttlemann, D., Carpenter, M., & Tomasello, M. (2009). Eighteen-month-old infants show false belief understanding in an active helping paradigm. *Cognition, 112,* 337–342.

Calarco, M. (2008). *Zoographies: The question of the animal from Heidegger to Derrida.* New York, NY: Columbia University Press.

Call, J., & Tomasello, M. (1999). A nonverbal false belief task: The performance of children and great apes. *Child Development, 70*(2), 381–395.

Call, J., & Tomasello, M. (2008). Does the chimpanzee have a theory of mind? 30 years later. *Trends in Cognitive Sciences, 12*(5), 187–192.

Cavalieri, P., & Singer, P. (Eds.). (1994). *Menschenrechte für die Große Menschenaffen: Das Great Ape Projekt.* München, Germany: Wilhelm Goldmann.

Conard, N. J. (2007). Cultural evolution in Africa and Eurasia during the middle and late pleistocene. In W. Henke & I. Tattersall (Eds.), *Handbook of paleoanthropology* (pp. 2001–2037). New York, NY: Springer.

Darwin, C. (2004). *The descent of man, and selection in relation to sex* (J. Murray, Ed.). London, England: Penguin Books. (Original work published 1879)

Davidson, D. (1982). Rational animals. *Dialectica, 36*(4), 317–327.

DeGrazia, D. (1996). *Taking animals seriously: Mental life and moral status.* Cambridge, England: Cambridge University Press.

DeGrazia, D. (2006). On the question of personhood beyond *Homo sapiens.* In P. Singer (Ed.), *In defense of animals. The second wave* (pp. 40–53). Oxford, England: Blackwell.

Diamond, J. (2006). *Der dritte Schimpanse: Evolution und Zukunft des Menschen.* Frankfurt am Main, Germany: Fischer.

Emery, N. J., & Clayton, N. S. (2001). Effects of experience and social context on prospective caching strategies by scrub jays. *Nature, 414,* 243–246.

Engels, E.-M. (2007). *Charles Darwin.* München, Germany: C. H. Beck.

Fouts, R. (2000, July/August). My best friend is a chimp. *Psychology Today, 223.* Retrieved from http://www.psychologytoday.com/articles/200007/my-best-friend -is-chimp

Fragaszy, D. M., & Perry, S. (Eds.). (2003). *The biology of traditions: Models and evidence.* Cambridge, England: Cambridge University Press.

Francione, G. L. (1995). *Animals, property, and the law.* Philadelphia, PA: Temple University Press.

Ganslandt, H. R. (1995). Menschenrechte. In J. Mittelstraß (Ed.), *Enzyklopädie Philosophie und Wissenschaftstheorie* (Vol. 2, pp. 846–847). Stuttgart, Germany: Metzler.

Gardner, R. A., & Gardner, B. T. (1975). Evidence for sentence constituents in the early utterances of child and chimpanzee. *Journal of Experimental Psychology— General, 104,* 244–267.

Gigon, O. (2002). Die philosophische Ethik der Griechen. In *Aristoteles: Die Nikoma- chische Ethik. Translation, commentaries and introduction* (pp. 53–75). München, Germany: dtv.

Goodall, J. (1964). Tool-using and aimed throwing in a community of free-living chimpanzees. *Nature, 201,* 1264–1266.

Gopnik, A., Slaughter, V., & Meltzoff, A. N. (1994). Changing your views: How under- standing visual perception can lead to a new theory of the mind. In C. Lewis & P. Mitchell (Eds.), *Children's early understanding of mind: Origins and development* (pp. 157–181). Hillsdale, NY: Erlbaum.

Gould, J. L., & Gould, C. G. (1999). *The animal mind.* New York, NY: Scientific American Library.

Grant, R. (1996). Culture. In P. B. Clarke & A. Linzey (Eds.), *Dictionary of ethics, theology and society* (pp. 206–212). New York, NY: Routledge.

Griffin, D. R. (1976). *The question of animal awareness: Evolutionary continuity of mental experience.* New York, NY: Rockefeller University Press.

Hare, B., Call, J., Agnetta, B., & Tomasello, M. (2000). Chimpanzees know what conspecifics do and do not see. *Animal Behaviour, 59,* 771–785.

Hare, B., Call, J., & Tomasello, M. (2001). Do chimpanzees know what conspecifics know? *Animal Behaviour, 61,* 139–151.

Hauser, M. D. (2001). *Wild minds: What animals really think.* London, England: Penguin Books.

Hermann, L. M., Richards, D. G., & Wolz, J. P. (1984). Comprehension of sentences by bottlenosed dolphins. *Cognition, 16,* 129–219.

Hernandez-Aguilar, R. A., Moore, J., & Rayne Pickering, T. (2007). Savanna chim- panzees use tools to harvest the underground storage organs of plants. *Proceedings of the National Academy of Science, 104*(49), 19210–19213.

Hilpert, K. (1998). Menschenrechte. In W. Korff, L. Beck, & P. Mikat (Eds.), *Lexikon der Bioethik* (Vol. 2, pp. 670–679). Gütersloh, Germany: Gütersloher Verlagshaus.

Hirata, S. (2006). Chimpanzee learning and transmission of tool use to fish for honey. In T. Matsuzawa, M. Tomonaga, & M. Tanaka (Eds.), *Cognitive development in chimpanzees* (pp. 201–213). Tokyo, Japan: Springer.

Hoad, T. F. (Ed.). (1991). *The concise Oxford dictionary of English etymology*. Oxford, England: Clarendon Press.

Hoffmann, L. (2007). Der Mensch und seine Sprache—eine anthropologische Skizze. In A. Redder (Ed.), *Diskurse und Texte. Festschrift für Konrad Ehlich zum 65 Geburtstag* (pp. 21–37). Tübingen, Germany: Stauffenburg.

Horner, V., & Whiten, A. (2005). Causal knowledge and imitation/emulation switching in chimpanzees (*Pan troglodytes*) and children. *Animal Cognition, 8,* 164–181.

Hülsken, C. (2001). *Training in der Theory of Mind-Forschung. Die Rolle von Kohärenz und Feedback in der Entwicklung einer naiven Alltagspsychologie*. Aachen, Germany: Shaker.

Hunt, G. R., & Gray, R. D. (2003). Diversification and cumulative evolution in New Caledonian crow tool manufacture. *Proceedings of the Royal Society of London, 270*(1517), 867–874.

Hutchins, M., Kleiman, D. G., Geist, V., & McDade, M. C. (2003). Mammals and humans: Mammals in zoos. In M. Hutchins, D. G. Kleiman, V. Geist, & M. C. McDade (Eds.), *Grzimek's animal life encyclopedia: Vol. 12. Mammals I* (2nd ed., pp. 203–212). Farmington Hills, MI: Gale Group.

Janik, V. M., Sayigh, L. S., & Wells, R. S. (2006). Signature whistle shape conveys identity information to bottlenose dolphins. *Proceedings of the National Academy of Sciences of the United States of America, 103*(21), 8293–8297.

Jantschke, F. (1997). Zoo- und Zirkustiere. In H. H. Sambraus & A. Steiger (Eds.), *Das Buch vom Tierschutz* (pp. 402–423). Stuttgart, Germany: Ferdinand Enke.

Kalof, L., & Fitzgerald, A. J. (Eds.). (2007). *The animals reader: The essential classic and contemporary writings*. Oxford, England: Berg.

Kalof, L., & Resl, B. (Eds.). (2007). *A cultural history of animals* (Vols. 1–6). Oxford, England: Berg.

Kaminski, J., Call, J., & Tomasello, M. (2008). Chimpanzees know what others know, but not what they believe. *Cognition, 109,* 224–234.

Kant, I. (2008). *Grundlegung zur Metaphysik der Sitten* (T. Valentiner, Ed.). Stuttgart, Germany: Reclam. (Original work published 1785/1786)

Kasten, H. (2005). *4–6 Jahre: Entwicklungspsychologische Grundlagen*. Weinheim, Germany: Beltz.

Kenward, B., Rutz, C., Weir, A. A. S., & Kacelnik, A. (2006). Development of tool use in New Caledonian crows: Inherited action patterns and social influence. *Animal Behaviour, 72,* 1329–1343.

Kenward, B., Weir, A. A. S., Rutz, C., & Kacelnik, A. (2005). Tool manufacture by naïve juvenile crows. *Nature, 433,* 121.

Klann-Delius, G. (1999). Sprachlernleistungen bei subhumanen Primaten. In *Spracherwerb* (pp. 81–85). Stuttgart, Germany: Metzler.

Klenner, H. (1990). Menschenrechte. In H. J. Sandkühler (Ed.), *Europäische Enzyklopädie zu Philosophie und Wissenschaften* (Vol. 3, pp. 366–372). Hamburg, Germany: Meiner.

Knight, A. (2007). The poor contribution of chimpanzee experiments to biomedical progress. *Journal of Applied Animal Welfare Science, 10*(4), 281–308.

Knight, A. (2008a). The beginning of the end for chimpanzee experiments? *Philosophy, Ethics & Humanities in Medicine, 3*(16). Retrieved from http://www.peh-med.com/content/3/1/16

Knight, A. (2008b). Non-animal methodologies within biomedical research and toxicity testing. *Alternatives to Animal Experimentation, 25*(3), 213–231.

Knight, A. (2008c). Systematic reviews of animal experiments demonstrate poor contributions toward human healthcare. *Reviews on Recent Clinical Trials, 3*(2). Retrieved from http://www.benthamdirect.org/pages/b_viewarticle.php?articleID=3148332

Krachun, C., Carpenter, M., Call, J., & Tomasello, M. (2009). A competitive nonverbal false belief task for children and apes. *Developmental Science, 12*(4), 521–535.

Krützen, M., Mann, J., Heithaus, M. R., Connor, R. C., Bejder, L., & Sherwin, W. B. (2005). Cultural transmission of tool use in bottlenosed dolphins. *Proceedings of the National Academy of Sciences of the United States of America, 102*(25), 8939–8943.

Lindl, T., Völkel, M., & Kolar, R. (2005). Tierversuche in der biomedizinischen Forschung. Eine Bestandsaufnahme der klinischen Relevanz von genehmigten Tierversuchsvorhaben: Nach 10 Jahren keine Umsetzung in der Humanmedizin nachweisbar. *Alternatives to Animal Experimentation, 3,* 143–151.

Lonsdorf, E. V. (2006). What is the role of mothers in the acquisition of termite-fishing behaviors in wild chimpanzees (*Pan troglodytes schweinfurthii*)? *Animal Cognition, 9,* 36–46.

Lurz, R. W. (Ed.). (2009). *The philosophy of animal minds.* Cambridge, England: Cambridge University Press.

Matsuzawa, T., Biro, D., Humle, T., Inoue-Nakamura, N., Tonooka, R., & Yamakoshi, G. (2001). Emergence of culture in wild chimpanzees: Education by master-apprenticeship. In T. Matsuzawa (Ed.), *Primate origins of human cognition and behaviour* (pp. 557–574). Tokyo, Japan: Springer.

McFarland, D. (2006). *Oxford dictionary of animal behavior.* Oxford, England: Oxford University Press.

McGrew, W. C., & Tutin, C. E. G. (1978). Evidence for a social custom in wild chimpanzees? *Man, 13,* 234–251.

Newen, A., & Bartels, A. (2007). Animal minds and the possession of concepts. *Philosophical Psychology, 20*(3), 283–308.

Onishi, K. H., & Baillargeon, R. (2005). Do 15-month-old infants understand false beliefs? *Science, 308,* 255–258.

Ouattara, K., Lemasson, A., & Zuberbühler, K. (2009). Campbell's monkeys concatenate vocalizations into context-specific call sequences. *Proceedings of the National Academy of Sciences of the United States of America, 106*(51), 22026–22031.

Pepperberg, I. M. (2002). *The Alex studies: Cognitive and communicative abilities of Grey parrots.* Cambridge, MA: Harvard University Press.

Pepperberg, I. M. (2008). *Alex and me.* New York, NY: Harper Collins.

Perler, D., & Wild, M. (2005). *Der Geist der Tiere. Philosophische Texte zu einer aktuellen Diskussion.* Frankfurt am Main, Germany: Suhrkamp.

Povinelli, D. J., & Vonk, J. (2003). Chimpanzee minds: Suspiciously human? *Trends in Cognitive Sciences, 7*(4), 157–160.

Premack, D., & Woodruff, G. (1978). Does the chimpanzee have a theory of mind? *The Behavioral and Brain Sciences, 4,* 515–526.

Reiss, D. (1990). The dolphin: An alien intelligence. In B. Bova & B. Preiss (Eds.), *First contact: The search for extraterrestrial intelligence* (pp. 31–40). New York, NY: New American Library.

Rogers, L. J., & Kaplan, G. (2004). All animals are *not* equal: The interface between scientific knowledge and legislation for animal rights. In C. R. Sunstein & M. C. Nussbaum (Eds.), *Animal rights: Current debates and new directions* (pp. 175–202). Oxford, England: Oxford University Press.

Rogoff, B. (2003). *The cultural nature of human development.* Oxford, England: Oxford University Press.

Sanz, C., Call, J., & Morgan, D. (2009). Design complexity in termite-fishing tools of chimpanzee (*Pan troglodytes*). *Biology Letters, 5,* 293–296.

Sanz, C., Morgan, D., & Gulick, S. (2004). New insights into chimpanzees, tools and termites from the Congo Basin. *The American Naturalist, 164,* 567–581.

Sanz, C. M., Schöning, C., & Morgan, D. B. (2009). Chimpanzees prey on army ants with specialized tool set. *American Journal of Primatology, 71,* 1–8.

Schütt, H. P. (Ed.). (1990). *Die Vernunft der Tiere.* Frankfurt am Main, Germany: Keip.

Seidenberg, M. S., & Petitto, L. A. (1979). Signing behaviour in apes: A critical review. *Cognition, 7,* 177–215.

Semaw, S. (2000). The world's oldest stone artefacts from Gona, Ethiopia: Their implications for understanding stone technology and patterns of human evolution between 2.6–1.5 million years ago. *Journal of Archaeological Science, 27*(12), 1197–1214.

Seyfarth, R. M., & Cheney, D. L. (1993, February). Wie Affen sich verstehen. *Spektrum der Wissenschaft, 2,* 88–95.

Shatz, M., Wellmann, H. M., & Silber, S. (1983). The acquisition of mental verbs: A systematic investigation of the first reference to mental state. *Cognition, 14,* 301–321.

Sommer, V. (2007). *Darwinisch Denken. Horizonte der Evolutionsbiologie.* Stuttgart, Germany: Hirzel.

Sturma, D. (2002). Person. In H. J. Sandkühler (Ed.), *Enzyklopädie Philosophie* [CD-ROM]. Hamburg, Germany: Meiner.

Taylor, A. H., Hunt, G. R., Holzhaider, J. C., & Gray, R. D. (2007). Spontaneous metatool use by New Caledonian crows. *Current Biology, 17,* 1504–1507.

Tietz, S., & Wild, M. (2006). Denken Tiere? *Information Philosophie, 3,* 14–26.

Tomasello, M., Call, J., & Hare, B. (2003a). Chimpanzees understand psychological states—The question is which ones and to what extent. *Trends in Cognitive Sciences, 7*(4), 153–156.

Tomasello, M., Call, J., & Hare, B. (2003b). Chimpanzees versus humans: It's not that simple. *Trends in Cognitive Sciences, 7*(4), 239–240.

Van Schaik, C. P., Ancrenaz, M., Borgen, G., Galdikas, B., Knott, C. D., Singleton, I., et al. (2003). Orangutan cultures and the evolution of material culture. *Science, 299*(102), 102–105.

Van Schaik, C. P., van Noordwijk, M. A., & Wich, S. A. (2006). Innovation in wild Bornean orangutans (*Pongo pygmaeus wurmbii*). *Behaviour, 143*, 839–876.

Warneken, F., & Tomasello, M. (2006). Altruistic helping in human infants and young chimpanzees. *Science, 311*(5765), 1301–1303.

Weir, A. A. S., Chappell, J., & Kacelnik, A. (2002). Shaping of tools in New Caledonian Crows. *Science, 297*, 981.

White, T. (2007). *In defense of dolphins: The new moral frontier.* Malden, MA: Blackwell.

Whiten, A. (2005). The second inheritance system of chimpanzees and humans. *Nature, 437*, 52–55.

Whiten, A., Goodall, J., McGrew, W. C., Nishida, T., Reynolds, V., Sugiyama, Y., et al. (1999). Cultures in chimpanzees. *Nature, 399*, 682–685.

Whiten, A., Horner, V., & de Waal, F. B. M. (2005). Conformity to cultural norms of tool use in chimpanzees. *Nature, 437*, 737–740.

Wild, M. (2008). *Tierphilosophie zur Einführung.* Hamburg, Germany: Junius.

Wimmer, H., & Perner, J. (1983). Beliefs about beliefs: Representation and constraining function of wrong beliefs in young children's understanding of deception. *Cognition, 13*, 103–128.

Wise, S. M. (2000). Rattling the cage: Toward legal rights for animals. Cambridge, MA: Perseus Books.

Workman, L., & Reader, W. (2004). *Evolutionary psychology: An introduction.* Cambridge, England: Cambridge University Press.

4 Opening the Door: Non-veterinarians and the Practice of Complementary and Alternative Veterinary Medicine

MEGAN SCHOMMER

Growing interest in complementary and alternative veterinary medicine (CAVM) has sparked a debate among veterinarians, who claim such therapeutic modalities fall under the purview of veterinary medicine, and non-veterinarians, who argue that several modalities do not require the rigorous training of a veterinarian to be performed safely. The veterinary profession must proactively redefine its definition of the practice of veterinary medicine in the face of increasing challenges to state practice acts. By looking to human medicine as a model for how to balance conventional and alternative modalities, the profession can develop a system that provides animal caregivers access to CAVM while still safeguarding animal health.

KEY WORDS: acupuncture, alternative, CAVM, complementary, ethics, medicine, veterinary

INTRODUCTION

In the spring of 2008, animal massage therapist Mercedes Clemens received a letter from the Maryland Board of Chiropractic Examiners ordering her to cease and desist from practicing massage on horses or any animals (Syeed, 2008). The order was accompanied by a letter from the State Board of Veterinary Medical Examiners (SBVME) detailing the state's veterinary practice act and warning that any non-veterinarians found to be in violation of the act "may face criminal prosecution for practicing veterinary medicine without a veterinary license" ("Massage," 2008). When Ms. Clemens brought suit against both the state's chiropractic board and the veterinary board to defend her right to practice massage on animals, the veterinary board issued another letter in which it clarified that although massage for the specific treatment of a specific disease or disorder would qualify as the practice of veterinary medicine, what Ms. Clemens was doing with horses would not be prohibited by the practice act. The board wrote that the lawsuit "does not contain a single allegation that she is offering—or advertising—her massage services for the purposes of treating or diagnosing disease or injury of horses. Thus, SBMVE regulatory oversight is not an issue at this time" ("Massage," 2008). Ms. Clemens's attorney responded, "The Veterinary Board's change in position simply acknowledges the obvious: limiting animal massage to licensed veterinarians makes no more sense than limiting human massage to medical doctors. Animal massage is a skill that requires some hands-on training and common sense around animals but not four years of veterinary school at a cost of $150,000" ("Massage," 2008).

Although the veterinary board would argue that its position was merely clarified, not changed, this declaration of success by Ms. Clemens's attorney illustrates a growing concern in veterinary medicine. Cases and legislation involving complementary and alternative veterinary medicine (CAVM) for animals are becoming more common, yet the strategies for addressing these issues vary widely, and the outcomes are not always clear (Macejko, 2008). These cases generally involve challenges or changes to state veterinary practice acts (VPAs), the statutes in each state that stipulate what constitutes the practice of veterinary medicine. In the spring of 2008, the Minnesota legislature passed an exemption to the state VPA that allows human chiropractors to practice on animals, provided they complete 210 additional hours of animal-specific training and animals are referred for chiropractic treatment by a veterinarian (State of Minnesota, 2008c). At the same time, Louisiana introduced legislation that would allow licensed physical therapists to work on animals following a health clearance by a veterinarian (Department of Legislative and Regulatory Affairs, 2008a). In 2006, Maryland approved legislation that allows licensed human acupuncturists to work on animals with veterinary oversight and animal-specific training (Department of Legislative and Regulatory Affairs, 2007). Also in 2006, a proposed bill in Arizona would have exempted a wide range of CAVM therapies, including acupressure, massage, nutritional counseling, and animal communication, from the state's VPA (Department of Legislative and Regulatory Affairs, 2006). Although a very small portion of veterinary medicine is devoted to complementary and alternative therapies (only 21 out of 1,667 practitioners in Minnesota registered with the American Veterinary Medical Association [AVMA] identified themselves as practicing CAVM; American

Veterinary Medical Association, 2009), CAVM is a hot topic in state legislatures because it represents a novel and undefined area of veterinary medicine.

THE CONFLICTS BETWEEN
VETERINARY PRACTICE ACTS AND CAVM

The National Center for Complementary and Alternative Medicine (2009) defines complementary and alternative medicine as a "group of diverse medical and health care systems, practices, and products that are not generally considered part of conventional medicine" (para. 1). Much of the recent legislation regarding CAVM has sought to add exemptions to state VPAs to allow non-veterinarians to practice CAVM modalities such as animal massage. Similarly, court cases regarding CAVM have involved non-veterinarians defending their right to work on animals, as in Mercedes Clemens's case. Currently, most states include CAVM therapies under the scope of veterinary medicine. As described by the American Veterinary Medical Law Association,

> the focus is not upon whether "alternative," "complementary," or "holistic," etc. is expressly mentioned in a state's statutory definition of the "practice of veterinary medicine" but, rather, upon whether the activity or endeavor being undertaken with regard to an animal involves, for example, diagnosis, treatment, correction, changing, alleviating, or preventing animal disease, illness, pain, deformity, defect, injury, or other physical, dental, or mental conditions of an animal. If the activity or endeavor does involve such, then it comes within the statutory definition of the "practice of veterinary medicine," unless specifically exempted elsewhere in that state's *veterinary practice act*. (American Veterinary Medical Law Association & Richard, 2004, p. 2)

The VPAs ensure that those offering animal health care services to the public are qualified and competent (Wilson, 2000). Veterinary boards certify that veterinarians have met minimum qualifying standards in order to be allowed to work with animals, but there are no uniform standards for assessing the competency of non-veterinary CAVM practitioners. Veterinarians can be disciplined or have their licenses revoked for harming animals, but "the only recourse an animal owner has against a layperson creating harm to an animal is litigation. There, only a finite amount of money may be collected, and the nonregulated layperson may not be prevented from working elsewhere, even if found guilty" (Osborne, 2008, p. 1197).

The VPAs' definitions of veterinary medicine have served the profession well so far because veterinarians have generally been the only option for people to turn to for safe, accurate, and effective health care for the animals in their care. In the past, the unauthorized practice of veterinary medicine or surgery usually involved laypeople trying to replace veterinarians by practicing surgery, diagnosing and treating animal diseases, or administering preventive treatments such as vaccines. However, today, there are many non-veterinarians trying to offer services not traditionally provided by veterinarians. By definition, complementary and alternative medicine (CAM) is "a group of diverse medical and health care systems, practices, and products that are not presently considered to be part of conventional medicine" (National Center for Complementary and Alternative Medicine, 2009). Non-veterinary CAM practitioners, from untrained laypeople to those highly trained in one particular modality such as doctors of chiropractic, are attempting to respond to consumer demand for CAVM therapies (Macejko, 2008). Many veterinarians argue that this trend is dangerous for animal and public health. CAVM practitioners argue that VPAs are unfairly limiting all types of therapies to veterinarians, and the current requirements are effectively a ban on CAVM modalities. The question facing veterinary medicine is whether all animal health care services require the level of training and skill of a veterinarian. Although some CAVM modalities are riskier than others, many VPAs paint all alternative medicine with a broad brush—if a modality is (or is advertised to be) therapeutic, it is considered the practice of veterinary medicine (American Veterinary Medical Law Association & Richard, 2004).

POTENTIAL COSTS OF BROAD VETERINARY PRACTICE ACTS

One could defend the vaguely worded VPAs and argue that all therapeutic treatments are and should remain under the definition of the practice of veterinary medicine. However, in 2003, veterinarian Dr. David Ramey observed,

> Given that most people providing alternative treatments to humans are not medical doctors, it is difficult to rationalize the position that those providing such treatments to animals must be veterinarians. Protests to the contrary from factions within the veterinary profession may be justifiably criticized as turf protection. If professionals are unable to demonstrate that CAVM practices must be applied by veterinarians, challenges to the veterinary practice acts should be expected to occur with increasing regularity. (p. 1681)

Indeed, Dr. Ramey was correct about challenges to VPAs. Legislatures and courts are increasingly agreeing with non-veterinarians that modalities such as massage should not be limited to veterinarians, despite protests from state veterinary medical associations and the AVMA. Following the removal of the word "human" from the phrase "human body" in the state acupuncture act, the Maryland attorney general issued a legal opinion that human acupuncturists could work on animals without being licensed veterinarians (Osborne, 2008). In April 2007, the governor of Colorado signed into law a bill allowing physical therapists to practice on animals (Brown, 2007). In the spring of 2008, chiropractors were exempted from the Minnesota VPA provided they receive additional animal-specific training and a referral from a veterinarian (Department of Legislative and Regulatory Affairs, 2008b).

The current trends in legislation provide evidence that if veterinary practice acts do not open the door to non-veterinary CAVM practitioners, these practitioners will force change through legal and governmental channels. The onus is on veterinarians to prove that CAVM modalities are unsafe if practiced by non-veterinarians, and in general, states are agreeing with lay practitioners rather than veterinarians. This trend is dangerous because it takes control of animal health decisions out of the hands of veterinarians and places veterinary medical associations on the defensive. Even in cases where veterinary boards successfully defend the practice act, they tend to do so at an ethical cost. In 2006, proposed legislation in Arizona would have allowed exemptions in the state VPA for laypeople practicing homeopathy, acupressure, animal communication, and a number of other CAVM modalities. The AVMA prepared a statement describing why each proposed exemption would be dangerous for animal and public health (Department of Legislative and Regulatory Affairs, 2006). Regarding animal communication, the AVMA wrote, "Even setting aside the fact that telepathic communication with animals is not scientifically proven, empowering individuals to practice 'animal communication' without any supervision leaves the door wide open for consumers to be taken advantage of and for animals to be potentially mistreated" (Animal Communication section, para. 1). Regarding flower essence therapy, the statement argued, "The specifically stated purpose of flower essence therapy and aromatherapy is to enhance health of animals. This is a function clearly designated to veterinarians in the practice act" (Acupressure section, bullet 2).

ETHICAL CONCERNS AND CAVM

The incorporation of CAVM modalities into the definition of "veterinary medicine" raises a number of ethical concerns for individual veterinarians and the profession as a whole. In an article about his "four principles" approach to medical ethics, Professor Raanan Gillon (1994) wrote, "We need to ensure that we can provide the benefits we profess (thus 'professional') to be able to provide" (p. 185). Although including CAVM modalities in a state's VPA does not necessarily oblige all veterinarians to practice such modalities, it does seem to imply that if animal caregivers wished to seek out such modalities, they would be able to find veterinarians who offer them. Yet veterinary schools in general offer very few courses about CAVM, and there is no professionally recognized board certification program in CAVM. Veterinarians are also obligated by the AVMA Guidelines for Complementary and Alternative Veterinary Medicine to critically evaluate the scientific evidence available before utilizing a CAVM modality (American Veterinary Medical Association, 2007), leading an ethical veterinarian to avoid modalities with no scientific evidence such as animal communication. If the profession is failing to provide the benefits professed in the AVMA's definition of "veterinary medicine," then the profession is not living up to its professional duties, and animal caregivers are left with little recourse if they desire alternative treatment modalities.

Dr. Bernard Rollin (2002), animal welfare philosopher and ethicist, has written about Aesculapian authority, the "uniquely powerful authority vested in those that society perceives as healers" (p. 1144). Aesculapian authority is what allows doctors to make patients (or patients' guardians, in the case of pediatricians or veterinarians) change their lifestyles, undergo painful surgical procedures, or remain bedridden for weeks. For all medical professionals, veterinarians included, this authority imbues a moral responsibility to take extreme care with what they tell patients (or patients' caregivers). As CAVM becomes more widespread and animal caregivers seek such modalities, it becomes tempting for veterinarians to give in to demands to provide such therapies, even in the absence of evidence that they are actually effective.

> Many clinicians have begun to provide such therapies for a variety of reasons. These include: "The clients demand them" and "They will get them from somewhere; it might as well be me." Yet the concept of Aesculapian authority is seriously impeded by such reasoning, for one of the sources of that authority is one's medical expertise, based in the best knowledge one can garner. If one prostitutes that authority to endorse non-remedies posing as remedies, it can well lead to erosion of that authority, particularly when the social pendulum swings, as it inevitably will, away from fascination with therapies that have no basis in proof of efficacy and are, in many cases, incompatible with what we know of nature. Like one's reputation for veracity, medical credibility, once lost, is difficult to regain. (Rollin, 2002, p. 1148)

When the AVMA's Department of Legislative and Regulatory Affairs (2006) argued that a bill in Arizona should include animal communication in the state's VPA, "even setting aside the fact that telepathic communication with animals is not scientifically proven" (Animal Communication section, para. 1), it attempted to argue that animal communication qualifies as the practice of medicine despite never having been shown to help animals. Through such actions, the AVMA runs the risk of assuring consumers that telepathic communication is a valid form of veterinarian medicine, and because of Aesculapian authority, consumers are less likely to question their veterinarians than non-veterinarians offering animal communication. This would seem to be counter to what the AVMA hoped to accomplish by limiting the practice of "animal communication" to veterinarians. Rather than attempting to limit the practice of baseless therapies by incorporating them into the state's practice act, the AVMA could have used Aesculapian authority to its advantage by creating strong statements advising animal caregivers against seeking such therapies. Dr. Rollin suggests that veterinarians should not dismiss clients' desires to seek CAVM therapies, nor should they offer to provide therapies that they know to be ineffective. Instead, he suggests that veterinarians should use Aesculapian authority to attempt to determine why caregivers are interested in such therapies. "More empathy in human dimensions of medicine," according to Rollin (2002), "may well help to end people's desperate search for magic cures" (p. 1149).

Writing on the subject of incorporating grooming parlors into veterinary clinics, veterinary ethicist and Tufts School of Veterinary Medicine professor Jerrold Tannenbaum (1989) argued that "these practitioners . . . will be assisting in the demise of the image of the veterinarian as a dignified provider of medical care. Poodle cuts, shampooing, colognes, and fancy ribbons do not belong in the same place in which momentous issues of life and death are confronted by a healer" (p. 245). Similarly, the incorporation of non-evidence-based modalities into the definition of veterinary medicine risks degrading the image of veterinary medicine as a whole. The profession cannot consider such modalities to be both "non-evidence-based" and "medicine" without weakening the definition of the practice of veterinary medicine itself. This creates a contradiction between the justifiable desire to safeguard the public and animal welfare and the profession's obligation to maintain the "skills and virtues that make up excellence in the practice of veterinary medicine" (C. Taliaferro, personal communication, November 7, 2009). This ethical contradiction also opens the veterinary profession to public charges of turf guarding and financial motivation.

If the public starts to view professional boards as self-serving, the profession risks the public trust necessary to be allowed to self-regulate. According to Jane Hern (2000), secretary of the Royal College of Veterinary Medicine, "professions which appear to look after their own will be looked on less favourably by government and the public generally . . . It might be said that the laity are striking back against the conspiracy which they perceived the professions to be guilty of" (p. 70).

HUMAN MEDICINE AS A MODEL FOR COOPERATION
BETWEEN PROFESSIONALS AND LAYPERSONS

The profession should not be forced to redefine the practice act in response to court cases or legislation, given that veterinarians are the best qualified to decide what should constitute the practice of veterinary medicine. Yet practice acts that are too broad leave the veterinary profession on shaky ethical ground when the acts are challenged. The profession should instead make the VPAs much more specific, including details about when, how, and why a particular non-veterinarian would be allowed to perform therapeutic treatments on animals. If the profession is proactive in opening the door to CAVM practitioners, rather than waiting for legislation or case law forced by CAM practitioners to determine what an exemption entails, it can have control of the provisions of each exemption. Creating a VPA that has a strong ethical foundation will also create a VPA that can stand up to challenges in court far more easily than what the American Veterinary Medical Law Association has called today's "broad and well-nigh all encompassing definition of the 'practice of veterinary medicine'" (American Veterinary Medical Law Association & Richard, 2004, p. 3).

Because CAM modalities are relatively new to veterinary medicine, veterinarians have no framework for coordinating animal health care with non-veterinarians. The human medical field has a much longer history of coordinating patient care among MDs and non-physician modalities such as chiropractic treatment, physical therapy, and massage. Although human and veterinary medicine are not and should not be considered directly comparable, the relationship between physicians and CAM practitioners could offer helpful insight into how veterinarians might relate to CAVM practitioners. For example, we can explore how the Physician Practice Act in Minnesota clarifies the relationships between various types of health care practitioners (State of Minnesota, 2008b). Human medicine organizes medical therapies into a hierarchy based on the amount of education required to practice and the relative risk involved in the practice of the therapy. At the top of the hierarchy are the most highly trained medical professionals, the medical doctors (MDs) or doctors of osteopathy (DOs). Below these professionals are members of other health care professions, including chiropractors, nurses, and acupuncturists. The professional levels are regulated by professional boards and are expected to act according to a professional code of ethics. Below these are members of specialized health care occupations, such as massage therapists or aromatherapists. Below these are people who work to promote general health and wellness, such as personal athletic trainers, yoga teachers, or dietary consultants. The high end of the hierarchy involves people who are in control of the riskiest aspects of health care, including diagnosing, performing surgery, or treating diseases. The low end of the hierarchy involves people who provide low-risk services that can be therapeutic but that are not sufficient for the sole treatment of disease or injury. This system allows for a high degree of cooperation among the various health care providers while ensuring the most invasive modalities have a relatively high degree of regulation and oversight. This system also allows many unlicensed CAM practitioners, such as massage therapists, to practice freely but with regulatory oversight that can prevent incompetent practitioners from being allowed to work in the state.

Veterinary medicine could divide CAVM therapies into a similar hierarchy based on the amount of specialized training required to safely perform the modality. Unlike the human system, we have to account for the fact that people most qualified to administer a particular modality on humans, such as a doctor of chiropractic (DC), have not been required to learn anything about animal anatomy or physiology. Further, the veterinary profession must build in safeguards to prevent animal caregivers from utilizing lay practitioners as a replacement for veterinary care instead of as adjunctive therapy. Some states, including Minnesota, have already developed a system that allows DCs to practice on animals while still having veterinary oversight and proving some competency in working on animals. Minnesota's VPA contains an exemption for licensed chiropractors who take 210 hours in animal-specific chiropractic training and requires a veterinary referral (State of Minnesota, 2008c). This veterinary oversight helps to protect animals from receiving chiropractic treatment inappropriately (i.e., getting a chiropractic adjustment for a "sore back" that actually is caused by abdominal pain) while still allowing the DC to work on the animal without being employed by the veterinarian. Further, because chiropractors are regulated by a professional board, chiropractors who provide incompetent care to an animal can face disciplinary action or risk the loss of their license by the chiropractic board (State of Minnesota, 2008a). The type of exemption devised for Minnesota animal chiropractic therapy opens the channels of communication about an adjunctive modality offered by fellow medical professionals, allowing veterinarians to "collaborate with other professionals in the quest for knowledge and professional development," as encouraged by the AVMA's (2009) Principles of Veterinary Medical Ethics (Professional Behavior section, para. J). However, this exemption still allows veterinarians to remain the primary gatekeepers of this therapeutic treatment for animals.

The second major concern when creating exemptions to allow non-veterinarians to work on animals is that animal caregivers will seek less expensive CAVM therapies as a replacement for veterinary medicine rather than as an adjunctive therapy. In order to ensure that therapies provided by non-veterinarians are adjunctive rather than used in place of conventional veterinary care, such practitioners should require their clients to provide evidence of a valid veterinarian-client-patient relationship (V-C-P-R). This requirement could also minimize the risk that an animal might present to a non-veterinarian with a zoonotic disease (a disease transmitted from animals to humans) by requiring evidence of appropriate preventive health care such as current vaccinations and regular fecal exams. More invasive therapies such as chiropractic treatments are more likely to cause harm to an animal, and thus the evidence of a V-C-P-R must be stronger than for less invasive therapies such as massage. The Minnesota VPA's exemption for chiropractors requires animal caregivers to obtain a referral from a veterinarian so that there is not only evidence of a valid V-C-P-R, but also a direct veterinary recommendation that chiropractic treatment is a safe and appropriate modality for that animal. Providing exemptions for non-veterinarians to have a role in animal health need not provide a means for animal caregivers to avoid utilizing veterinary care altogether.

CONCLUSION

Rather than increasingly having to defend the practice act, it would be in the best interest of veterinarians, animals, and the public for veterinary boards to proactively redefine their practice acts such that they are both legally and ethically defensible. The recent challenges to state VPAs regarding CAVM modalities are just one symptom of a larger issue that, left unresolved, will continue to fester in animal and veterinary communities. If the profession is proactive, we can ensure that animals, their caregivers, and their veterinarians have access to alternative modalities while still maintaining adequate veterinary involvement to ensure the health and safety of animals and the public.

Acknowledgments

Special thanks to all those whose insightful thoughts and discussions helped me in exploring this complex topic: Veterinarians Keum Hwa Choi, Margie Garrett, Lynelle Graham, Donn Griffith, Shelly Lenz, Marcia Martin, Richard Palmquist, Jim Sinning, Lisa Tuzo, James Wilson, Julie Wilson, and Susan Wynn; veterinary technician Lisa Garrity; animal massage therapist Dawn Brown Cook; philosophy professor Charles Taliaferro; classmates and colleagues Kate O'Conor, Rebecca Abrams, and Sara Shepard; and husband Christopher Schommer. Thanks also to the Society for Veterinary Medical Ethics and Waltham for sponsoring the student essay scholarship contest that led to the creation of this article.

References

American Veterinary Medical Association. (2007, November). *AVMA guidelines for complementary and alternative medicine.* Retrieved from http://www.avma.org /issues/policy/comp_alt_medicine.asp

American Veterinary Medical Association. (2008, April). *Principles of veterinary medical ethics of the AVMA.* Retrieved from http://www.avma.org/issues/policy /ethics.asp

American Veterinary Medical Association. (2009). *AVMA member directory.* Retrieved from http://www.avma.org/myavma/directory/search.asp

American Veterinary Medical Law Association & Richard, K. (2004, October 7). *The law and complementary & alternative medicine.* Retrieved from American Holistic Veterinary Medical Association website: http://ahvma.org/images/pdf_files /whitepaper-cavm.pdf

Brown, J. (2007, April 16). Animal protections pass house. *Denver Post.* Retrieved from http://www.denverpost.com

Department of Legislative and Regulatory Affairs. (2006, February). *State legislative resources.* Retrieved on March 30, 2009, from American Veterinary Medical Association website: http://www.avma.org/advocacy/state/issues/la_legis_bill_ smplanalysis.asp

Department of Legislative and Regulatory Affairs. (2007, January 16). *State legislative resources.* Retrieved on March 30, 2009, from American Veterinary Medical Association website: http://www.avma.org/advocacy/state/legislative_updates /legislative_update_070116.asp

Department of Legislative and Regulatory Affairs. (2008a, April 14). *State legislative resources.* Retrieved on March 30, 2009, from American Veterinary Medical Association website: http://www.avma.org/advocacy/state/legislative_updates /legislative_update_080414.asp

Department of Legislative and Regulatory Affairs. (2008b, May 14). *State legislative resources.* Retrieved on March 30, 2009, from American Veterinary Medical Association website: http://www.avma.org/advocacy/state/legislative_updates/legislative_update_080515.asp

Gillon, R. (1994, July 16). Medical ethics: Four principles plus attention to scope. *British Medical Journal, 309,* 184–188.

Hern, J. (2000). Professional conduct and self-regulation. In G. Legood (Ed.), *Veterinary ethics: An introduction* (pp. 63–73). New York, NY: Continuum.

Macejko, C. (2008, December 1). State boards wage war on lay persons practicing veterinary medicine. *DVM Newsmagazine.* Retrieved from http://veterinarynews.dvm360.com

Massage therapist sues Maryland state vet board—the state vet board responds. (2008, July 11). *The Equiery.* Retrieved from http://www.equiery.com/VetLawsuit/VetLawsuit.htm

National Center for Complementary and Alternative Medicine. (2009, January 9). *What is complementary and alternative medicine?* Retrieved from http://nccam.nih.gov/health/whatiscam

Osborne, M. (2008). Scope-of-practice laws draw attacks. *Journal of the American Veterinary Medical Association, 233,* 1194–1197.

Ramey, D. (2003). Regulatory aspects of complementary and alternative medicine. *Journal of the American Veterinary Medical Association, 222,* 1679–1682.

Rollin, B. (2002). The use and abuse of Aesculapian authority in veterinary medicine. *Journal of the American Veterinary Medical Association, 220,* 1144–1149.

State of Minnesota. (2008a). *Chiropractic practice act.* Minnesota Statutes Chapter 148. Retrieved from https://www.revisor.leg.state.mn.us/data/revisor/statute/2008/148/2008–148.pdf

State of Minnesota. (2008b). *Physician practice act.* Minnesota Statutes Chapter 147. Retrieved from https://www.revisor.leg.state.mn.us/data/revisor/statute/2008/147/2008–147.pdf

State of Minnesota. (2008c). *Veterinary practice act.* Minnesota Statutes Chapter 156. Retrieved from https://www.revisor.leg.state.mn.us/data/revisor/statute/2008/156/2008–156.pdf

Syeed, N. (2008, August 11). Md. woman sues state for right to massage horses. *Associated Press.* Retrieved from LexisNexis Academic Universe.

Tannenbaum, J. (1989). *Veterinary ethics.* Baltimore, MD: Williams and Wilkins.

Wilson, J. (2000). *Contracts, benefits, and practice management for the veterinary profession.* Yardley, PA: Priority Press.

5 An Evaluative Review of Theories Related to Animal Cruelty

ELEONORA GULLONE

The two dominant theories relating to animal cruelty are critically reviewed. These are (1) the violence graduation hypothesis and (2) the deviance generalization hypothesis. The outcomes indicate very high consistency with the broader antisocial behavior and aggression literature, which is large and very robust. This strongly supports the validity of the animal cruelty theory proposals. Proposals that animal cruelty is one of the earliest indicators of externalizing disorders and that it is a marker of development along a more severe trajectory of antisocial and aggressive behaviors are supported. The implications of these conclusions are discussed.

KEY WORDS: animal cruelty, human aggression, antisocial behavior, comorbidity, violence graduation hypothesis, deviance generalization hypothesis

The purpose of this article is to provide an evaluative review of the two major theoretical perspectives related to the etiology of animal cruelty: the violence graduation hypothesis and the deviance generalization hypothesis. The article begins by providing a definition of animal cruelty.

ANIMAL CRUELTY DEFINED

Among the most often cited definitions of animal cruelty is that put forth by Frank Ascione, who defined it as "socially unacceptable behavior that intentionally causes unnecessary pain, suffering, or distress to and/or the death of an animal" (Ascione, 1999, p. 51). Others (e.g., Felthous & Kellert, 1986) define *substantial cruelty to animals* as a behavior pattern that deliberately, repeatedly,

Journal of Animal Ethics 4(1): 37–57

and unnecessarily causes hurt to vertebrate animals in such a way that is likely to cause them serious injury. Brown (1988) defined cruelty as "unnecessary suffering knowingly inflicted on a sentient being (animal or human)" (p. 3) and argued that suffering may be of a physical type. That is, it may be the sensation of pain, or it may be distress. It may also be psychological hurt, such as would be the case with maternal deprivation.

Summarizing the different views on animal cruelty, Dadds, Turner, and McAloon (2002) noted that most definitions include a behavioral dimension that can include acts of omission (e.g., neglect) or acts of commission (e.g., beating; cf. Brown, 1988). Another key characteristic is the indication that the behavior occurred purposely—that is, with deliberateness and without ignorance. An additional definitional criterion is that the behavior brings about physical and/ or psychological harm. Incorporating these definitional criteria, Dadds (2008) defined animal cruelty as a repetitive and proactive behavior (or pattern of behavior) intended to cause harm to sentient creatures.

Given these considerations, the definition of animal cruelty adopted herein is as follows:

> Animal cruelty is behavior performed repetitively and proactively by an in-
> dividual with the deliberate intention of causing harm (i.e., pain, suffering,
> distress, and/or death) to an animal with the understanding that the animal
> is motivated to avoid that harm. Included in this definition are both physical
> harm and psychological harm. As with the literature on human aggression,
> animal cruelty at the more extreme end of the aggression dimension (e.g.,
> burning while alive, torture, murder, rape, assault as compared to teasing,
> hitting, tormenting), should be considered a violent subtype of animal cruelty.

This conceptualization of animal cruelty is relevant to the predominant theoretical perspectives that have been put forth regarding its etiology. These perspectives are reviewed in the following section.

THEORETICAL PERSPECTIVES OF ANIMAL CRUELTY

The Violence Graduation Hypothesis

Several research studies published predominantly in the 1970s to 1990s inves-
tigated the proposal that animal cruelty in childhood is predictive of violence toward humans in adulthood. These studies (e.g., Felthous & Yudowitz, 1977; Kellert & Felthous, 1985; Merz-Perez, Heide, & Silverman, 2001; Ressler, Burgess, & Douglas, 1988) typically involved examination of the childhood histories of adult criminals and psychiatric patients. Their findings provided support

for a significant association between violence in adulthood and animal cruelty, including severe animal torture and killing, in childhood and adolescence.

In much of their work, Felthous and Kellert (Felthous, 1980; Felthous & Kellert, 1986; Kellert & Felthous, 1985) compared the retrospective reports of aggressive and nonaggressive criminals with those of noncriminals. For example, their 1985 study involved results based on personal interviews with 152 criminals and noncriminals (32 aggressive criminals, 18 moderately aggressive criminals, 50 nonaggressive criminals, and 52 noncriminals). They found that 25% of aggressive criminals reported five or more incidents of animal cruelty during their childhood, compared to less than 6% of moderately aggressive or nonaggressive criminals.

In 1987, these same researchers published a review of 15 controlled studies in which they examined "whether the scientific literature supports an association between a pattern of repeated, substantial cruelty to animals in childhood and later violence against people that is serious and recurrent" (Felthous & Kellert, 1987, p. 710). On the basis of their review, they concluded that "the literature suggests an association between a pattern of cruelty to animals in childhood or adolescence and a pattern of dangerous and recurrent aggression against people at a later age" (Felthous & Kellert, 1987, p. 716).

Based on such work, the violence graduation hypothesis (VGH) was proposed. According to this hypothesis, animal cruelty may be a form of rehearsal for human-directed violence. In developmental terms, it has been proposed that animal cruelty in childhood is an incremental step toward violence directed at humans. The Humane Society of the United States (1997) coined the term "first strike" to refer to this association. In support of this proposal, animal welfare societies in particular have drawn upon cases of highly publicized serial killers who were abusive toward animals in their childhood.

Other research that has been argued to show support for the VGH includes the work by Tingle, Barnard, Robbins, Newman, and Hutchinson (1986). This study compared the childhood and adolescent experiences of rapists and pedophiles to determine whether the two types of offenders are best grouped separately. Although this was not the focus of the study, the results showed that there were high frequencies of animal cruelty in both groups, with nearly half of the rapists and more than one quarter of the pedophiles having harmed animals as children.

In their study involving 45 violent and 45 nonviolent inmates in a maximum-security prison, Merz-Perz et al. (2001) found that violent inmates reported animal cruelty in their childhoods at a rate three times greater than the nonviolent inmates. When cruelty toward companion animals, as compared to cruelty toward other animals, was examined, the difference between the two groups was even greater, with 26% of the violent group reporting companion animal cruelty compared to 7% of the nonviolent group.

In a review related to a more specifically defined sample of 11 youth involved in 9 incidents of multiple school shootings, Verlinden, Hersen, and Thomas (2000) found that of the 11 perpetrators involved, 5 (45%) had histories of alleged animal cruelty. Also in relation to a very specifically defined sample of convicted serial murderers, Wright and Hensley (2003) reported that out of 354 cases of serial murder, 75 perpetrators (21%) had committed cruelty to animals during their childhood.

In an examination involving 261 inmates from medium- and high-security prisons, Tallichet and Hensley (2004) found support for the proposal that repeated acts of animal cruelty in childhood or adolescence are predictive of subsequent violent crime. In a replication of this study, Hensley, Tallichet, and Dutkiewicz (2009) examined survey data of 180 inmates from a medium- and maximum-security prison. As predicted, they found that recurrent acts of childhood animal cruelty were predictive of later recurrent acts of violence toward humans.

In other research, Gleyzer, Felthous, and Holzer (2002) compared 48 criminal defendants with a history of substantial animal cruelty and a matched sample of defendants without a history of animal cruelty, to investigate whether animal cruelty was associated with a diagnosis of antisocial personality disorder in adulthood. They found support for the hypothesized relationship between a history of childhood cruelty to animals and such a diagnosis in adulthood. They also found that a diagnosis of antisocial personality disorder or the presence of antisocial personality traits was statistically significantly more prevalent in the animal cruelty group.

In addition to the research investigations examining the link between childhood animal cruelty and adult violence toward humans, there is support for the relationship in the histories of adults who are habitually violent, such as multiple murderers and serial killers. These data are reviewed next.

Federal Bureau of Investigation Work

According to Brantley, now retired from the Federal Bureau of Investigation's Investigative Support Unit, animal cruelty is prominent in the histories of people who are habitually violent. Their histories also reveal violence toward other children and adults, as well as the destruction of property (Lockwood

& Church, 1996). The connection between cruelty to animals and aggression against humans was first acknowledged by the Federal Bureau of Investigation (FBI) in the late 1970s when 36 multiple murderers were interviewed. Brantley (2007) provided a checklist of risk indicators for future violence. This list includes characteristics that are descriptive of what are otherwise referred to as externalizing disorders. These disorders are defined by personality traits that are disinhibitory in nature. Examples include low frustration tolerance, aggression, impulsivity, irritability, arrest history, early adjustment problems, juvenile delinquency, chemical abuse, and alcohol abuse.

A number of high-profile mass and serial murder cases are cited as support for the violence graduation hypothesis (Petersen & Farrington, 2007), including the cases of Kip Kinkel and Luke Woodham, each of whom was responsible for a school shooting. Both were also known to have been cruel to animals. The highly publicized Columbine High School shootings carried out by Eric Harris and Dylan Klebold resulted in the killing of 12 students and a teacher. More than 20 other people were also injured. Both males were known to brag about mutilating animals (PETA, 2003). In April 1996, Martin Bryant was responsible for one of Australia's most terrible mass murders. He killed a total of 35 people in a 19-hour rampage in Port Arthur, Tasmania. At 11 years old, he was found to have tortured and harassed animals. It was also reported that he tormented his baby sister. Animal cruelty is highly prominent in the histories of serial killers as well (Lockwood & Hodge, 1998).

Although the validity of accounts of serial killers and mass murderers can be criticized on the basis that such accounts are secondhand and retrospective in nature, it is noteworthy that these cases have substantial commonalities, including a strong suggestion of the presentation of callous-unemotional traits and pathological behavior.

Evaluation of the Violence Graduation Hypothesis

The research and other data cited as support for the VGH have been criticized as methodologically limited (e.g., Beirne, 2004). The proposed limitations include that the research tends to be retrospective in nature and is primarily based on the self-reports provided by institutionalized individuals. Self-reports have the problem of potentially being biased, and retrospective reporting has the limitation of possible recall error. Researchers have called for longitudinal research that follows children through to adulthood in order to soundly investigate the hypothesis. It has also been argued that research is needed to rule out the possibility that the relationship between animal cruelty and human aggression is the result of other variables or a third shared factor (Flynn, 2011), such as antisocial traits.

Perhaps the most significant limitation is that the majority of studies have investigated the cruelty connection in highly aggressive and incarcerated criminals, thereby limiting the generalizability of the hypothesis. Consequently, within this theoretical framework, there is the tendency to ignore possible correlations between animal cruelty and other less severe forms of antisocial behavior or criminal behavior (cf. Arluke, Levin, Luke, & Ascione, 1999).

In a recent study (Alys, Wilson, Clarke, & Toman, 2009), the problem of restricted sampling was addressed by comparing three groups of male adults. The first group comprised an incarcerated sample of male homicidal sex offenders with a mean age of around 35 years, the second group comprised 20 male sex offender outpatients with an average age of 45 years, and the third group comprised 20 male students enrolled in an introductory psychology university course with an average age of 35 years. Participants responded to questions about childhood or adolescent cruelty to animals and about other antisocial behavior including stealing, destruction of property, and cruelty to children. They also responded to questions about child abuse experiences and paternal alcoholism. The results revealed that all three groups significantly differed from each other. The homicidal sex offenders committed significantly more animal cruelty in their younger years compared to each of the other two groups. The differences were particularly marked between the homicidal sexual offenders (nearly all of whom reported being cruel to animals) and the university students (none of whom reported animal cruelty). There was also a significant difference between the non-homicidal sex offenders and the university students, with the former group reporting animal cruelty during their childhood and adolescent years. Although this study addressed the limitation of biased sampling, it is based on the criticized methods of self-report and retrospective reporting.

Despite its critics, the VGH has continued to attract research interest (Hensley, Tallichet, & Dutkiewicz, 2009) with several more recent studies arguing support for the hypothesis (e.g., Merz-Perez et al., 2001; Merz-Perez & Heide, 2004; Tallichet & Hensley, 2004; Verlinden et al., 2000; Wright & Hensley, 2003). However, it is noteworthy that, as recommended by Felthous and Kellert (1987), recent work has highlighted the importance of assessing recurrent, rather than isolated, acts of childhood animal cruelty when examining the association between childhood animal cruelty and later acts of interpersonal violence. It is also noteworthy that such a position is consistent with the definition of conduct disorder given in the *Diagnostic and Statistical Manual of Mental*

Disorders. The manual states that for a diagnosis of conduct disorder, there must be a repetitive and persistent pattern of at least one criterion behavior from those listed (one of which is "has been physically cruel to animals") over a period of six months.

Also of relevance are the research findings regarding childhood onset versus adolescent onset of antisocial behavior; these findings have indicated that individuals in the childhood-onset group present with the more severe forms of antisocial behavior. Indeed, consistent with claims made by the VGH, most violent individuals with a childhood onset of antisocial behavior have a developmental history characterized by an escalation in the severity of aggression (e.g., Farrington, 1991; Loeber & Hay, 1997). Also of relevance, the childhood-onset group has been referred to as the life-course persistent group.

Moreover, it is within the childhood-onset group that children with callous-unemotional traits are generally classified. Callous-unemotional traits form a prominent part of psychopathy character traits in adults (Cleckley, 1976; Hare, 1993). Individuals characterized by callous-unemotional traits lack a sense of guilt and empathy, and they callously use others for their own gain (Frick & White, 2008). At least three dimensions have consistently emerged in the conceptualization of psychopathy in adults: (1) callous-unemotional traits, (2) an interpersonal style characterized by arrogance as well as deceitful and manipulative behavior, and (3) an impulsive and irresponsible behavioral style that includes poor planning and a tendency toward boredom or need for stimulation.

Of note, callous-unemotional traits have demonstrated stability from childhood to early adolescence and adulthood (Lynam, Caspi, Moffitt, Loeber, & Stouthamer-Loeber, 2007). Particularly noteworthy is the finding that callous-unemotional traits in childhood are predictive of later antisocial behavior and psychopathy (Blonigen, Hicks, Kruger, Patrick, & Iacono, 2006; Frick & Viding, 2009).

Given that the majority of studies claiming support for the VGH have been based on institutionalized individuals who have committed aggressive or violent crimes, it is most likely that these individuals can best be classified as being on the life-course persistent trajectory. It is therefore reasonable to argue that the majority of VGH studies are reporting the same pattern of life-course persistent aggression and escalation typical of the severe end of the antisocial spectrum, as has been consistently documented in the broader antisocial behavior literature (Farrington, 1991; Loeber & Hay, 1997).

Also of note, Frick et al. (1993) found that along with fighting (first appearing at an average age of 6 years), bullying (7 years), and assaulting (7.5 years), animal cruelty (6.5 years) was one of the earliest-appearing indicators of conduct disorder. Most importantly, Frick and colleagues found that "cruelty to animals" was one of several items that discriminated between individuals who fell on the destructive end of the conduct disorder severity dimension and those who fell on the nondestructive end. Of relevance to the current discussion, research outside of VGH supports the argument that childhood animal cruelty is one of several significant markers of the development of a more aggressive or antisocial individual. For example, childhood animal cruelty has been found to significantly discriminate between clinical and subclinical conduct problem behaviors (Gelhorn, Sakai, Price, & Crowley, 2007). Children diagnosed with a conduct disorder who are cruel to animals have been found to have more severe conduct problems than children diagnosed with conduct disorder who are not cruel to animals (Luk, Staiger, Wong, & Mathai, 1999). Consistent findings were reported in a study involving 131 children aged 6 to 13 years, conducted by Dadds, Whiting, and Hawes (2006). The study findings suggest that cruelty to animals may be an early manifestation of antisocial behavior shown by a subgroup of children who develop conduct problems associated with low empathy and callous-unemotional traits. In other words, cruelty to animals during the childhood years may be a marker for the development of more severe conduct problems.

In sum, the criticisms directed at this research have in large part caused the validity of this theory to be questioned. However, the preceding review highlights that the findings of the research conducted within this framework are in fact consistent with much of the general aggression research, particularly supporting conclusions regarding individuals classified at the more severe end of the antisocial spectrum, including those who display callous-unemotional traits. The argument that violence graduates with age from less to more severe for people who show aggressive behaviors early in development is consistent with research looking at the childhood-onset group of aggressive individuals. Those individuals with childhood-onset aggression who also display callous-unemotional traits are most likely to display a life-course trajectory and to engage in behaviors characteristic of the more severe end of the antisocial spectrum.

Thus, the argument that these individuals graduate from animal abuse in childhood to human violence in adulthood is consistent with the findings related to the behaviors of individuals at this more severe end of the antisocial spectrum. Based on the general aggression literature and the research specifically examining the VGH, it is reasonable to propose that a pattern of repeated animal cruelty in young children is one behavioral marker, and perhaps a particularly important behavioral marker, of a life-course of persistent and escalating severity of aggressive acts.

Nevertheless, the pattern of association between animal cruelty and human-directed criminal and antisocial behavior is broader than that depicted by the VGH. There is evidence that many human-directed antisocial behaviors occur concurrently in time with animal cruelty behaviors. There is also evidence that animal cruelty is associated with antisocial behaviors at the lower end of the severity spectrum, including, for example, drug abuse and property damage. Although the VGH does not address these associations, the second framework, to be discussed in the next section, does address these associations.

The Deviance Generalization Hypothesis

The second framework of focus is the deviance generalization hypothesis (DGH). The argument put forth within this hypothesis is consistent with the conceptualization of aggression and antisocial behavior. Over the past decade, it has become increasingly clear that aggressive behaviors mostly occur within the context of other antisocial behaviors, including lying, stealing, destruction of property, burglary, sexual assault, and other violent crimes (Hartup, 2005). Given the co-occurrence between aggressive behavior, most notably physical aggression, and other forms of antisocial behavior such as illicit drug use, it has been deemed necessary to broaden the focus of research in the area and include aggression within the broader class of antisocial behaviors (Dodge, Coie, & Lynam, 2006). Accordingly, Rutter (2003) proposed that an adequate conceptualization of the antisocial behavior construct must encompass a large range of socially disapproved behaviors. This is most strongly true at the severe end of the antisocial behavior spectrum (Dishion, French, & Patterson, 1995; Farrington, 1991; Lynam, 1996).

In contrast to research examining the VGH, support for the DGH also comes from research that has *not* targeted institutionalized or aggressive subtypes of criminal offenders. This research is consistent with current thinking that aggressive behaviors including animal cruelty constitute a subset of behaviors classified within the antisocial behavior spectrum (Frick & Viding, 2009).

Of particular importance in evaluations of the validity of the DGH is the finding from the broader antisocial behavior literature that the greater the frequency and variety of antisocial acts, the stronger the prediction that the individual is engaged in more serious forms of antisocial behavior, including violence (Dishion et al., 1995; Farrington, 1991). This has specific relevance to the argument and research finding that repeated acts of animal cruelty are associated with violence that is serious and recurrent (e.g., Felthous & Kellert, 1987). It is also consistent with findings that individuals who are cruel to animals are more likely than those who are not to be engaged in a variety of other crimes (cf. Arluke et al., 1999; Gullone, 2012; Gullone & Clarke, 2008).

The literature relating to the DGH that is reviewed in this section has been organized into a number of subsections, including discussion related to (1) the conceptualization of conduct disorder, antisocial personality disorder, and psychopathy; (2) empirical support for the co-occurrence between animal cruelty and other criminal behaviors; (3) empirical support for the co-occurrence between family violence and animal cruelty; and finally (4) research that has examined the links between bullying and animal cruelty as well as that examining the important role played by the witnessing of aggression.

Conduct Disorder, Antisocial Personality Disorder, and Psychopathy

As previously noted, diagnostic criteria for conduct disorder in the third edition of the *Diagnostic and Statistical Manual* (American Psychiatric Association, 1987) and subsequent revised versions include animal cruelty as one diagnostic criterion. It is particularly noteworthy that in their meta-analysis of child conduct problem behaviors, Frick et al. (1993) reported a median age of 6.5 years for the occurrence of the first incident of animal cruelty along with other aggressive behaviors (i.e., fighting, bullying, assaulting others), thus indicating that animal cruelty appears as one of the earliest indicators of conduct disorder. It is listed as such in the next-to-most recent version of the *Diagnostic and Statistical Manual of Mental Disorders* (DSM-IV-TR; American Psychiatric Association, 2000). Further, as many as 25% of children diagnosed with conduct disorder display cruelty to animals. As previously noted, cruelty to animals is one of several items that discriminates between the destructive and nondestructive categories, with animal cruelty falling within the destructive category (Frick et al., 1993).

In other research, Mellor, Yeow, Mamat, and Mohd Hapidzal (2008) conducted an investigation with 379 Malaysian children aged 6 to 12 years, enabling examination of the relationship between animal cruelty and disordered behavior in another culture. As has been found in other research (e.g., Ascione, 1993; Dadds, Whiting, & Hawes, 2006; Frick et al., 1993), the results indicated that children's animal cruelty was associated with externalizing difficulties, including conduct disorders and hyperactivity.

In their analysis of a National Epidemiological Survey data set including a nationally representative sample of 43,093 U.S. respondents, Gelhorn et al. (2007) found that cruelty to animals (assessed with the item "hurt or be cruel to an animal or pet on purpose") significantly discriminated between those with clinical and subclinical conduct problem behaviors. Specifically, 5.5% of males in the subclinical group compared to 18% of males in the conduct disorder group endorsed the item of animal cruelty. The comparative statistics for females were lower but equally discriminating (2.2% vs. 6.2%).

Consistent findings were reported by Luk et al. (1999) in their comparison study of 141 clinic-referred children presenting with at least one definite conduct disorder symptom apart from animal cruelty and a community sample of 36 children, all aged between 5 and 12 years. Forty children in the clinic-referred group (out of 141, 28%), compared to one child from the community sample (3%), were rated as "sometimes" or "definitely" being cruel to animals. As noted earlier, children in the animal cruelty group were found to have more severe conduct problems than the comparison group and were more likely to be male.

Also, the older children in the animal cruelty group had a highly elevated self-perception. Luk and colleagues (1999) proposed that the elevated self-worth of the children who were cruel to animals was suggestive of the presence of callous-unemotional traits (c.f. Frick, O'Brien, Wootton, & McBurnett, 1994), given that such traits manifest as behavior characterized not only by lack of guilt and empathy but also by superficial charm. This finding is consistent with research by Frick and Dickens (2006) with antisocial youth. In their research they also found that callous-unemotional traits were predictive of a higher severity and stability of aggressive and antisocial behavior (Frick & Dickens, 2006). In contrast, antisocial youth without callous-unemotional traits showed less aggressive behavior.

Evidence that callous-unemotional traits and psychopathy may be particularly predictive of animal cruelty behaviors is in keeping with findings of research that has investigated relationships between animal cruelty and other criminal behaviors. According to Lynam (1996), psychopathy is characterized by more crimes than is true for the average criminal offender and also by more types of crimes. Such findings are reflective of the criminal behavior profiles of people who are cruel to animals. Such a profile is also reflective of particularly severe and violent antisocial adults (Blair, Peschardt, Budhani, Mitchell, & Pine, 2006).

In a controlled study aimed at identifying risk factors for abuse and interpersonal violence among an urban population, Walton-Moss, Manganello, Frye, and Campbell (2005) compared 845 women who had experienced abuse in the past two years with a control group of non-abused women from the same metropolitan area. Risk factors predicting perpetration of interpersonal violence included being a high school dropout, being in fair or poor mental health, having a problem with drugs or alcohol, and committing companion animal cruelty.

In the more recent investigation by Vaughn and colleagues (2009), the correlates of lifetime animal cruelty, including conduct disorder and other disorders, were examined. The 2001–2002 data set comprised data from a nationally representative sample of 43,093 non-institutionalized U.S. residents aged 18 years or older. Data were collected via interview by trained interviewers using a validated interview schedule (Grant, Harford, Dawson, & Pickering, 1995).

Among the sociodemographic variables assessed, being male predicted a higher prevalence of animal cruelty, as did being younger and from a lower socioeconomic background. The findings showed that the prevalence of antisocial behaviors was higher among those with a lifetime history of animal cruelty than among those without such a history. The most prevalent antisocial behaviors among those who were cruel to animals were crimes that included the robbing or mugging of another person. Other more prevalent behaviors were setting fires on purpose, harassing and threatening someone, and forcing someone to have sex.

In additional analyses, the data revealed that animal cruelty was uniquely associated with disorders characterized by low self-control, including lifetime alcohol use, pathological gambling, conduct disorder, and a number of personality disorders, including obsessive-compulsive personality disorder and histrionic personality disorder. Indeed, the most common psychiatric disorders among people with a history of animal cruelty were conduct disorder, antisocial personality disorder (or a family history of antisocial personality disorder), and lifetime nicotine dependence, as well as lifetime alcohol use. Supporting the role played by developmental family experiences, animal cruelty was also associated with a family history of antisocial behavior.

Criminal Behavior and Animal Cruelty

The research by Coston and Protz (1998) is supported by other research showing a correlation between criminal behaviors and animal cruelty (e.g., Vaughn et al., 2009). These researchers sought to examine the overlap between animal cruelty and other crimes by cross-referencing cases of individuals in a county in North Carolina who had been investigated for animal cruelty in 1996 with 911 calls two years earlier and one year later. They found 1,016 matches for crimes investigated two years earlier than 1996. The resulting reports were for sexual assault (40%), mental health request (23%), assault (22%), animal cruelty (6%), missing person (5%), and domestic violence (4%). One-third of the individuals had been arrested for criminal offenses other than animal cruelty during this earlier period.

The number of matches one year later was 754, and the reports related to creating a disturbance (32%), domestic violence (31%), assault (16%), missing person (6%), man with a gun (5%), animal cruelty (4%), mental health (2%), sexual assault (2%), and drugs (1%). One-third had been arrested, and 10% were convicted for assault, domestic violence, and drug possession.

Although the aim of their study was to examine the VGH, Arluke et al. (1999) found support for the DGH. As with the studies described previously, they investigated the relationship between criminality and animal cruelty. To overcome some of the limitations of past research, they obtained their data from official records of criminality rather than through self-report from institutionalized individuals. They also included a noncriminal comparison group. Their method included identifying adults who had been prosecuted for at least one incident of animal cruelty between 1975 and 1986, and their data were extracted from the records of the Massachusetts Society for the Prevention of Cruelty to Animals.

The researchers defined and identified cruelty as cases "where an animal has been intentionally harmed physically (e.g., beaten, stabbed, shot, hanged, drowned, stoned, burned, strangled, driven over, or thrown)" (Arluke et al., 1999, p. 966). This resulted in the identification of 153 participants, of whom 146 were male. The sample had a mean age of 31 years, and 58% were younger than 21. With regard to the demographics of the abused animals, the largest proportion was dogs (69%), followed by cats (22%), and the remaining were birds, free-living animals, horses, or farmed animals. Their control group comprised individuals matched to the animal cruelty group on sex, socioeconomic status, age, and street of residence in the same year as the cruelty incident. The details for the control group were obtained from municipal voting lists. Following this, computerized criminal records were used to track criminal records from the state's criminal justice records system. This was done for both groups. Criminal offenses were classified into five groups: (1) violent, (2) property-related, (3) drug-related, (4) public disorder, and (5) other.

The study results indicated that animal abusers were significantly more likely than non–animal abusers to be involved in other forms of criminal behavior, including violent offenses. As many as 70% of those who were cruel to animals also committed at least one other offense, compared with 22% of the control group participants. The differences ranged from 11% for the control group and 44% for the abusive group on property-related crimes to 12% for the control group and 37% for the abusive group on public disorder–related crimes. For violent crimes, the two groups differed substantially (7% and 37% for the control and abusive groups, respectively; Arluke et al., 1999).

Based on their findings, the authors concluded that animal cruelty appears to be one of many antisocial behaviors displayed by individuals, ranging from property to personal crimes (Arluke et al., 1999). Of significance is the fact that this research study included a non-institutionalized sample of people who were cruel to animals. Thus, the finding that a single known act of animal cruelty was predictive of participation in other criminal offenses is particularly compelling.

To examine whether Australian data would support Arluke et al.'s (1999) findings of deviance generalization, Gullone and Clarke (2008) obtained data from the Statistical Services Division of Victoria Police for *all recorded alleged offenses* in Victoria, Australia, for the years 1994 to 2001 (inclusive). Data for the equivalent time frame (classified into the same categories) were also separately obtained *only for alleged animal cruelty offenders*.

The data for *all alleged offenders* revealed that although offenses against the person constituted a relatively small proportion of the total number of crimes at an average of 7.7% of all crimes over the eight-year period, the percentage *only for the alleged animal cruelty offenders* was markedly higher at 25% (see Table 1). This category of offenses included such crimes as homicide, rape, assault, abduction/kidnap, and harassment. Importantly, these statistics are remarkably similar to those reported by Arluke et al. (1999).

There were also differences between the group of all alleged offenders and the alleged animal cruelty offenders for the remaining three categories, but they were not as great. Of note, the category "offenses against property" is the only one that has a higher percentage for all offenders than for only animal cruelty offenders (see Table 1).

TABLE 1: Comparative Percentages of Crimes by Category for All Alleged Offenders and Only Alleged Animal Cruelty Offenders Based on Victoria Police Data for the Years 1994 to 2001

Category of offense	All offenders	Animal cruelty offenders
Offenses against the person	7.7	25.0
Offenses against property	80.7	48.4
Drug offenses	3.8	6.7
Other offenses	7.7	19.8

From these data it appears that there is a greater likelihood that people alleged to have been cruel to animals will engage in offenses against the person, including violent crimes, when compared to all alleged offenders. They are also more likely to be involved in miscellaneous offenses (i.e., "Other offenses") and drug-related offenses ("Drug offenses"). The drug-offenses difference is not surprising given the reported findings of Vaughn and colleagues (2009), which showed that among the most prevalent antisocial behaviors of those who were cruel to animals were "lifetime nicotine dependence" and "lifetime alcohol use disorder."

Of note, when broken down by age and sex, the data across the different crime categories showed that for all alleged offenders, as well as for only animal cruelty offenders, the offenders were characteristically male. Also, the most frequent ages for all alleged offenders during the years recorded were between 12 and 35 years, for both males and females, but particularly for males. For both males and females the peak ages were between 18 and 25 years. In examination of age and sex trends only for alleged animal cruelty offenders, the same peak in frequency between the ages of 18 and 25 years was found, for both males and females. Thus, as is consistent with reported findings in the broader antisocial behavior literature, there were markedly more males identified among all alleged offenders and also among alleged animal cruelty offenders only. Males were also overrepresented across all age categories when researchers looked at the whole database and also at only the animal cruelty database. The particular importance of these statistics is their demonstration of demographic similarity between adults who engage in criminal behaviors of various types, particularly violent behaviors, and adults who are cruel to animals. Such data not only provide support for a link between antisocial behaviors, particularly aggression directed at other people and that directed at animals; they also indicate that animal cruelty can be usefully conceptualized within a human aggression/antisocial behavior framework.

On the basis of the preceding work, it can be concluded that there is substantial empirical evidence that animal cruelty co-occurs with other antisocial or criminal behaviors. This finding is consistent with evidence from the broader antisocial behavior literature showing that aggressive behaviors mostly occur within the context of other antisocial behaviors, including lying, stealing, destruction of property, burglary, sexual assault, and other violent crimes (see Gullone, 2012). Additionally, the work by the FBI reported in the previous section provides support for co-occurrence at the more extreme end of the antisocial behavior continuum.

Family Violence and Animal Cruelty

Additional support for the DGH comes from research demonstrating comorbidity between animal cruelty and domestic or family violence. One of the most consistently replicated findings in the animal cruelty literature is a significant co-occurrence between family or domestic violence and animal cruelty. This research has found that more than 50% of all abused women have companion animals, and in as many as 50% of cases, the animals are abused by the perpetrators of the domestic violence. Motivations for the abuse include hurting and/or controlling the women or their children. The research has also consistently found that concern for the safety of their companion animals keeps many women (and their children) from leaving or staying separated from their abusers. It can be argued that when it occurs within the family home, animal cruelty is a symptom of a deeply dysfunctional family (Lockwood & Hodge, 1998).

One of the earliest studies to investigate the relationship between family environment and animal cruelty was the UK study by Hutton (1983/1998), which reported RSPCA cruelty data for a community in England. The data showed that out of 23 families with a history of animal cruelty, 82% had also been identified by human social services as having children who were at risk of abuse or neglect.

In more recent years, several studies have investigated the relationship between family violence and animal cruelty (e.g., Ascione, 1998; Ascione et al., 2007; Daniell, 2001; Faver & Cavazos, 2007; Flynn, 2000; Quinslick, 1999; Volant, Johnson, Gullone, & Coleman, 2008). These studies have been conducted across several countries, including the United States, Canada, and Australia. Of note, the findings are remarkably consistent across the studies despite their differences in parameters, such as country where the study was conducted, sample size, and methodology used. Findings include that between 11.8% and 39.4% of women have reported that the perpetrator threatened to hurt or kill their companion animals. Between 25.6% (Flynn, 2000) and 79.3% (Quinslick, 1999) of women reported that the perpetrator had *actually* hurt or killed their companion animal(s). Many of the studies examining animal cruelty within abusive families have also reported that between 18% (Ascione, 1998) and 48% (Carlisle-Frank, Frank, & Nielsen, 2004) of women have delayed leaving their violent situation out of fear that their companion animal(s) would be harmed or killed if they were to leave.

A limitation of these studies, with few exceptions (e.g., Ascione et al., 2007; Volant et al., 2008), is that they did not include a comparison group of women who were not in a violent family situation. In a study by Ascione and colleagues

(2007), 5% of non-abused women reported companion animal cruelty, and in Volant's study (2008), 0% reported companion animal cruelty. The latter study involved a group of 102 women recruited through 24 domestic violence services in the state of Victoria and a non–domestic violence comparison group (102 women) recruited from the community. The findings included that 46% of women in the domestic violence sample reported that their partner had threatened to hurt or kill their companion animal, compared with 6% of women in the community sample.

The focus of studies examining the relationship between family violence and companion animal cruelty has predominantly been on determining (1) the prevalence of companion animal cruelty within physically violent relationships and (2) the prevalence of women who delay leaving their violent relationship for fear of harm befalling their companion animals in their absence, as well as the length of the delay. A smaller number of studies have investigated motivations underlying the companion animal cruelty in the context of family violence. On the basis of these studies, it appears that the predominant motivation is one of control. For example, in his qualitative study involving 10 women seeking refuge from domestic violence, Flynn (2000) found that batterers use animal cruelty to intimidate, to hurt, or to control their partners.

However, not all batterers are cruel to animals. To determine whether batterers who are cruel to their companion animals differ from those who are not, Simmons and Lehmann (2007) investigated the reports of 1,283 female companion-animal caregivers who were seeking refuge from partner abuse. They found that batterers who were cruel to animals (not all battered animals were companion animals) used more forms of violence than those who were not. Specifically, batterers who were cruel to animals had higher rates of sexual violence, marital rape, emotional violence, and stalking. They also used more controlling behaviors, including isolation, male privilege, blaming, intimidation, threats, and economic abuse. The differences were even greater for those who killed a companion animal compared to those who did not abuse animals.

A study by Loring and Bolden-Hines (2004) involved 107 women who had been emotionally and physically abused and who were referred to a family violence center. Each of the women had committed at least one illegal behavior, and 72 (62%) of the women had cared for companion animals in the previous year or during the year in which the study was conducted. As many as 54 (75%) of the 72 women reported actual or threatened companion animal cruelty, and of these 54 women, 24 reported that they had been coerced into committing an illegal act through threats or actual harm to their companion animal(s).

A more recent study by DeGue and DiLillo (2009) involving 860 university students from three U.S. universities showed that about 60% of participants who witnessed or perpetrated animal cruelty as a child also retrospectively reported experiences of child maltreatment or domestic violence. The study results also showed that those who had been sexually or physically abused or neglected as children were those most likely to report that they had been cruel to animals as children.

Bullying and Animal Cruelty in Youth

In addition to being linked with abusive childhood experiences, animal cruelty has been shown to co-occur with bullying behaviors. Reinforcing the link, both animal cruelty and bullying have been related to later antisocial behaviors and antisocial personality disorder (Gelhorn et al., 2007). Not surprisingly, there are also conceptual similarities between animal cruelty and bullying behaviors, including overlapping definitional criteria. For example, bullying has been defined as behavior that is intended to hurt the victim and that is characterized by a power imbalance, an unjust use of power, enjoyment by the aggressor, and a general sense of being oppressed on the part of the victim (Rigby, 2002). It is generally agreed that a definition of bullying needs to include an intention to inflict verbal, physical, or psychological harm; a victim who does not provoke the bullying behaviors; and occurrences in familiar social groups (Baldry, 1998; Baldry & Farrington, 2000; Griffin & Gross, 2004; Gumpel & Meadan, 2000).

Though explicit in definitions of bullying but not in definitions of animal cruelty, there is a clear power imbalance where the perpetrator is more powerful than the victim and uses this power to inflict physical, emotional, or psychological harm on the victim. Also, both animal cruelty and bullying behaviors are predominantly observed in male populations. Males have rates of animal cruelty four times higher than those of females (Flynn, 1999) and are more likely than females to engage in bullying behaviors (Baldry, 1998; Bosworth, Espelage, & Simon, 1999; Smith & Myron-Wilson, 1998; Veenstra et al., 2005). Additionally suggestive of overlapping processes between animal cruelty and bullying is their appearance within a close developmental time frame (Frick et al., 1993). Despite this strong conceptual overlap, animal cruelty and bullying behaviors have for the most part been researched separately.

The exceptions include a study by Baldry (2005), who examined the prevalence of animal cruelty, bullying behaviors, and being a victim of bullying in an Italian sample of children and adolescents aged 9 to 12 years. Her results showed that girls and boys who had engaged in direct bullying behaviors were twice as likely as their non-bullying peers to have been cruel to animals. Engagement in animal cruelty by boys was predicted by their direct victimization at school and indirect bullying, whereas engagement in animal cruelty by girls was predicted by their exposure to animal cruelty and by their experience of verbal abuse by their fathers.

Involving a school-based sample of 249 adolescents (105 males, 144 females) ranging in age from 12 to 16 years, Gullone and Robertson (2008) investigated relationships between self-reported animal cruelty and bullying. Significant positive relationships were found between bullying and animal cruelty. Both behaviors were also found to correlate significantly with bullying victimization, witnessing of animal cruelty, and family conflict.

A 2007 study by Henry and Sanders involved 185 undergraduate university males studying psychology. The researchers justified their decision to include only males in their study on the basis that rates of animal cruelty are substantially lower among females. Applying a retrospective reporting methodology, the study aimed to investigate the relationships between self-reports of animal cruelty and bullying as well as being a victim of bullying. They also investigated whether the relationship varied depending on the frequency of animal cruelty or the individual's classification of bully, victim, or bully/victim. They hypothesized that the relationship between bullying and animal cruelty would be strongest for those who had been involved in multiple acts of animal cruelty rather than isolated acts. They also hypothesized that the relationship would be strongest for those in the bully/victim group, given research suggesting that this group has the highest level of maladjustment.

The findings indicated a marked distinction between those who had been involved in a single act of animal cruelty and those who had been involved in multiple acts. Those who reported multiple acts of animal cruelty were more likely to be classified into the bully/victim group than those involved in a single act of animal cruelty. The authors concluded that their findings support the proposal that animal cruelty may sometimes constitute displaced aggression. They also concluded that high rates of bullying and of victimization are predictive of multiple acts of animal cruelty and vice versa.

In summary, research has investigated the co-occurrence of a number of antisocial behaviors, including aggressive or violent behaviors. Such research has provided support for the DGH. Disordered functioning characteristic of conduct disorder, antisocial personality disorder, and psychopathy has been found to include animal cruelty among other aggressive behaviors. Behaviors that are characteristic of disordered functioning have also been found to co-occur with animal cruelty. For example, children who bully are also more likely to be cruel to animals. People who commit crimes, particularly violent crimes, including partner or child abuse, are more likely to be cruel to animals than are people who have not committed these other crimes. At the more extreme end of the antisocial behavior continuum, FBI work has shown that animal cruelty is a prominent behavior in the profiles of violent criminals.

CONCLUSION

In conclusion, this article has reviewed the two predominant frameworks for understanding the connections between animal cruelty and human aggression, violence, and antisocial behavior more generally. Through review of the relevant research, it has been demonstrated that the VGH and the DGH are valid proposals supported by the empirical work that has investigated them. Moreover, with findings from the broader antisocial and aggressive behavior literature taken into account, it has been demonstrated that many of the criticisms that have been directed at the animal cruelty research, particularly the VGH research, do not compromise the validity of the reported findings. Indeed, the findings of the animal cruelty research are overwhelmingly consistent with findings from the extensive and solid evidence provided by the broader aggression and antisocial behavior literature. As is currently accepted, aggressive and violent behaviors commonly co-occur with other antisocial behaviors. It follows that animal cruelty is an aggressive and violent behavior that cannot logically be separated from other aggressive and violent behaviors or indeed from other deviant behaviors.

It can therefore be confidently concluded that, in addition to being one of the earliest indicators of externalizing disorders, including conduct disorder, animal cruelty is a marker of development along a more severe trajectory of antisocial and aggressive behaviors (Frick et al., 1993; Luk et al., 1999). Thus, its early identification provides an optimal opportunity for engaging preventative strategies. As such, it is of significant importance for health care professionals.

Furthermore, the significant co-occurrence between animal cruelty and other antisocial behaviors indicates that animal cruelty is yet another marker of antisocial or aggressive behavior that can be classified along the externalizing behavior spectrum. It logically follows that lawmakers and policy makers must act on this vast body of research. Laws need to be developed that acknowledge the relationship and similarities between different types of abuse and violence, including animal cruelty. Based on the empirical information available, there exists no possible justification for relegating animal cruelty offenses to the "less important" category. Moreover, there is no justification for punishing violent criminals significantly more leniently or—as often happens—not at all if the victim of the violent crime is an animal as opposed to a human being. Indeed, there is a high statistical probability that the victims of the violent or antisocial individual are both animal and human. Thus, recognition of the importance of animal cruelty will undoubtedly benefit not only the animal victims but the whole of society.

References

Alys, L., Wilson, J.C., Clarke, J., & Toman, P. (2009). Developmental animal cruelty and its correlates in sexual homicide offenders and sex offenders. In A. Linzey (Ed.), *The link between animal abuse and human violence* (pp. 145–162). Eastbourne, England: Sussex Academic Press.

American Psychiatric Association. (1987). *Diagnostic and statistical manual of mental disorders* (3rd ed.). Washington, DC: Author.

American Psychiatric Association. (2000). *Diagnostic and statistical manual of mental disorders* (4th ed., text rev.). Washington, DC: Author.

Arluke, A., Levin, J., Luke, C., & Ascione, F. (1999). The relationship of animal abuse to violence and other forms of antisocial behavior. *Journal of Interpersonal Violence, 14*, 963–975.

Ascione, F. R. (1993). Children who are cruel to animals: A review of research and implications for developmental psychopathology. *Anthrozoos, 6*, 226–247.

Ascione, F. R. (1998). Battered women's reports of their partners' and their children's cruelty to animals. *Journal of Emotional Abuse, 1*, 119–133.

Ascione, F. R. (1999). The abuse of animals and human interpersonal violence: Making the connection. In F. Ascione & P. Arkow (Eds.), *Child abuse, domestic violence, and animal abuse: Linking the circles of compassion for prevention and intervention* (pp. 50–61). West Lafayette, IN: Purdue University Press.

Ascione, F. R., Weber, C. V., Thompson, T. M., Heath, J., Maruyama, M., & Hayashi, K. (2007). Battered pets and domestic violence: Animal abuse reported by women experiencing intimate violence and by nonabused women. *Violence Against Women, 13*, 354–373.

Baldry, A. C. (1998). Bullying among Italian middle school students: Combining methods to understand aggressive behaviors and victimisation. *School Psychology International, 19*, 361–374.

Baldry, A. C. (2005). Animal abuse among preadolescents directly and indirectly victimized at school and at home. *Criminal Behavior and Mental Health, 15*, 97–110.

Baldry, A. C., & Farrington, D. P. (2000). Bullies and delinquents: Personal characteristics and parental styles. *Journal of Community & Applied Social Psychology, 10*, 17–31.

Beirne, P. (2004). From animal abuse to interhuman violence? A critical review of the progression thesis. *Society & Animals, 12,* 39–65.

Blair, R. J. R., Peschardt, K. S., Budhani, S., Mitchell, D. G. V., & Pine, D. S. (2006). The development of psychopathy. *Journal of Child Psychology and Psychiatry, 47,* 262–275.

Blonigen, D. D., Hicks, B. M., Kruger, R. F., Patrick, C. P., & Iacono, W. G. (2006). Continuity and change in psychopathic traits as measured via normal-range personality: A longitudinal-biometric study. *Journal of Abnormal Psychology, 115,* 85–95.

Bosworth, K., Espelage, D. L., & Simon, T. R. (1999). Factors associated with bullying behavior in middle school students. *Journal of Early Adolescence, 19,* 341–362.

Brantley, A. C. (2007, September). *The use of animal cruelty evidence in dangerousness assessments by law enforcement.* First International Academic Conference on the Relationship between Animal Abuse and Human Violence, Oxford Centre for Animal Ethics, Oxford, England.

Brown, L. (1988). *Cruelty to animals: The moral debt.* London, England: Macmillan.

Carlisle-Frank, P., Frank, J. M., & Nielsen, L. (2004). Selective battering of the family pet. *Anthrozoos, 17,* 26–42.

Cleckley, H. (1976). *The mask of sanity.* St. Louis, MO: Mosby.

Coston, C., & Protz, C. M. (1998). Kill your dog, beat your wife, screw your neighbour's kids, rob a bank? A cursory look at an individual's vat of social chaos resulting from deviance. *Free Inquiry in Creative Sociology, 26,* 153–158.

Dadds, M. R. (2008). Conduct problems and cruelty to animals in children: What is the link? In F. R. Ascione (Ed.), *The international handbook of animal abuse and cruelty: Theory, research, and application* (pp. 111–131). West Lafayette, IN: Purdue University Press.

Dadds, M. R., Turner, C. M., & McAloon, J. (2002). Developmental links between cruelty to animals and human violence. *Australian & New Zealand Journal of Counselling, 35,* 363–382.

Dadds, M. R., Whiting, C., & Hawes, D. J. (2006). Associations among cruelty to animals, family conflict, and psychopathic traits in childhood. *Journal of Interpersonal Violence, 21,* 411–429.

Daniell, C. (2001, Spring). Ontario SPCA's women's shelter survey shows staggering results. *The Latham Letter,* 16–17.

DeGue, S., & DiLillo, D. (2009). Is animal cruelty a "red flag" for family violence? Investigating co-occurring violence toward children, partners, and pets. *Journal of Interpersonal Violence, 24,* 1036–1056.

Dishion, T. J., French, D. C., & Patterson, G. R. (1995). The development and ecology of antisocial behavior. In D. Cicchetti & D. J. Cohen (Eds.), *Developmental psychopathology, Vol. 2: Risk, disorder, and adaptation* (pp. 421–471). Oxford, England: Wiley.

Dodge, K. A., Coie, J. D., & Lynam, D. (2006). Aggression and antisocial behavior in youth. In N. Eisenberg, W. Damon, & R. M. Lerner (Eds.), *Handbook of child psychology* (6th ed., Vol. 3, pp. 719–788). Hoboken, NJ: Wiley.

Farrington, D. P. (1991). Childhood aggression and adult violence: Early precursors and later life outcomes. In D. J. Peplar & H. K. Rubin (Eds.), *The development and treatment of childhood aggression* (pp. 5–29). Hillsdale, NJ: Erlbaum.

Faver, C. A., & Cavazos, A. M. (2007). Animal abuse and domestic violence: A view from the border. *Journal of Emotional Abuse, 7,* 59–81.

Felthous, A. R. (1980). Aggression against cats, dogs and people. *Child Psychiatry & Human Development, 10*(3), 169–177.

Felthous, A. R., & Kellert, S. R. (1986). Violence against animals and people: Is aggression against living creatures generalized? *Bulletin of the American Academy of Psychiatry & the Law, 14,* 55–69.

Felthous, A. R., & Kellert, S. R. (1987). Childhood cruelty to animals and later aggression against people: A review. *American Journal of Psychiatry, 144*(6), 710–717.

Felthous, A. R., & Yudowitz, B. (1977). Approaching a comparative typology of assaultive female offenders. *Psychiatry, 40,* 270–276.

Flynn, C. P. (1999). Exploring the link between corporal punishment and children's cruelty to animals. *Journal of Marriage & the Family, 61,* 971–981.

Flynn, C. P. (2000). Why family professionals can no longer ignore violence toward animals. *Family Relations: Interdisciplinary Journal of Applied Family Studies, 49,* 87–95.

Flynn, C. P. (2011). Examining the links between animal abuse and human violence. *Crime, Law and Social Change, 55,* 453–468.

Frick, P. J., & Dickens, C. (2006). Current perspectives on conduct disorder. *Current Psychiatry Reports, 8,* 59–72.

Frick, P. J., Lahey, B. B., Loeber, R., Tannenbaum, L., et al. (1993). Oppositional defiant disorder and conduct disorder: A meta-analytic review of factor analyses and cross-validation in a clinic sample. *Clinical Psychology Review, 13,* 319–340.

Frick, P. J., O'Brien, B. S., Wootton, J. M., & McBurnett, K. (1994). Psychopathy and conduct problems in children. *Journal of Abnormal Psychology, 103,* 700–707.

Frick, P. J., & Viding, E. (2009). Antisocial behavior from a developmental psychopathology perspective. *Development and Psychopathology, 21,* 1111–1131.

Frick, P. J., & White, S. F. (2008). Research review: The importance of callous-unemotional traits for developmental models of aggressive and antisocial behavior. *Journal of Child Psychology and Psychiatry, 49,* 359–375.

Gelhorn, H. L., Sakai, J. T., Price, R. K., & Crowley, T. J. (2007). DSM-IV conduct disorder criteria as predictors of antisocial personality disorder. *Comprehensive Psychiatry, 48,* 529–538.

Gleyzer, R., Felthous, A. R., & Holzer, C. E. (2002). Animal cruelty and psychiatric disorders. *Journal of the American Academy of Psychiatry & the Law, 30,* 257–265.

Grant, B. F., Harford, D. A., Dawson, D. A., & Pickering, R. P. (1995). The Alcohol Use Disorder and Associated Disabilities Interview Schedule (AUDADIS): Reliability of alcohol and drug modules in a general population sample. *Drug and Alcohol Dependence, 39,* 37–44.

Griffin, R. S., & Gross, A. M. (2004). Childhood bullying: Current empirical findings and future directions for research. *Aggression and Violent Behavior, 9*, 379–400.

Gullone, E. (2012). *Animal cruelty, antisocial behavior and aggression: More than a link*. Hampshire, England: Palgrave Macmillan.

Gullone, E., & Clarke, J. (2008). Human-animal interactions: The Australian perspective. In F. Ascione (Ed.), *The international handbook of theory and research on animal abuse and cruelty* (pp. 305–335). West Lafayette, IN: Purdue University Press.

Gullone, E., & Robertson, N. (2008). The relationship between bullying and animal abuse in adolescents: The importance of witnessing animal abuse. *Journal of Applied Developmental Psychology, 29*, 371–379.

Gumpel, T. P., & Meadan, H. (2000). Children's perceptions of school-based violence. *British Journal of Educational Psychology, 70*(3), 391–404.

Hare, R. D. (1993). *Without conscience: The disturbing world of the psychopaths among us*. New York, NY: Guilford Press.

Hartup, W. W. (2005). The development of aggression. In R. E. Tremblay, W. W. Hartup, & J. Archer (Eds.), *Developmental origins of aggression* (pp. 3–22). New York, NY: Guilford Press.

Henry, B. C., & Sanders, C. E. (2007). Bullying and animal abuse: Is there a connection? *Society & Animals, 15*, 107–126.

Hensley, C., Tallichet, S. E., & Dutkiewicz, E. L. (2009). Recurrent childhood animal cruelty: Is there a relationship to adult recurrent interpersonal violence? *Criminal Justice Review, 34*, 248–257.

Humane Society of the United States (1997). First strike. Retrieved from http://www.hsus.org/firststrike/factsheets/index.html

Hutton, J. S. (1998). Animal abuse as a diagnostic approach in social work: A pilot study. In R. Lockwood & F. R. Ascione (Eds.), *Cruelty to animals and interpersonal violence: Readings in research and application* (pp. 415–420). West Lafayette, IN: Purdue University Press. (Original work published 1983)

Kellert, S. R., & Felthous, A. R. (1985). Childhood cruelty toward animals among criminals and noncriminals. *Human Relations, 38*(12), 1113–1129.

Lockwood, R., & Church, A. (1996, Fall). Deadly serious: An FBI perspective on animal cruelty. *HSUS News*, 27–30.

Lockwood, R., & Hodge, G. R. (1998). The tangled web of animal abuse: The links between cruelty to animals and human violence. In R. Lockwood & F. R. Ascione (Eds.), *Cruelty to animals and interpersonal violence: Readings in research and application* (pp. 77–82). West Lafayette, IN: Purdue University Press.

Loeber, R., & Hay, D. (1997). Key issues in the development of aggression and violence from childhood to early adulthood. *Annual Review of Psychology, 48*, 371–410.

Loring, M. T., & Bolden-Hines, T. A. (2004). Pet abuse by batterers as a means of coercing battered women into committing illegal behavior. *Journal of Emotional Abuse, 4*, 27–37.

Luk, E. S., Staiger, P. K., Wong, L., & Mathai, J. (1999). Children who are cruel to animals: A revisit. *Australian and New Zealand Journal of Psychiatry, 33,* 29–36.

Lynam, D. R. (1996). Early identification of chronic offenders: Who is the fledgling psychopath? *Psychological Bulletin, 120,* 209–234.

Lynam, D. R., Caspi, A., Moffitt, T. E., Loeber, R., & Stouthamer-Loeber, M. (2007). Longitudinal evidence that psychopathy scores in early adolescence predict adult psychopathy. *Journal of Abnormal Psychology, 116,* 155–165.

Mellor, D., Yeow, J., Mamat, N. H., & Mohd Hapidzal, N. F. (2008). The relationship between childhood cruelty to animals and psychological adjustment: A Malaysian study. *Anthrozoos, 21,* 363–374.

Merz-Perez, L., & Heide, K. M. (2004). *Animal cruelty: Pathway to violence against people.* Walnut Creek, CA: AltaMira Press.

Merz-Perez, L., Heide, K. M., & Silverman, I. J. (2001). Childhood cruelty to animals and subsequent violence against humans. *International Journal of Offender Therapy and Comparative Criminology, 45,* 556–573.

People for the Ethical Treatment of Animals (PETA). (2003). Animal abuse and human abuse: Partners in crime. Retrieved from http://www.peta.org/mc/factsheet _display.asp?ID=132

Petersen, M. L., & Farrington, D. P. (2007). Cruelty to animals and violence to people. *Victims & Offenders, 2,* 21–43.

Quinslick, J. A. (1999). Animal abuse and family violence. In F. R. Ascione & P. Arkow (Eds.), *Child abuse, domestic violence, and animal abuse: Linking the circles of compassion for prevention and intervention* (pp. 168–175). Lafayette, IN: Purdue University Press.

Ressler, R. K., Burgess, A. W., & Douglas, J. E. (1988). *Sexual homicide: Patterns and motives.* Lexington, MA: Lexington Books.

Rigby, K. (2002). Bullying in childhood. In P. K. Smith & C. H. Craig (Eds.), *Blackwell handbook of childhood social development* (pp. 549–568). Malden, MA: Blackwell.

Rutter, M. (2003). Commentary: Causal processes leading to antisocial behavior. *Developmental Psychology, 39,* 372–378.

Simmons, C. A., & Lehmann, P. (2007). Exploring the link between pet abuse and controlling behaviors in violent relationships. *Journal of Interpersonal Violence, 22,* 1211–1222.

Smith, P. K., & Myron-Wilson, R. (1998). Parenting and school bullying. *Clinical Child Psychology and Psychiatry, 3,* 405–417.

Tallichet, S. E., & Hensley, C. (2004). Exploring the link between recurrent acts of childhood and adolescent animal cruelty and subsequent violent crime. *Criminal Justice Review, 29,* 304–316.

Tingle, D., Barnard, G. W., Robbins, L., Newman, G., & Hutchinson, D. (1986). Childhood and adolescent characteristics of pedophiles and rapists. *International Journal of Law and Psychiatry, 9,* 103–116.

Vaughn, M. G., Fu, Q., DeLisi, M., Beaver, K. M., Perron, B. E., Terrell, K., et al. (2009). Correlates of cruelty to animals in the United States: Results from the

National Epidemiologic Survey on Alcohol and Related Conditions. *Journal of Psychiatric Research, 43*, 1213–1218.

Veenstra, R., Lindenberg, S., Oldehinkel, A. J., De Winter, A. F., Verhulst, F. C., & Ormel, J. (2005). Bullying and victimization in elementary schools: A comparison of bullies, victims, bully/victims, and uninvolved preadolescents. *Developmental Psychology, 41*, 672–682.

Verlinden, S., Hersen, M., & Thomas, J. (2000). Risk factors in school shootings. *Clinical Psychology Review, 20*, 3–56.

Volant, A. M., Johnson, J. A., Gullone, E., & Coleman, G. J. (2008). The relationship between domestic violence and animal abuse: An Australian study. *Journal of Interpersonal Violence, 23*(9), 1277–1295.

Walton-Moss, B. J., Manganello, J., Frye, V., & Campbell, J. C. (2005). Risk factors for intimate partner violence and associated injury among urban women. *Journal of Community Health: The Publication for Health Promotion and Disease Prevention, 30*, 377–389.

Wright, J., & Hensley, C. (2003). From animal cruelty to serial murder: Applying the graduation hypothesis. *International Journal of Offender Therapy and Comparative Criminology, 47*, 71–88.

6 Risk Factors for the Development of Animal Cruelty

ELEONORA GULLONE

Research shows that animal cruelty shares many of the etiologial pathways and risk factors that have been shown for other aggressive behaviors. The shared etiology not only aids understanding of the co-occurrence that has been documented between animal cruelty and other aggressive and antisocial crimes, it also highlights the dangers over and above those to animals that are lurking where animal cruelty offenders remain unidentified and their crimes remain unsanctioned. This article reviews current understandings about the development of antisocial behaviors, including human aggression, and animal cruelty behaviors. Available research leads one to ask, when individuals have been found to be guilty of animal cruelty, what other aggressive behaviors might they be guilty of? For young children, one must ask, are they victims of child abuse, are they living in circumstances of domestic violence, and/or what is the aggression or violence that they may have been witness to? Animal cruelty and most aggressive behaviors from the later childhood years onward are indicators of non-normative development. Early detection of such behaviors can provide a valuable opportunity to engage in preventative intervention for young people or for appropriate sanctions to be applied for adults. Such interventions would be beneficial for all, humans and animals alike.

KEY WORDS: animal cruelty, aggression, antisocial behavior, witnessing of violence, family and parenting experiences, cognitive factors, empathy, emotion regulation.

INTRODUCTION

Research shows that animal cruelty shares many of the etiologial pathways and risk factors that have been shown for other aggressive human behaviors. The shared etiology not only aids understanding of the co-occurrence that has been documented between animal cruelty and other aggressive and antisocial

Journal of Animal Ethics 4(2): 61–79

crimes (Gullone, 2012), it also highlights the dangers over and above those to animals that are lurking where animal cruelty offenders remain unidentified and their crimes remain unsanctioned.

Prior to discussing the risk factors that predict the development of animal cruelty, definitions of the constructs that are central to this review will be discussed. Of particular note is the conceptualization that has evolved over the past decade that aggressive behaviors mostly occur within the context of other antisocial behaviors, including lying, stealing, destruction of property, burglary, sexual assault, and other violent crimes (Hartup, 2005). Significant co-occurrence has been noted between aggressive behavior, most notably physical aggression, and other forms of antisocial behavior. Much empirical work (e.g., Farrington, 1991), has shown that "the frequency and variety of antisocial acts are the best predictors of more serious forms of antisocial behavior, including violence" (Dishion, French, & Patterson, 1995, p. 422).

Thus, animal cruelty and other aggressive behaviors are specific forms of antisocial behaviors that have been shown to co-occur along with other forms of antisocial behaviors. However, other antisocial behaviors can primarily be differentiated from human aggression and animal cruelty behaviors on the basis that these latter behaviors have as their fundamental motivation the deliberate intention to cause harm or injury to other sentient beings. This is clearly indicated in the following definitions.

DEFINING HUMAN AGGRESSION

According to Dodge, Coie, and Lynam (2006), aggression can be defined as behavior that aims to harm or injure another or others. Similar definitions have been put forth by others. For example, Anderson (2002) has defined aggression as behavior performed by a person (the aggressor) with the immediate intention of harming another person (the victim). The perpetrator (aggressor) must believe that the behavior will harm the victim and that the victim is motivated to avoid that intended harm.

DEFINING ANIMAL CRUELTY

Nonhuman animal definitions, not surprisingly, share many of the features that are common to definitions of aggression toward humans. Summarizing the different views on animal cruelty, Dadds, Turner, and McAloon (2002) noted that most definitions include a behavioral dimension that can include acts of omission (e.g., neglect) or acts of commission (e.g., beating) (see also Brown, 1988). Another key characteristic is indication that the behavior occurred purposely, that is, with deliberateness and without ignorance. An additional definitional criterion is that the behavior brings about physical and/or psychological harm. Incorporating these definitional criteria, Dadds (2008) defined animal cruelty as a repetitive and proactive behavior (or pattern of behavior) intended to cause harm to sentient creatures.

Gullone (2012) has elaborated further upon Dadds's definition. According to Gullone, animal cruelty can be defined as:

> Behavior performed repetitively and proactively by an individual with the deliberate intention of causing harm (i.e., pain, suffering, distress and/or death) to an animal with the understanding that the animal is motivated to avoid that harm. Included in this definition are both physical harm and psychological harm.

Given shared manifestations as reflected in their definitions, it is not at all surprising that animal cruelty and aggressive behaviors should share risk factors and etiological pathways of development.

RISK FACTORS FOR THE DEVELOPMENT OF ANIMAL CRUELTY

Consistent with the broader literature on aggressive and other antisocial behavior, empirical studies examining factors that are predictive of animal cruelty include a number of constitutional or biological risk factors and individual difference risk factors. Being male has been a consistently demonstrated risk factor across the developmental spectrum (Arluke & Luke, 1997; Coston & Protz, 1998). Age is another important constitutional variable (Arluke & Luke, 1997; Gullone & Clarke, 2008). Environmental factors have also been shown to be important. These factors include microenvironments that can also be referred to as proximal environments, such as a child's family and parenting experiences (e.g., Kellert & Felthous, 1985; Rigdon & Tapia, 1977; Tapia, 1971). Also included are macro-environments, which are considered to be more distal environments, such as cultural attitudes and norms (Flynn, 1999a).

In a recent review, Flynn (2011) listed what he considers to be the leading predictive factors of children's animal cruelty. These include "a) being a victim of physical or sexual abuse, b) witnessing violence between one's parents, and c) witnessing parents or peers harm animals" (p. 455). Other predictors of animal cruelty that Flynn included were the experiences of being bullied or the behavior of bullying. The research examining the proposed risk factors for the development of animal cruelty behaviors will be reviewed beginning with biological and maturational variables.

Temperamental Predisposition

Differences in temperament (defined as an internal disposition that influences relatively stable styles of behaving over time and across situations; Schwartz, Wright, Shin, Kagan, & Rauch, 2003) have been reported to be important predictors. It is noteworthy that biological predispositions are just that—predispositions. It is their interaction with environmental factors (such as family and parenting experiences—to be reviewed in the next section) that is of most significance in understanding their etiological role.

One particularly relevant constellation of temperamental predispositions is referred to as callous-unemotional traits. In particular, experiences of abuse or neglect in childhood interfere with otherwise normative development. Such childhood experiences have been shown to serve as incubators of callous-unemotional trait development in predisposed individuals (Anderson & Bushman, 2002; Repetti, Taylor, & Seeman, 2002).

Individuals characterized by callous-unemotional traits lack a sense of guilt and empathy and callously use others for their own gain (Frick & White, 2008). Research with antisocial youth has shown that callous-unemotional traits are predictive of a higher severity and stability of aggressive and antisocial behavior (Frick & Dickens, 2006). Youth who present callous-unemotional traits tend to be less responsive to cues of punishment and tend toward a reward-dominant style. This contrasts with antisocial youth without callous-unemotional traits who tend to show less aggressive behavior and whose behavior tends to be reactive rather than proactive (Frick and Dickens, 2006).

Sex Differences

A second important factor shown to be an important risk factor for animal cruelty is sex (and gender). Consistent with the broader antisocial behavior literature showing that there are marked sex differences with males outnumbering females on aggressive tendencies by a ratio of around 10 to 1 (Loeber & Hay, 1997), research has shown that males are more likely to be cruel to animals. This is true for childhood (Baldry, 2005), adolescence (Thompson & Gullone, 2006), and adulthood (Gullone & Clarke, 2008). Of note, Flynn (1999a; 1999b) found that not only were males more likely to commit animal cruelty, they were also more likely to witness it.

Investigating a childhood community sample involving 268 girls and 264 boys (aged 9 to 12 years), Baldry (2005) found that 35.9% of girls reported abusing animals compared with 45.7% of boys. The investigation by Thompson and Gullone (2006) involving 281 adolescents, aged between 12 and 18 years, found that males scored significantly higher than females on two different self-report animal cruelty questionnaires. In their study, Gullone and Robertson (2008) also found that boys scored higher on measures of animal cruelty compared to girls.

Studies examining animal cruelty in adults have also found a higher prevalence among men compared to women. For example, in an investigation of all animal cruelty cases prosecuted in Massachusetts between 1975 and 1996, Arluke and Luke (1997) found that approximately 97% of the perpetrators were male. Similarly, in Gullone and Clarke's (2008) report of Australian data for all recorded offenses in Victoria for the years spanning 1994 to 2001, when broken down by age and sex, the data showed that across crime categories including animal cruelty, offenders were characteristically male. Males were also found to be overrepresented across all age categories but most particularly between the ages of 18 and 35 years, indicating the importance of maturational period or age.

Age Differences

As has been found for other forms of violence, late adolescence and early adulthood are the ages that are most typical for perpetrating animal cruelty for males and females, albeit with a markedly higher prevalence in males. For example, Arluke and Luke (1997) reported that the average age for committing animal cruelty was 30 years. They also found that just over one quarter of the offenders were adolescents and more than half (56%) were under 30 years. In their Australian study, Gullone and Clarke (2008) reported consistent findings in their examination of all recorded offenses in the state of Victoria during the years between 1994 and 2001. In addition to being male, most offenders for all offenses including animal cruelty, against the person, against property, and for drugs were aged between 18 and 35 years. When looking only at animal cruelty offenses, there was a peak between 18 and 25 years.

In a study of 28 convicted and incarcerated male sexual homicide perpetrators, Ressler, Burgess, and Douglas (1988) found that prevalence of cruelty to animals was 36% in childhood and 46% in adolescence. Of note, in their study Arluke and Luke (1997) also found differences depending on age in the type of animal abused. Adults were more likely to be cruel to dogs while adolescents were more likely to kill cats. The type of cruelty also differed with shooting animals being more characteristic of adult animal cruelty and beating being more characteristic of adolescent animal cruelty.

The finding that there are age differences in the propensity to be cruel to animals is not surprising given the profound differences that are associated with different developmental milestones. Not only does physical strength increase as children mature, cognitive functioning and emotion regulation also develop. Emotion regulation involves processes that enable us to be aware of our emotions as well as processes that enable us to monitor, evaluate, and change our emotions in order to achieve our goals in a manner that is appropriate for the particular situation. In addition to the maturation of cognitive and emotion processes with age, environmental experiences will vary in their intensity of impact depending on developmental stage, as has been shown for the witnessing of animal cruelty. This will be discussed in the next section.

Witnessing of Violence and Animal Cruelty

Research has consistently demonstrated the importance of witnessing aggression for the development of aggressive behavior (e.g., Cummings, 1987; Davies, Myers, Cummings, & Heindel, 1999; Margolin & Gordis, 2000; Maughan & Cicchetti, 2002). A number of studies investigating the relationship between animal cruelty and family violence have also examined children's witnessing of animal cruelty and children's engagement in animal cruelty. These studies have shown that between 29% and 75% of children in violent families have witnessed animal cruelty and between 10% and 57% have engaged in animal cruelty. Parental reports of animal cruelty in normative samples of children (children who do not come from violent homes) are typically around 10% or lower (Ascione et al., 2007).

In her 2005 study, Baldry found that youth who witnessed violence between family members, or who witnessed harm to animals, were three times more likely to be cruel to animals compared to peers without such experiences. Currie (2006) also reported a significant relationship between the witnessing of aggressive behavior (domestic violence) and animal cruelty via parent report. Mothers' reports regarding their children's animal cruelty were compared, which included a group of 94 children (47 mothers) with a history of domestic violence and 90 children (45 mothers) without a history of domestic violence. According to the mother reports, exposed children were more likely to be cruel to animals compared to children who had not been exposed to violence. Additional support for this relationship was reported by DeGue and DiLillo

(2009), who found that those participants who had witnessed animal cruelty were eight times more likely than those who had not, to perpetrate animal cruelty.

In research specifically examining the relationship between children's aggressive behaviors and their witnessing of domestic violence, Baldry (2003) found that children who engaged in bullying behaviors were 1.8 times more likely to have been exposed to domestic violence than those who were not. Similarly, in their study of 281 (113 males; 168 females) school-based adolescents ranging in age between 12 and 18 years, Thompson and Gullone (2006) found that those who reported witnessing animal cruelty on at least one occasion also reported significantly higher levels of engaging in animal cruelty, compared to youth who did not witness animal cruelty. Particularly noteworthy is their finding that witnessing a stranger abusing an animal predicted *lower* levels of animal cruelty. This contrasted with the finding that witnessing animal cruelty by a friend, relative, parent, or sibling predicted *higher* levels of cruelty (Thompson & Gullone, 2006).

Hensley and Tallichet (2005) reported similar findings to those of Thompson and Gullone (2006). They not only found that inmates who reported witnessing animal cruelty were more likely to frequently be cruel to animals but also that those who witnessed a family member or a friend hurt or kill animals were more likely to commit animal cruelty with even greater frequency. The findings of these studies are consistent with Bandura's vicarious learning theory (1983), which proposes that observation of behavior is more likely to lead to performance of the observed behavior if the model has a meaningful relationship with the observer; in other words, if the model is a *significant* other. Also, consistent with Henry's (2004a) findings, it is noteworthy that those who were younger when they first witnessed someone hurt or kill animals were more likely to commit animal cruelty more frequently.

Further indicating the important aetiological role of witnessing cruelty is the study by Gullone and Robertson (2008) in which the possible pathways of acquisition for bullying and for animal cruelty behaviors were investigated. It was found that each type of behavior was significantly predicted by the witnessing of animal cruelty. Thus, this study supports the coexistence of animal directed aggression and human directed aggression in youth. As with Baldry's (2005) results, it also further demonstrates the importance of observational learning (Bandura, 1978). In this case, the observation of animal cruelty as a pathway for the development of different aggressive behaviors was demonstrated.

Others (e.g., Flynn, 1999b; 2000; Henry, 2004b; Hensley & Tallichet, 2005) have examined this relationship by asking undergraduate students or imprisoned males about their childhood experiences and behaviors. A study by Henry (2004a) involved 169 university students who were asked about exposure to, and perpetration of, animal cruelty. Results indicated that animal cruelty was witnessed on at least one occasion by 50.9% of participants. Also, the witnessing of animal cruelty before the age of 13 years was associated with higher perpetration rates (32%) compared to the witnessing of animal cruelty at 13 years or later (11.5%).

Witnessing significant others, such as parents, abusing animals has been demonstrated to play a large role in attitude formation for a child, contributing to the development of beliefs that aggressive and violent behaviors are somewhat normative, thereby supporting the development of what has been, in the general aggression literature, referred to as *normative beliefs* (Anderson & Huesmann, 2003). As has been consistently reported in the human aggression literature, children's beliefs about aggression are correlated with those of their parents (Huesmann, Eton, Lefkowitz, & Walder, 1984) as well as those of their peers (Huesmann & Guerra, 1997).

While research has shown that witnessing significant others behave in an aggressive manner serves as a powerful pathway of acquisition, observing media violence also has a significant effect on attitudes and behaviors (Anderson & Huesmann, 2003). A large and robust body of research has consistently shown that exposure to media violence predicts an increase in aggressive thoughts, desensitization to later violence exposure, and reductions in physiological arousal following violence exposure. It also predicts an increased acceptance and endorsement of violent behavior (Anderson & Huesmann, 2003; Anderson et al., 2010; Greeson & Williams, 1986; Hansen & Hansen, 1990). There is strong empirical evidence indicating that exposure to real life or media violence plays a strong role in the formation of cognitions related to aggression and violence (Flynn, 1999b), as well as the development of aggressive behavior (e.g., Baldry, 2005; Becker, Stuewig, Herrera, & McCloskey, 2004; Currie, 2006; Gullone & Roberston, 2008; Margolin & Gordis, 2000; Thompson & Gullone, 2006).

In sum, these studies demonstrate the importance of witnessing animal cruelty (i.e., an aggressive behavior) for the learning of, and engagement in, aggressive behavior. Children who witness or directly experience violence or aggression have been documented to be more likely to develop ways of thinking and behaving that support aggression (Guerra, Huesmann, & Spindler, 2003) and a tendency to behave aggressively (Anderson & Huesmann, 2003). Given that studies have consistently reported that children exposed to domestic violence are more likely to engage in acts of animal cruelty than children who have not been exposed to domestic violence (Baldry, 2005; Flynn, 2000; Hensley & Tallichet, 2005), it can be concluded that witnessing or experiencing violence and/or aggression are important pathways for the development of these behaviors.

Of course, it is not only the witnessing of aggression and violence that contributes to the learning of behavior and to the formation of attitudes and beliefs; the actual experiencing of behavior is likely to contribute to learning and attitude formation even more powerfully. Therefore, it is not at all surprising that a relationship has been found between children's experiences of abuse and neglect and their engagement in animal cruelty. The next section will review the research looking at the relationships between family and parenting experiences and children's animal cruelty.

Family and Parenting Experiences

Across different assessment methodologies, including retrospective reporting, a significant relationship between the experiencing of abuse in childhood (mostly within the family environment) and engagement in animal cruelty has emerged. Other factors placing children at risk of developing aggressive and antisocial behaviors, including animal cruelty behaviors, are those that characterize *risky families* (Repetti et al., 2002).

Characteristics of risky families include: overt family conflict, expressions of negative affect, and low nurturance and warmth. Risky parents are cold, unsupportive, or neglectful. Risky parenting and risky family environments leave children vulnerable to the development of psychological and physical disorders. It is important to emphasize the interactional role played by both environment and biology. While certain biologically based characteristics, such as temperament, are predictive of development along an antisocial behavior trajectory, children whose aggression increases as they develop, rather than following the normative decreasing pathway, may also be expressing a learned survival behavior for their particular circumstance. This is highlighted by research showing the intergenerational transmission of aggression.

In the earliest published investigation of the etiology of animal cruelty by children, Tapia (1971) reported an analysis of 18 child cases of cruelty to animals selected from the clinic files of the Child Psychiatry Section of the University of Missouri's School of Medicine. In all selected cases, cruelty to animals was either the chief complaint or one of the referring complaints. Among the cases, there was a high male prevalence. The children were of normal intelligence and young in age, spanning from 5 to 15 years with half of the cases being between

8 and 10 years. A chaotic home environment with aggressive parental models was the most common factor across the cases. On the basis of the case analysis, Tapia concluded that cruelty to animals occurs in conjunction with other hostile behavior including bullying, fighting, lying, stealing, and destructiveness, and that a chaotic home environment, together with aggressive parent models, are common factors.

In 1977, Rigdon and Tapia conducted a follow-up study of Tapia's (1971) study in an attempt to determine whether the presence of cruelty to animals as a significant clinical feature provides information that is of prognostic value. The original data reported in 1971 were collected between two and nine years prior to the published study. Five of the original 18 children were not able to be located for this follow-up study. The detailed case-by-case analysis revealed that of the 13 cases followed up, eight were still cruel to animals as many as nine years later. The authors concluded that "most of these children are the products of a chaotic home situation with aggressive parents who administered harsh corporal punishment" and that "the most effective form of therapy seemed to be removal from or a significant change in the chaotic home environment" (p. 36).

In other research, Deviney, Dickert, and Lockwood (1983) studied 53 families who had companion animals in their home and who met New Jersey legal criteria for child abuse and neglect. They found that compared to the general population, there were higher rates of animal cruelty in families where there was substantiated child abuse or neglect. Observations during home interviews revealed that companion animals were abused or neglected in 60% of these families. When the sample was classified according to type of abuse (physical abuse—40%; sexual abuse—10%; neglect—58%), in an alarming 88% of families displaying physical abuse, cruelty to animals was also present. As many as two thirds of the companion animals in these homes were abused by the fathers in the family, and one third were abused by the children in the family.

In their work comparing criminal (aggressive versus nonaggressive) and noncriminal retrospective reports of childhood experiences and abuse behaviors, Kellert and Felthous found that domestic violence and, particularly, paternal abuse and alcoholism, were common factors among aggressive criminals who had a history of childhood animal cruelty (Felthous, 1980; Felthous & Kellert, 1986; Kellert & Felthous, 1985). According to Kellert and Felthous (1985), the family and childhood experiences of many of the aggressive criminals were particularly violent. The domestic violence in the families of the aggressive criminals was most strongly characterised by paternal violence. Of note, three quarters of the aggressive criminals reported repeated and excessive child abuse compared to 31% of the nonaggressive criminals and 10% of the noncriminals. Among the nonaggressive criminals and noncriminals who were cruel to animals, reports of being physically abused as children were common. As many as 75% of noncriminals who reported experiences of parental abuse also reported being cruel to animals.

In a study by Ressler, Burgess, Hartman, Douglas, and McCormack (1986), 36 convicted sexually oriented killers were interviewed about their childhood histories. The offenders who were sexually abused in childhood or adolescence were significantly more likely than those who were not abused to report a number of aggressive behaviors including cruelty to animals, cruelty to other children, and assaultive behavior toward adults.

In research examining the relationships between childhood experiences and animal cruelty, Miller and Knutson (1997) compared the self-reports of 314 inmates in a corrections department with those of a group of undergraduate university students. They found modest associations between animal cruelty and punitive and acrimonious childhood histories. On this basis, the authors concluded that there is an association between punitive childhood histories and antisocial behavior.

Also based on retrospective self-reports, Flynn's (1999b) study involved 267 undergraduate students. The results showed a relationship between corporal punishment by parents and the perpetration of animal cruelty. Those who had perpetrated animal cruelty were physically punished more frequently before their teenage years compared to those who had never been cruel to an animal. Also, more than half of male teenagers who were hit by their fathers reported perpetrating animal cruelty.

Ascione, Friedrich, Heath, and Hayashi (2003) also examined the associations between children's cruelty to animals and physical abuse. In addition, they looked at the relationship between animal cruelty and parental physical fighting. Three groups of children (sexually abused group; psychiatric sample with no sexual abuse group; control group) aged between 6 and 12 years were involved in the study. Cruelty to animals was associated with a history of abuse, and the association was stronger for children who had been physically abused and for those who had witnessed domestic violence.

A more recent study by Duncan, Thomas, and Miller (2005) yielded converging findings through the assessment of charts of boys (aged 8 to 17 years) with conduct problems. The children's histories were also examined to identify the occurrence of physical child abuse, sexual child abuse, paternal alcoholism, paternal unavailability, and domestic violence. Children were grouped according to whether they had or had not been cruel to animals. The study found that children who were cruel to animals were twice more likely to have been physically and/or sexually abused or to have been exposed to domestic violence compared to children who were not cruel to animals.

In sum, these findings of research examining the relationships between childhood animal cruelty and parenting and family experiences are consistent with those from the larger literature relating to the development of antisocial behavior. Such research, for example, has shown that within homes where there is greater family instability, more conflict, and problematic parenting strategies (i.e., physical punishment), children are more likely to develop along the trajectory of childhood-onset antisocial behavior, also noted as being the more problematic trajectory with regard to stability of aggression and severity of aggression.

As victims of abuse, children experience a sense of powerlessness that, at a very basic level, is likely to be experienced as a threat to survival. Identifying with their abuser enables a transformation from a sense of powerlessness to one of being in control (Marcus-Newhall, Pederson, Carlson, & Miller, 2000). For children, those who are more vulnerable than themselves are likely to be small animals. Thus, it is the animals who are the vulnerable others to whom aggression can be displaced.

Displacement of Aggression

Displaced aggression constitutes a form of aggression against others (human or nonhuman animals) who did not play a direct role in the precipitating event (Marcus-Newhall et al., 2000; Pederson, Gonzales, & Miller, 2000). Displaced aggression increases if the target of such aggression provides even a minor trigger or the slightest of provocations (e.g., a dog barking). Displaced aggression also increases if the target can be perceived to be a member of a disliked out-group (Anderson & Huesmann, 2003) or as having less social value (e.g., a nonhuman animal).

There are instances when animal cruelty by children constitutes the displacement of aggression from humans to animals that occurs through children's identification with their abuser. Indeed, displaced aggression has been included as one of the nine motivations for animal cruelty reported by Kellert and Felthous (1985).

In addition to environmental variables including family and parenting influences, research has examined the important role played by cognitive constructs in better understanding the development of antisocial and aggressive behaviors. Such constructs include *knowledge structures* and *aggressive scripts*.

Cognitive Errors, Aggressive Cues, and Exposure to Violence

Cognitive structures are proposed to develop largely as a consequence of learning experiences. It would be expected, therefore, that individuals who experience or observe abuse in their formative years learn aggressive behaviors, hostile perceptions, attributions, and expectation biases. They are also more likely to learn callous attitudes and processes to enable disengagement from normative empathic reactions, which would otherwise serve as aggression inhibitors.

Thus, in environments that are sympathetic to antisocial behaviors, the development of aggressive scripts and normative beliefs related to aggression is promoted. Over time, through genetic and experiential or environmental factors, individuals develop neural pathways associated with these knowledge structures and behavioral scripts. Once stored in memory, these structures and scripts influence information processing, perceptions, and behavior (Anderson, 2002; Huesmann, 1988).

Knowledge Structures

Knowledge structures influence perception at multiple levels and in complex ways. They influence judgements and behavior, and they incorporate emotions. For example, when a knowledge structure containing the emotion of anger is activated, anger will be experienced. Highlighting the broad-ranging role played by knowledge structures in everyday life, Anderson and Bushman (2002) note that knowledge structures influence the situations that an individual will seek out as well as those that they will avoid.

With increased use and over time, knowledge structures tend to become automatic in their influence and increasingly function outside of conscious awareness (Schneider & Shiffrin, 1977; Todorov & Bargh, 2002). Also, over time, knowledge structures become much more rigid and resistant to change. In relation to aggression-related knowledge structures, it is generally agreed upon that the hardening begins to take place at around age 8 or 9. Another important cognitive construct is referred to as a *script*.

Script Theory

Script theory was proposed by Huesmann (1986). Scripts are proposed to define situations and also to guide behavior. Once scripts have been learned, they are available for retrieval at subsequent times as guides for behavior. Scripts have been defined as "sets of particularly well-rehearsed, highly associated concepts in memory" (Anderson & Bushman, 2002, p. 31). They involve causal links, goals, and action plans. The processing of social cues is guided by scripts that are stored in memory and are the evolved representational product of experience. They influence selective attention to cues, the perception of stimuli, and the consequent decisions made on the basis of those perceptions. Script theory has proven useful for explaining the generalization of learning processes across different situations as well as the automization of perception-judgement-decision-behavioral processes (Anderson & Bushman, 2002).

Huesmann (1988) proposed that during the early developmental years, children acquire *memory scripts*, which influence their perception of acceptable actions and their likely consequences. Research has shown that the most accessible social scripts for both aggressive children and adults are aggressive ones (Anderson & Huesmann, 2003). When compared to nonaggressive children, aggressive children are more likely to attend to aggressive social cues (Gouze, 1987). Aggressive children are also less likely to rely on external cues but more on their own stereotypes (Dodge & Tomlin, 1987) and they are more likely to describe their social relationships using such constructs (Stromquist & Strauman, 1991).

Shedding some light on the ways in which particular experiences can influence the development of particular information processing pathways, and consequently the selective attention to particular cues, Pollak and Tolley-Schell (2003) found that physically abused children are more likely to attend to angry faces selectively and to demonstrate reduced attention to happy faces. Such children also demonstrate difficulty disengaging from angry faces. Of additional concern, it is not only children who are abused or who directly experience violence who develop beliefs and scripts that support aggression and a tendency to behave violently but also children who witness abuse or violence (Anderson & Huesmann, 2003).

In sum, cognitive constructs including knowledge structures and behavioral scripts are useful for understanding why, when compared to nonaggressive individuals, aggressive individuals are more likely to perceive hostility in situations even where there is none. This tendency, referred to as a hostile attribution bias, is particularly pronounced in ambiguous situations (Anderson & Bushman, 2002; Crick & Dodge, 1994; Dodge et al., 2006). In relation to animal cruelty, aggressive children may be more likely to attribute hostile intentions to animals since cues provided by animals are often more ambiguous than those provided by humans (Dadds, 2008). Such misattribution can also explain adult aggression toward animals. Although empirical research is required to confirm such processes, they are a logical extension of the hostile attribution bias findings in relation to humans.

In addition to the cognitive constructs involved in understanding the underlying processes of aggressive and antisocial behaviors, there are processes underpinned more strongly by emotions, which will be discussed in the next section.

THE DEVELOPMENT OF EMPATHY
AND EMOTION REGULATION

A number of emotion-related processes play a role that is specifically relevant to aggressive behavior (Lemerise & Arsenio, 2000). Of particular relevance are the emotion-related competencies and strategies involved in regulating emotions.

From as early as 1 year of age, aggression, particularly peer-directed aggression, becomes evident. By the time children have begun school, their aggression levels begin to decrease. Some theorize that this decrease coincides with an increase in interpersonal skills and emotion regulation competencies including effortful control (Anderson & Huesmann, 2003; Eisenberg, Champion, & Ma, 2004; Keenan & Shaw, 1997). Other developing abilities at this time include perspective-taking (Selman, 1980), empathy (Zahn-Waxler, Radke-Yarrow, & King, 1979), and emotion processing (Schultz, Izard, & Bear, 2004). According to Ascione, Thompson, and Black (1997), motivations driving young children's animal cruelty including *curiosity* and *exploration* likely occur as a consequence of younger children not yet having internalized society's values regarding the appropriate treatment of animals.

It is not surprising that the development of empathy and emotion regulation competencies predicts a decrease in aggressive behaviors while the compromised development of these competencies places children at risk of developing antisocial behaviors, including engaging in animal cruelty. Moreover, those children most at risk are likely to be that subgroup of children with conduct disorders who also present callous-unemotional traits and an inability to experience guilt (Hastings, Zhan-Waxler, Robinson, Usher, & Bridges, 2000; Luk, Staiger, Wong, & Mathai, 1999). These children tend to initiate and engage in persistent antisocial acts, including displays of aggression toward both people and animals (Miller, 2001). At this extreme end of the antisocial behavior continuum, a lack of empathy and guilt in addition to an interpersonal style characterized by callousness are predictive of psychopathy (Frick & White, 2008).

Thus, while low levels of empathy constitute a risk factor for antisocial and aggressive behavior (McPhedran, 2009), higher levels of empathy can be a protective factor against the development of these behaviors. Empathic and prosocial youths are more inclined to treat their companion animals humanely (Poresky, 1990; Vidovic, Stetic, & Bratko, 1999). Several empirical studies have demonstrated the importance that empathy has for interpersonal relationships and behaviors, including those with animals. For example, Poresky's (1990) study assessed the relationship between bonds with companion animals and empathy levels among 38 children ranging in age from 3 to 6 years. As expected, children who had a strong bond with their companion animal scored higher on empathy than children who did not have companion animals.

In a related study, Vidovic et al. (1999) assessed companion animal ownership and socio-emotional development among a sample of 826 youths ranging in age from 10 to 15 years. Participants who scored higher than average on a companion animal attachment scale yielded significantly higher scores on both empathy and prosocial orientation than those who scored lower than average. A more recent study involving 381 13- to 18-year-olds by Thompson and Gullone (2008) yielded supporting findings. These researchers examined the associations between empathy and prosocial behaviors as well as empathy and antisocial behaviors. Behaviors toward humans and nonhuman animals were investigated. As predicted, low empathy was found to be a significant predictor of antisocial behaviors and high empathy was found to be a significant predictor of prosocial behaviors toward both humans and nonhuman animals.

CONCLUSION

In conclusion, what is most apparent from this review is that the risk factors, not surprisingly, for animal cruelty are not different than those for other aggressive and antisocial behaviors. What is also clear is that the co-occurrence of animal cruelty with other antisocial and aggressive behaviors is cause for significant concern in a number of regards. When a child or adolescent is found to have abused an animal, one needs to consider not only what other aggressive behaviors this individual might be engaged in, but also what might be happening in this individual's life. Is the individual a victim of child abuse or domestic violence? Has the individual witnessed aggression or violence?

A relatively recent study conducted by Vaughn and colleagues (2009) is one of the largest and most comprehensive studies to investigate risk factors that has been conducted to date. Given that there has been a relationship demonstrated between bullying and animal cruelty, Vaughn et al. also included bullying as a variable in their study. The study, which was conducted in the United States, was based on data derived from the first two waves of a national epidemiologic survey regarding alcoholism and related disorders. The results showed a number of risk factors to be significant.

For bullying, the risk factors included: being made to do chores that were too difficult or dangerous; threatening to hit or throw something; pushing, shoving, slapping, or hitting; and hitting that left bruises, marks, or injuries. For animal cruelty, the risk factors included swearing and saying hurtful things, having a parent or other adult living within the home that went to jail or prison, and being fondled or touched in a sexual way by an adult/other person.

Of significance is the finding that cruelty to animals was significantly associated with *all assessed* antisocial behaviors. Specifically, strong associations were found between animal cruelty and lifetime alcohol use disorders; conduct, antisocial, obsessive-compulsive, and histrionic personality disorders; pathological gambling; and a family history of antisocial behavior.

On the basis of their findings, Vaughn et al. (2009) concluded that:

> Cruelty to animals is associated with elevated rates observed in young, poor, men with family histories of antisocial behavior and personal histories of conduct disorder in childhood, and antisocial, obsessive-compulsive and histrionic personality disorders, and pathological gambling in adulthood. Given these associations, and the widespread ownership of pets and animals, effective screening of children, adolescents and adults for animal cruelty and appropriate mental health interventions should be deployed. (Abstract)

Animal cruelty has also been identified as one of the earliest indicators of what are referred to as externalizing disorders, including conduct disorder as well as a predictor of the development of aggression along a more severe trajectory (Frick et al., 1993; Luk et al., 1999). Striving for its early identification would therefore seem to be of significant priority as such would provide an optimal opportunity for engaging preventative strategies.

The focus of preventative strategies should be guided by the risk factors reviewed in this work. Processes involved in the development of aggressive behaviors, most particularly the development of cognitive structures such as normative beliefs and aggressive scripts through exposure to antisocial behaviors, need also to be addressed at a broader, community level. Given the pivotal roles for aggression learning played by witnessing cruelty, exposure to aggressive models, and media violence, concern is warranted also with regard to legalized aggressive behaviors such as hunting, attending rodeos, and fishing. On the basis of the reviewed research, it is reasonable to conclude that legalized aggression has an influence on young people's development of relevant cognitive structures and consequent aggressive behaviors. This would particularly be the case for individuals with a vulnerable disposition (e.g., a temperament characterized by callous-unemotional traits) toward the development of such behaviors or those within a vulnerable environment or "risky" family.

Moreover, labelling certain aggressive behaviors as entertainment or sport because they are targeting particular species and others as antisocial because they are targeting other species, such as companion animals, is incongruous. Mixed and confusing messages are communicated when cruelty is legalized in relation to some practices and species, such as confined farming practices for pork production, but outlawed for other species on the basis of the argument that they cause suffering.

For most individuals, the potential psychological discomfort caused by such conflicting messages may be managed through the use of cognitive mechanisms (e.g., vilifying the recipients, obscuring personal agency, or cognitively reconstructing the conduct) that enable individuals to disengage self-sanctions for engaging in reprehensible behavior (Bandura, 1983). However, for young people whose attitudes are undergoing processes of formation, such contradiction and inconsistency can only serve as barriers to the development of empathy and compassion. It follows that if we cultivate a culture of compassion toward our nonhuman citizens, current and future generations will benefit through reduced antisocial and violent behavior toward all sentient beings.

References

Anderson, C. A. (2002). Aggression. In E. Borgatta & R. Montgomery (Eds.), *The encyclopedia of sociology* (2nd ed., pp. 68–78).), New York, NY: MacMillan.

Anderson, C. A., & Bushman, B. J. (2002). Human aggression. *Annual Review of Psychology, 53,* 27–51.

Anderson, C. A., & Huesmann, L. R. (2003). Human aggression: A social-cognitive view: In M. A. Hogg & J. Cooper (Eds.), *The Sage Handbook of Social Psychology* (pp. 296–323). Thousand Oaks, CA: Sage Publications Inc.

Anderson, C. A., Shibuya, A., Ihori, N., Swing, E. L., Bushman, B. J., Sakamoto, A., & Salee, M. (2010). Violent video game effects on aggression, empathy, and prosocial behavior in Eastern and Western countries: A meta-analytic review. *Psychological Bulletin, 136,* 151–173.

Arluke, A., & Luke, C. (1997). Physical cruelty toward animals in Massachusetts, 1975–1996. *Society and Animals, 5,* 195–204.

Ascione, F. R., Friedrich, W. N., Heath, J., & Hayashi, K. (2003). Cruelty to animals in normative, sexually abused, and outpatient psychiatric samples of 6- to 12-year-old children: Relations to maltreatment and exposure to domestic violence. *Anthrozoos, 16*, 194–212.

Ascione, F. R., Thompson, T. M., & Black, T. (1997). Childhood cruelty to animals: Assessing cruelty dimensions and motivations. *Anthrozoos, 10*, 170–179.

Ascione, F. R., Weber, C. V., Thompson, T. M., Heath, J., Maruyama, M., & Hayashi, K. (2007). Battered pets and domestic violence: Animal abuse reported by women experiencing intimate violence and by nonabused women. *Violence Against Women, 13*, 354–373.

Baldry, A. C. (2003). Animal abuse and exposure to interparenteral violence in Italian youth. *Journal of Interpersonal Violence, 18*(3), 258–281.

Baldry, A. C. (2005). Animal abuse among preadolescents directly and indirectly victimized at school and at home. *Criminal Behavior and Mental Health, 15*, 97–110.

Bandura, A. (1978). Social learning theory of aggression. *Journal of Communication,* Summer, 12–29.

Bandura, A. (1983). *Psychological mechanisms of aggression.* In R. G. Geen & E. I. Donnerstein (Eds.), *Aggression: Theoretical and empirical reviews* (Vol. 1, pp. 1–40). New York, NY: Academic Press.

Becker, K. D., Stuewig, J., Herrera, V. M., & McCloskey, L. A. (2004). A study of firesetting and animal cruelty in children: Family influences and adolescent outcomes. *Journal of the American Academy of Child & Adolescent Psychiatry, 43*, 905–912.

Brown, L. (1988). *Cruelty to animals: The moral debt.* London, England: Macmillan.

Coston, C., & Protz, C. M. (1998). Kill your dog, beat your wife, screw your neighbour's kids, rob a bank? A cursory look at an individual's vat of social chaos resulting from deviance. *Free Inquiry in Creative Sociology, 26*, 153–158.

Crick, N. R., & Dodge, K.A. (1994). A review and reformulation of social information processing mechanisms in children's adjustment. *Psychological Bulletin, 115*, 74–101.

Cummings, E. M. (1987). Coping with background anger in early childhood. *Child Development, 58*, 976–984.

Currie, C. L. (2006). Animal cruelty by children exposed to domestic violence. *Child Abuse & Neglect, 30*, 425–435.

Dadds, M. R. (2008). Conduct problems and cruelty to animals in children: What is the link? In F. R. Ascione (Ed.), *The international handbook of animal abuse and cruelty: Theory, research, and application* (pp. 111–131). West Lafayette, IN: Purdue University Press.

Dadds, M. R., Turner, C. M., & McAloon, J. (2002). Developmental links between cruelty to animals and human violence. *Australian & New Zealand Journal of Counselling, 35*, 363–382.

Davies, P. T., Myers, R. L., Cummings, E. M., & Heindel, S. (1999). Adult conflict history and children's subsequent responses to conflict: An experimental test. *Journal of Family Psychology, 13*, 610–628.

DeGue, S., & DiLillo, D. (2009). Is animal cruelty a "red flag" for family violence? Investigating co-occurring violence toward children, partners, and pets. *Journal of Interpersonal Violence, 24*, 1036–1056.

Deviney, E., Dickert, J., & Lockwood, R. (1983). The care of pets within child abusing families. *International Journal for the Study of Animal Problems, 4*, 321–329.

Dishion, T. J., French, D. C., & Patterson, G. R. (1995). The development and ecology of antisocial behavior. In D. Cicchetti & D. J. Cohen (Eds.), *Developmental psychopathology: Vol. 2. Risk, disorder, and adaptation* (pp. 421–471). Oxford, England: John Wiley & Sons.

Dodge, K. A., Coie, J. D., & Lynam, D. (2006). Aggression and antisocial behavior in youth. In N. Eisenberg, W. Damon, & R. M. Lerner (Eds.), *Handbook of child psychology, Vol. 3. Social, emotional, and personality development* (6th ed., pp. 719–788). Hoboken, NJ: John Wiley & Sons Inc.

Dodge, K. A., & Tomlin, A. (1987). Utilization of self-schemas as a mechanism of attributional bias in aggressive children. *Social Cognition, 5*, 280–300.

Duncan, A., Thomas, J. C., & Miller, C. (2005). Significance of family risk factors in development of childhood animal cruelty in adolescent boys with conduct problems. *Journal of Family Violence, 20*, 235–239.

Eisenberg, N., Champion, C., & Ma, Y. (2004). Emotion-related regulation: An emerging construct. *Merrill-Palmer Quarterly, 50*, 236–259.

Farrington, D. P. (1991). Childhood aggression and adult violence: Early precursors and later life outcomes. In D. J. Peplar & H. K. Rubin (Eds.), *The development and treatment of childhood aggression* (pp. 5–29). Hillsdale, NJ: Erlbaum.

Felthous, A. R. (1980). Aggression against cats, dogs and people. *Child Psychiatry & Human Development, 10*(3), 169–177.

Felthous, A. R., & Kellert, S. R. (1986). Violence against animals and people: Is aggression against living creatures generalized? *Bulletin of the American Academy of Psychiatry & the Law, 14*, 55–69.

Flynn, C. P. (1999a). Animal abuse in childhood and later support for interpersonal violence in families. *Society and Animals, 7*, 161–172.

Flynn, C. P. (1999b). Exploring the link between corporal punishment and children's cruelty to animals. *Journal of Marriage & the Family, 61*, 971–981.

Flynn, C. P. (2000). Why family professionals can no longer ignore violence toward animals. *Family Relations: Interdisciplinary Journal of Applied Family Studies, 49*, 87–95.

Flynn, C. P. (2011). Examining the links between animal abuse and human violence. *Crime, Law and Social Change, 55*, 453–468.

Frick, P. J., & Dickens, C. (2006). Current perspectives on conduct disorder. *Current Psychiatry Reports, 8*, 59–72.

Frick, P. J., Lahey, B. B., Loeber, R., Tannenbaum, L., Van Horn, Y., Christ, M. A. G., Hart, E. A., & Hanson, K. (1993). Oppositional defiant disorder and conduct disorder: A meta-analytic review of factor analyses and cross-validation in a clinic sample. *Clinical Psychology Review, 13*, 319–340.

Frick, P. J., & White, S. F. (2008). Research review: The importance of callous-unemotional traits for developmental models of aggressive and antisocial behavior. *Journal of Child Psychology and Psychiatry, 49*, 359–375.

Gouze, K. R. (1987). Attention and social problem solving as correlates of aggression in preschool males. *Journal of Abnormal Child Psychology, 15*, 181–197.

Greeson, L. E., & Williams, R. A. (1986). Social implications of music videos for youth: An analysis of the content and effects of MTV. *Youth and Society, 18*, 177–189.

Guerra, N. G., Huesmann, L. R., & Spindler, A. (2003). Community violence exposure, social cognition, and aggression among urban elementary school children. *Child Development, 74*, 1561–1576.

Gullone, E. (2012). *Animal cruelty, antisocial behavior and aggression: More than a link.* Hampshire, England: Palgrave Macmillan Ltd.

Gullone, E., & Clarke, J. (2008). Human-animal interactions: The Australian perspective. In F. Ascione (Ed.), *The international handbook of theory and research on animal abuse and cruelty* (pp. 305–335). West Lafayette, IN: Purdue University Press.

Gullone, E., & Robertson, N. (2008). The relationship between bullying and animal abuse in adolescents: The importance of witnessing animal abuse. *Journal of Applied Developmental Psychology, 29*, 371–379.

Hansen, C. H., & Hansen, R. D. (1990). Rock music videos and antisocial behavior. *Basic and Applied Social Psychology, 11*, 357–369.

Hartup, W. W. (2005). The development of aggression. In R. E. Tremblay, W. W. Hartup, & J. Archer (Eds.), *Developmental origins of aggression* (pp. 3–22). New York, NY: Guilford Press.

Hastings, P. D., Zahn-Waxler, C., Robinson, J., Usher, B., & Bridges, D. (2000). The development of concern for others in children with behavior problems. *Developmental Psychology, 36*, 531–546.

Henry, B. C. (2004a). Exposure to animal abuse and group context: Two factors affecting participation in animal abuse. *Anthrozoos, 17*, 290–305.

Henry, B. C. (2004b). The relationship between animal cruelty, delinquency, and attitudes toward the treatment of animals. *Society & Animals, 12*, 185–207.

Hensley, C., & Tallichet, S. E. (2005). Animal cruelty motivations: Assessing demographic and situational influences. *Journal of Interpersonal Violence, 20*, 1429–1443.

Huesmann, L. (1986). Psychological processes promoting the relation between exposure to media violence and aggressive behavior by the viewer. *Journal of Social Issues, 42*, 125–139.

Huesmann, L. (1988). An information processing model for the development of aggression. *Aggressive Behavior, 14*, 13–24.

Huesmann, L. R., Eton, L. D., Lefkowitz, M. M., & Walder, L. O. (1984). Stability of aggression across time and generations. *Developmental Psychology, 20*, 1120–1134.

Huesmann, L. R., & Guerra, N. G. (1997). Children's normative beliefs about aggression and aggressive behavior. *Journal of Personality and Social Psychology, 72*, 408–419.

Keenan, K., & Shaw, D. (1997). Developmental and social influences on young girls' early problem behavior. *Psychological Bulletin, 121,* 95–113.

Kellert, S. R., & Felthous, A. R. (1985). Childhood cruelty toward animals among criminals and noncriminals. *Human Relations, 38*(12), 1113–1129.

Lemerise, E. A., & Arsenio, W. F. (2000). An integrated model of emotion processes and cognition in social information processing. *Child Development,* 107–118.

Loeber, R., & Dishion, T. (1983). Early predictors of male delinquency: A review. *Psychological Bulletin, 93,* 68–99.

Luk, E. S., Staiger, P. K., Wong, L., & Mathai, J. (1999). Children who are cruel to animals: A revisit. *Australian and New Zealand Journal of Psychiatry, 33,* 29–36.

Marcus-Newhall, A., Pederson, W. C., Carlson, M., & Miller, N. (2000). Displaced aggression is alive and well: A meta-analytic review. *Journal of Personality and Social Psychology, 78,* 670–689.

Margolin, G., & Gordis, E. B. (2000). The effects of family and community violence on children. *Annual Review of Psychology, 51,* 445–479.

Maughan, A., & Cicchetti, D. (2002). Impact of child maltreatment and interadult violence on children's emotion regulation abilities and socioemotional adjustment. *Child Development, 73,* 1525–1542.

McPhedran, S. (2009). A review of the evidence for associations between empathy, violence, and animal cruelty. *Aggression and Violent Behavior, 14,* 1–4.

Miller, C. (2001). Childhood animal cruelty and interpersonal violence. *Clinical Psychology Review, 21*(5), 735–749.

Miller, K. S., & Knutson, J. F. (1997). Reports of severe physical punishment and exposure to animal cruelty by inmates convicted of felonies and by university students. *Child Abuse and Neglect, 21,* 59–82.

Pollak, S. D., & Tolley-Schell, S. A. (2003). Selective attention to facial emotion in physically abused children. *Journal of Abnormal Psychology, 112,* 323–338.

Poresky, R. H. (1990). The young children's empathy measure: Reliability, validity and effects of companion animal bonding. *Psychological Reports, 66,* 931–936.

Repetti, R. L., Taylor, S. E., & Seeman, T. E. (2002). Risky families: Family social environments and the mental and physical health of offspring. *Psychological Bulletin, 128,* 330–366.

Ressler, R. K., Burgess, A. W., & Douglas, J. E. (1988). *Sexual homicide: Patterns and motives.* Lexington, MA: Lexington Books.

Ressler, R. K., Burgess, A. W., Hartman, C. R., Douglas, J. E., & McCormack, A. (1986). Murderers who rape and mutilate. *Journal of Interpersonal Violence, 1,* 273–287.

Rigdon, J. D., & Tapia, F. (1977). Children who are cruel to animals: A follow-up study. *Journal of Operational Psychiatry, 8,* 27–36.

Schneider, W., & Shiffrin, R. M. (1977). Controlled and automatic human information processing: I. Detection, search and attention. *Psychological Review, 84,* 1–66.

Schultz, D., Izard, C. E., & Bear, G. (2004). Children's emotion processing: Relations to emotionality and aggression. *Development and Psychopathology, 16,* 371–387.

Schwartz, C. E., Wright, C. I., Shin, L. M., Kagan, J., & Rauch, S. L. (2003). Inhibited and ininhibited infants "grown up": Adult amygdalar response to novelty. *Science, 300*(5627), 1952–1953.

Selman, R. L. (1980). *The growth of interpersonal understanding: Developmental and clinical analyses.* New York, NY: Academic Press.

Stromquist, V. J., & Strauman, T. J. (1991). Children's social constructs: Nature, assessment, and association with adaptive versus maladaptive behavior. *Social Cognition, 9,* 330–358.

Tapia, F. (1971). Children who are cruel to animals. *Child Psychiatry & Human Development, 2,* 70–77.

Thompson, K. L., & Gullone, E. (2006). An investigation into the association between the witnessing of animal abuse and adolescents' behavior toward animals. *Society and Animals, 14,* 223–243.

Todorov, A., & Bargh, J. A. (2002). Automatic sources of aggression. *Aggression and Violent Behavior, 7,* 53–68.

Vaughn, M. G., Fu, Q., DeLisi, M., Beaver, K. M., Perron, B. E., Terrell, K., et al. (2009). Correlates of cruelty to animals in the United States: Results from the National Epidemiologic Survey on Alcohol and Related Conditions. *Journal of Psychiatric Research, 43,* 1213–1218.

Vidovic, V. V., Stetic, V. V., & Bratko, D. (1999). Pet ownership, type of pet and socio-emotional development of school children. *Anthrozoos, 12,* 211–217.

Zahn-Waxler, C., Radke-Yarrow, M., & King, R. A. (1979). Child rearing and children's prosocial initiations toward victims of distress. *Child Development, 50*(2), 319–330.

7 The Neoteny Barrier: Seeking Respect for the Non-Cute

MARK J. ESTREN

A foundational human attraction to mammalian neoteny may be crucial for preservation of our own species, but it can be counterproductive in relationships between humans and other animals. The deeply rooted human psychological attraction to and preference for anthropomorphically viewed neotenic characteristics explains why some animals, whether endangered or not, receive far more public attention and scientific study than others. An understanding of the neoteny barrier makes it possible to find ways around it: The barrier may not be possible to break, but it can be modified by scientific awareness of its existence and an alteration of public perception of value to include animals who would not, in neotenic terms, be considered cute.

Anyone looking for an improved relationship between humans and other animals runs quickly, if unknowingly, into a blockage that seems at first insuperable: the neoteny barrier. Humans generally are more attracted to animals who retain infantile characteristics into adulthood. This is, at bottom, a biological imperative derived from the appearance of human babies, with their proportionately larger heads and eyes and, as they age slightly, their unsteady gait. Human attraction to neotenic animals relates directly to nurturing and species-propagating instincts for our own kind and also explains why, for example, we find a penguin's waddle amusingly endearing.

There are two possible evolutionary explanations for our focus on neoteny: We may be born with an aesthetic sense that causes us to favor juvenile morphological traits, or our genes may tell us to favor whatever traits our offspring happen to have (Gould, 1980b). In either case, the effect is the same: The animals to whom we feel the greatest attraction are those whom we deem, because of their morphology, to be cute.

This preference is all-pervasive and largely unconscious. And it is not confined to humans. The existence in other mammals of infants with big, widely

Journal of Animal Ethics 2(1): 6–11

spaced eyes, a button nose, and a mouth set low in the face explains why lactat-
ing mothers of one species, such as dogs, have been known to nurse infants of
another, such as cats (Angier, 2010).

The well-intentioned desire to have humans treat other animals with greater
respect can collide head-on with neotenic preferences, which permeate society
to an extent that is rarely acknowledged. In Japan, for example, the ubiquitous
Hello Kitty appears on more than 20,000 products made or licensed by Sanrio,
which owns the character. Hello Kitty is such a phenomenon because she "needs
protection," says Boston University sociologist Merry White. "She's not only
adorable and round, she's also mouthless and can't speak for herself" (quoted
in Garger, 2007).

Cartoon characters, created out of nothingness from artists' minds, provide a particularly clear example of the ubiquity of neotenic preference. Pixar
Studios carefully made Remy, the star of its animated movie *Ratatouille,* blue,
fluffy, and snub-nosed, more like an animated plush toy than a real rat. In this
approach, Pixar was following in the footsteps of its corporate parent, Walt
Disney Company, where Mickey Mouse evolved during half a century to have
a bigger head, bigger eyes, and larger cranial vault than he originally possessed—plus limbs that appeared shorter and thus more "babyish" to human
viewers because they were covered with clothing (Gould, 1980a).

Similar evolution is readily seen in other animal-based cartoon characters.
Betty Boop, the curvy flapper-era animated star, originated as a dog with long
ears but did not really take off in popularity until she was redrawn in her much
more familiar shape, with huge head, tiny button nose, and great big eyes—all
neotenic characteristics (Bogin, 1999). And in Walt Kelly's famous comic strip
Pogo, no fewer than three major characters underwent significant neotenic
transformation. Pogo Possum himself originally had a very long snout and
close-together eyes; over time, the snout shortened significantly, and the eyes
became bigger and wider. Porkypine originally looked much like a real porcu-
pine and walked on all fours, later attaining upright posture, quills more closely
resembling unruly hair, and wide eyes. And P. T. Bridgeport, the pompous circus
character named for P. T. Barnum and the city of Bridgeport, Connecticut, with
which both Barnum and Kelly were associated, metamorphosed most rapidly:
"It was not many days after the introduction of P. T. Bridgeport that I decided
to change the model. The first seemed a little unpleasant to me" (Kelly, 1959,
p. 44). The "unpleasant" character had jowls and close-set eyes; the changed
one, a round and puffy face and much larger eyes spaced farther apart.

In everyday life, human preference for the neotenic plays out constantly:
People tend to find squirrels cute and their close relatives, rats, abhorrent;

koalas, despite their prickly personalities, are considered so adorable that the United States has labeled the koala a threatened species even though Australia says it is not (Endangered and Threatened Wildlife and Plants, 2000)—whereas the koala's closest living relative, the short-legged, pig-faced, beady-eyed wombat, garners little attention or interest.

There may be distinct evaluative benefits to the human preference for neoteny, paralleling as it does the phylogenetic history of our species: "There he stands—our vertical, hunting, weapon-toting, territorial, neotenous, brainy naked ape, a primate by ancestry and a carnivore by adoption, ready to conquer the world" (Morris, 1967, p. 97).

But the strong human attraction to neoteny must be of the greatest concern to anyone seeking more-ethical treatment of all animals. Humans' neotenic preferences are mammal-specific: Little outcry is heard from nonscientists about the remarkable axolotl, a neotenic mole salamander that lives only in the Xochimilco area of central Mexico, where fewer than 1,200 are thought to survive (Walker, 2009). The axolotl, with tiny eyes, prominent gills, and slimy skin, does not possess the sort of neoteny to which humans are generally attracted. And yet it was to describe the retention of larval features in the Mexican axolotl that the word "neoteny" was originally coined.[1]

Other "unattractive" animals, endangered or not, also tend to engender scorn, sometimes masquerading as humor, from scientists and the public alike—with the result that they are demeaned in terms of their "worthiness," and attempts to preserve them become an uphill battle.

A straightforward web search readily turns up headlines such as "10 Endangered Species That Are Too Ugly to Live," "Ugly Endangered Species," and "Who Wants to Save an Ugly Animal?" Some such sites are well-meaning, arguing that even "ugly" animals deserve to live. But the patronizing nature of this anthropomorphic evaluation of animal appearance does as much harm as good, substituting human attitudes toward cuteness—which are based on neotenic characteristics of human babies and other mammals—for an objective consideration of the importance of each species within its ecological niche.

Indeed, so deep are human response patterns to animals with particular characteristics that scientists breeding animals for friendliness have found themselves with ones who also appear, to human eyes, cuter. In Russia's famous multi-decade fox-farm experiment,

> selecting which foxes to breed based solely on how well they got along with humans seemed to alter their physical appearance along with their dispositions. After only nine generations, the researchers recorded fox kits born with floppier ears. Piebald patterns appeared on their coats. By this time the

foxes were already whining and wagging their tails in response to a human presence, behaviors never seen in wild foxes. (Ratliff, 2011)

The neoteny barrier is a significant real-world problem, even among scientists. A recent study of conservation scientists' efforts found that

> the scientific investment per species differed greatly between groups—the mean number of papers per threatened large mammal eclipsed that of threatened reptiles, birds, small mammals, and amphibians by 2.6-, 15-, 216-, and more than 500-fold, respectively. Thus, in the eyes of science, all species are not created equal. A few species commanded a great proportion of scientific attention, whereas for many species information that might inform conservation is virtually nonexistent. (Trimble & Van Aarde, 2010, p. 886)

What is to be done? Recognition of the prejudicial nature of human response to animals is not in itself sufficient. People's preference for mammalian neoteny is far too deeply rooted to be mitigated, much less eliminated, by reasoned argument alone. But a two-pronged approach, one for scientists and one for the public at large, may provide reason for hope—and has, to a limited extent, already begun.

Within the scientific community, rationality and a form of enlightened self-interest have their place. It is incumbent on those conservationists who are aware of human predisposition toward animals with neotenic features to draw the attention of their colleagues to less-studied animals with a less overtly "cute" appearance. A suggestion that research-related rewards, and even funding, might be more readily forthcoming for work on animals whose appearance makes them less frequently studied would not be out of place.

Scientists respond well to research findings, and there is increasing awareness of the disparity between species needing protection and those receiving it—a divergence attributable in part to neoteny and also to other elements of attractiveness, as anthropomorphically defined (see, e.g., Frynta, 2010).

Daniel Frynta, an ecologist at Charles University in Prague, has studied the retention and breeding of animals in zoos and has determined that a zoo-kept animal must have particular characteristics: "It's got to be big. It's got to be cute. It's got to behave or look humanlike. If a critter is colorful, we like it. We also like it when zoo denizens play and speak and travel in family groups" (quoted in Eveleth, 2010). The reasons for this, Frynta says, are largely economic, not scientific: "Zoos full of endangered but ugly animals will never make money" (quoted in Eveleth, 2010). Increasing awareness of this reality may well raise the hackles and thus modify the research thrust of scientists, including those who, however unwittingly, themselves contribute to the minimization of the importance of "ugly" species by focusing their investigative attention on neotenic and otherwise anthropomorphically attractive ones.

And the "importance" argument provides a bridge between matters of concern to scientists and those of significance to the general public. An animal whom many people consider repulsive or frightening may gain popular backing once the animal's usefulness to humans is made clear: Our self-interest overcomes our visceral aversion. Thus, the Year of the Snake in China (2001) brought a new appreciation of the reptiles, who are deemed a delicacy, after farmers became more fully aware of serpents' crucial role in controlling rodents: "The intensive hunting of wild snakes caused the mouse population to explode, with devastating consequences for crops" ("China Snake Craze," 2001).

Similarly, the dull-brown, small-finned, long-bodied, long-snouted opossum pipefish (*Microphis brachyurus lineatus*)—listed in the United States as a "species of concern" for more than a decade—is anything but cute from a human perspective, but it is an important indicator of habitat quality in tropical and subtropical aquatic habitats, whose health in turn gives humans important information about the quality of our own environment (Buczynski, 2010). Emphasizing the usefulness of species to humans can overcome the fact that the species are not attractive to most people. A few educational programs that take just this approach are already in existence or under development.[2] They can even be extended over time to include animals who are neither attractive nor directly useful to humans—but who are nevertheless worthy of protection. This is precisely what EDGE (Evolutionarily Distinct and Globally Endangered),[3] a program of the Zoological Society of London, is attempting to do, basing its approach on the importance of phylogenetic diversity (Isaac, 2007).

In addition to these efforts, there is something to be said for encouraging a kind of contrarianism-of-appearance focus among scientists and the lay public alike. We humans have ourselves, through selective breeding, engineered animals who would scarcely be considered "cute" by neotenic standards, such as the Sphynx (Canadian hairless) cat, a breed that has existed for less than half a century. What is important is that such human-created "ugly" animals quickly develop followings of people who insist that they are, in a sense, beautiful.[4] Indeed, the aforementioned axolotl is fancied as an interesting aquarium denizen and is kept as such by people in many countries.

No one would suggest that human standards of beauty can be easily changed; indeed, an understanding of neoteny argues that they cannot foundationally be changed at all. But the adaptability of humans to new circumstances is among our species' most salient characteristics, and if we cannot escape our attraction to neotenic mammalian animals, there is some evidence that we can expand our definition of attractiveness to encompass animals who would not, at first glance, be deemed "cute." To the extent that we can do this, the animals will benefit from our willingness to see them in a new light, and we ourselves will gain a valuable perspective on some of the other inhabitants of our planet.

Notes

1. By German zoologist Julius Kollmann. See Kollmann (1885).
2. See, for example, http://www.pbs.org/wnet/nature/lessons/u-g-l-y-ive-got-a-great-alibi/lesson/423/
3. http://www.edgeofexistence.org/conservation/default.php
4. See, for example, http://www.sphynxcat.com

References

Angier, N. (2010, August 9). A masterpiece of nature? Yuck! *New York Times*.

Bogin, B. (1999). *Patterns of human growth*. Cambridge, England: Cambridge University Press.

Buczynski, B. (2010, April 29). Endangered faces: Top 3 ugly species and why they deserve protection too. *TENTHMIL*. Retrieved from http://tenthmil.com/campaigns/policy/_endangered_faces_top_3_ugly_species_and_why_they_deserve_protection_too

China snake craze threatens crops. (2001, January 28). *BBC News*. Retrieved from http://news.bbc.co.uk/2/hi/asia-pacific/1141525.stm

Endangered and Threatened Wildlife and Plants: Final Determination of Threatened Status for the Koala. 65 Fed. Reg. 26762 (2000).

Eveleth, R. (2010, December 8). Zoo illogical: Ugly animals need protection from extinction, too. *Scientific American*. Retrieved from http://www.scientificamerican.com/article.cfm?id=zoo-illogical-ugly-animal

Frynta, D., et al. (2010, September 7). Being attractive brings advantages: The case of parrot species in captivity. *PLoS One*.

Garger, I. (2007, March 1). Global psyche: One nation under cute. *Psychology Today*.

Gould, S. J. (1980a). A biological homage to Mickey Mouse. In *The panda's thumb* (chapter 9).

Gould, S. J. (1980b). *The panda's thumb: More reflections in natural history*. New York, NY: Norton.

Isaac, N. J. B., et al. (2007, March). Mammals on the EDGE: Conservation priorities based on threat and phylogeny. *PLoS One*.

Kelly, W. (1959). *Ten ever-lovin' blue-eyed years with Pogo*. New York, NY: Simon & Schuster.

Kollmann, J. (1885). Das Ueberwintern von europäischen Frosch—und Tritonlarven und die Umwandlung des mexikanischen axolotl. *Verhandlungen der Naturforschenden Gesellschaft in Basel, 7,* 387–398.

Morris, D. (1967, December 22). The naked ape. *Life, 63*(25), 94–108.

Ratliff, E. (2011, March). Taming the wild. *National Geographic, 219*(3), 34–59.

Trimble, M. J., & Van Aarde, R. J. (2010, June). Species inequality in scientific study. *Conservation Biology, 24,* 886–890.

Walker, M. (2009, August 26). Axolotl verges on wild extinction. *BBC Earth News.* Retrieved from http://news.bbc.co.uk/earth/hi/earth_news/newsid _8220000/8220636.stm

8 "Pets or Meat"? Ethics and Domestic Animals

GRACE CLEMENT

We treat companion animals according to one set of guidelines and so-called "meat animals" according to an opposing set of guidelines, despite the apparently significant similarities between the animals in question. I consider moral justifications offered for this disparity of treatment and show that this paradox reveals a mistake in our moral thinking. Generally, we group animals used in farming and free-living animals together as subject to the ethic of justice and distinguish both from companion animals, who are subject to the ethic of care. I argue that animals used in farming, like companion animals, should be understood as within the sphere of care.

KEY WORDS: ethic of justice, ethic of care, companion animals, domestic animals, animals used in farming

In Michael Moore's movie *Roger and Me,* a roadside sign in economically depressed Flint, Michigan, advertised "Rabbits or Bunnies, Pets or Meat for Sale." This scene, intended to illustrate the plight of Flint residents as a result of the choices of General Motors executives, also illustrates the plight of domestic animals as a result of the choices of humans. An animal can equally be categorized as meat or as a companion animal—as a friend or as a meal—not based on the qualities of the animal, but based simply on human preferences.

The "Pets or Meat" sign is an unusual and jarring example of a common phenomenon in which similar animals can be categorized either as meat or as companions. For instance, dogs and pigs are similar in a number of ways (in intelligence, sociality, sentience, etc.) that at least seem to be morally relevant. Both are also domestic social animals who are largely dependent on human care for their survival and well-being. Yet despite their similarities, dogs and pigs are, in general, treated very differently. There is widespread agreement that companion animals should have their basic needs met, and many of us think we

Journal of Animal Ethics 1(1): 46–57

should go much farther than that, treating our dogs as valued members of the family. On the other hand, pigs—and especially pigs used in factory farms—are treated as mere means to human ends. Whatever minimal care they receive, we do not take care of pigs used in factory farms for their own sakes. As Daniel Engster (2006) puts it, "the care provided to these animals is so inadequate as to seem the very antithesis of caring: in many cases, it seems to approximate a form of torture" (p. 530). In short, we treat companion animals according to one set of guidelines and treat meat animals according to an opposing set of guidelines, despite the great similarities between these animals in ways that would appear to be morally significant.

This article is a reflection on this paradox, which James Serpell (1996) calls the "paradox of pigs and pets." How can this kind of disparity of treatment make moral sense? *Does* it make moral sense? What can we learn from the fact that the same or similar animals are so differently treated? In this article I consider justice-oriented and care-oriented ways of making sense of this kind of disparity of treatment and show that neither ethic alone nor the usual interpretation of how the two ethics should collaborate succeeds in making sense of the disparity. Indeed, this paradox reveals a mistake in our moral thinking. We cringe at the "Pets or Meat" sign not just because it denies that rabbits have rights or even because it reveals a lack of caring or sensitivity, but because it draws our attention to the odd contradiction in how we conceive and carry out the treatment of comparable or, in this case, even identical animals. Reflecting on the "Pets or Meat" sign should provoke us to rethink the scopes of the ethics of justice and care and our moral categorizations of animals.

JUSTICE OR CARE

It is not difficult to account for the fact that companion animals and "meat" animals are treated so differently. We develop close relationships with some animals, which makes us feel responsible for their care. On the other hand, we have little or no relationship to many other animals, which makes us feel little or no moral obligations toward them. As a result, we find it natural and normal to regard any of our interests and purposes as taking precedence over the interests and purposes of "meat" animals. This disparity of treatment can be defended by a moral theory giving weight to social distance, which proposes that what is morally relevant is not the characteristics possessed by beings, but the social relations and networks to which they belong. Such an approach is defended by Lawrence Becker (1989), who argues that our moral responsibilities are greatest to those closest to us and gradually decrease with social distance: "When hard choices have to be made, one is expected to rank the interests of one's family over those of friends, those of friends over those of neighbors, those of neighbors over those of strangers" (Dombrowski, 1997, p. 101). We employ similar logic in our treatment of animals, as we rank the interests of companion animals over the interests of animals we do not know. We love and care for our companion animals while we regard other animals as merely a means to produce meat for our consumption, usually without a thought or care regarding the cost to them.

But there are important questions about whether our relationships or our related feelings are morally decisive or even morally relevant. Although a moral ranking of relationships by social distance may seem an obvious choice, it is in some ways morally arbitrary. This is because existing social categories or relationships may be deeply immoral. For instance, I may experience myself—and my society may define me—as socially more connected to other white people than to black people, but that certainly does not justify my giving moral preference to whites over blacks. To simply prioritize family over friends over neighbors over strangers is much too simple. Even if relationships do make a moral difference, social categories are not givens but must themselves be the subject of moral reflection.

Leading philosophical proponents of animal rights go even further than this, arguing that our relationships and our feelings are *not* morally relevant and that taking our relationships and our feelings so seriously gets in the way of recognizing what *is* morally relevant. Because we do not know or like the pigs in a factory farm, we tend to overlook the fact that, with respect to morally relevant qualities such as intelligence and sentience, pigs and dogs are quite similar. Each being with the capacity for rationality or self-awareness or with the capacity for sentience has his or her own moral status and is entitled to a certain level of moral consideration. Thus, if dogs and pigs have roughly similar levels of these morally relevant capacities, then they are entitled to similar rights. Of course, not all justice theories defend animal rights; some argue that animals lack moral rights. If animals, or particular animals, *lack* the basic capacities judged necessary to have rights—such as language or self-consciousness—then those animals cannot be said to have rights. In reflecting on the "Pets or Meat" sign, however, I wish to focus on the justice-oriented arguments of animal *advocates*, given that these arguments often focus on disparities of treatment between beings of similar morally relevant qualities in order to reveal common mistakes in our moral thinking.

Although justice-based animal advocates criticize disparate treatment of similar animals, they do *not* claim that we should take care of animals used in farming the way many of us take care of our companion dogs. But this is because they claim that not even dogs are entitled to be taken care of the way many of us take care of our dogs. Instead, it is at our own discretion that we give our companion dogs special privileges, or much more than they are morally owed. Such theorists do not exactly criticize people for their devotion to their companion animals, but neither do they take this devotion to be especially morally significant for understanding our moral responsibilities to animals. They regard it as an expression of emotion, and they see themselves as seeking a rational, not an emotional, basis for their moral claims. In their view, emotion is partial, whereas reason is objective, and morality must have an objective basis.

For instance, Peter Singer argues that looking at the human–companion animal relationship objectively reveals that the morally important fact is not one's relationship with or love for a particular dog, but the good aspects of dog-existence. Maximizing this good does not preclude painlessly killing one dog and "replacing" that dog with another (Singer, 1999, p. 89). To most of us, this "replaceability" position might seem the epitome of moral insensitivity; to Singer, it is the logical consequence of thinking through—in a way unclouded by emotion—what morality requires. We can also see Singer's (1992) view of emotional attachment to companion animals in this passage in which he recalls what he and his wife told a dog lover about their attitude toward animals:

> We tried to explain that we were interested in the prevention of suffering and misery; that we were opposed to arbitrary discrimination; that we thought it was wrong to inflict needless suffering on another being. . . . Otherwise, we said, we were not especially "interested in" animals. Neither of us had ever been inordinately fond of dogs, cats, or horses in the way that many people are. We didn't "love" animals. We simply wanted them treated as the independent sentient beings that they are. (p. ii)

Thus, the important moral questions from a justice perspective are about the capacities or characteristics of different species of animals and what they require of us, rather than about our personal relationships with specific animals.

Justice approaches, whether in favor of or opposed to animal rights, hold that dogs and pigs are quite similar in morally relevant ways. Strictly speaking, then, our beloved companion dogs are due no more than anonymous pigs in a factory farm, and anonymous pigs are due no less than companion dogs. Whatever rights animals do have (if they have rights) tend to give rise to *negative* duties, that is, the obligation *not to violate* animals. On this view, there is no right to be taken care of. Although we may choose to devote ourselves to the well-being of a dog (or a pig), there is no moral obligation to do so. In response to the "Pets or Meat" sign, the justice perspective would find the "meat" option the morally important one, with different justice theorists drawing different conclusions about whether we violate animals when we treat them as meat-producers. The "pets" option is, from this perspective, just an optional extra and thus outside the realm of the obligations that define morality.

The ethic of care defines morality very differently. On this view, our sympathetic responsiveness to animals *is* morally significant, and caring personal relationships are the paradigmatic moral relations. Thus, when care theorists address questions of animal ethics, they often begin with and focus on relationships between humans and their companion animals. For instance, in her book *Speaking from the Heart: A Feminist Perspective on Ethics* (1992), the care ethicist Rita Manning discusses some of the moral questions arising in her own life with animals: After adopting a dog with a strong desire to roam, should one confine the dog or allow him to live the "roaming" life he so desperately seeks? What are one's responsibilities to a horse who can't be ridden anymore, given that meeting the needs of a horse is a demanding and costly enterprise (p. 126)?

So, according to the ethic of care, one-on-one relationships are of special moral significance. What is less clear, from this perspective, is whether human–animal relationships *count* as caring relationships. Although there are care ethicists such as Manning who discuss caring for companion animals, they are in the minority. The most prominent philosophical care ethicists, including Virginia Held (2006) and Joan Tronto (1993), have not addressed the implications of the ethic of care for nonhuman animals in their work. Although the ethic of care regards humans as social beings whose identities are developed through relations with others, these others are generally assumed to be humans. Similarly, some care ethicists have examined the political implications of the ethic of care, but they have regarded the political world as an exclusively human realm.

On the other hand, those care ethicists, such as Manning and Nel Noddings (2003), who do examine care in human–animal relations, do not tend to regard the ethic of care as politically relevant. From this perspective, caring is necessarily a one-on-one relation, and the political realm is *not* about one-on-one relations. For some this means that the political realm is governed by an alternative ethic, the ethic of justice, whereas for others it means that the political realm is beyond the realm of ethics entirely. But in almost all work on the ethic of care, it is implied, if not exactly stated, that the ethic of care cannot govern human–animal relations outside the realm of our relationships with companion animals. As Manning (1992) writes, "I think there are important differences between animals raised for food and animals that are primarily companion animals. My hunch is that tending cattle and pigs doesn't provide the same complex relationship and concern for nature that tending companion animals does" (p. 129).

Manning's (1992) implication is that it may not even make sense to "care" for animals raised for food. She reflects on her sister and brother-in-law's decision to buy a piglet with the intention of raising him for food. She reports that the family took loving care of the pig until it was time to slaughter him and that "they spoke of him with affection even as they lifted his flesh to their mouths" (p. 129). Is there something contradictory about this attempt to combine an ethic of care with an ethic of use? Manning seems ambivalent about this, saying that one "cannot be acting to further the interests of an animal by killing it and eating it," but also that one "can give an animal care that is sensitive to its interests up to the moment of slaughter" (p. 130). Is there an important moral difference between slaughtering an anonymous pig used in factory farming and slaughtering the family's companion animal? Manning's discussion leads one to reflect on these questions, but she does not offer her own answers to them, implying that these answers are beyond the reach of the ethic of care.

Thus, the ethic of care can embrace the idea that we have special moral responsibilities to our companion animals, but it takes no clear stand on our responsibilities to animals with whom we have no one-on-one relationship. It is able to make sense of the "Pets or Meat" sign by concluding that it may be morally appropriate to care for a rabbit or to make her into a meal, depending on whether we are willing to develop a one-on-one relationship with her. Although it would seem uncaring to slaughter and eat a companion animal, the same animal who is not made a companion is beyond the realm of care. Thus, from the care perspective, it is the "pets" option that is morally significant, and the "meat" option is left unsettled.

Both the ethic of justice and the ethic of care focus so exclusively on one sphere of human–animal interactions that, despite their differences, the two ethics can easily be thought of as complementary. On this view we owe care to those animals with whom we have one-on-one relationships, and we owe only justice to other animals beyond the personal sphere. Whether justice allows us to treat animals as meat-producers is contested, but the categorization of animals, and ethics, into distinct categories is widely accepted, and it means that the paradoxical "Pets or Meat" sign does not necessarily represent a moral problem. Some animals—such as rabbits—could be in either category and thus could justifiably receive very different sorts of treatment.

RETHINKING THE SPHERES

As we have seen, the ethics of justice and care are easily thought of as governing distinct realms of human–animal interactions. On this view, the ethic of justice governs our interactions with animals with whom we have no one-on-one relationship, whereas the ethic of care governs our interactions with animals with whom we do have such relationships. In what follows, however, I want to show that this interpretation of the spheres of justice and care oversimplifies matters in important ways. I do not take issue here with the basics of the ethic of justice with regard to our moral obligations to free-living animals; nor do I take issue here with the basics of the ethic of care with regard to our moral responsibilities to our companion animals. But I show that the case of animals used in farming—animals who are neither companion animals nor free-living animals—is a more difficult matter and that our moral obligations to these animals are the key to thinking through the paradox implicit in the "Pets or Meat" sign.

Let us begin by asking *why* we have the responsibility to take care of our companion animals. Once we answer this question, we should be able to determine whether the same justification applies to animals used in farming. Although social distance certainly matters, we cannot say that we have special responsibilities to those closest to us simply because they *are* closest to us or simply because we choose to accept these responsibilities. These claims would preclude the possibility that obligations to care for distant others can *ever* outweigh obligations to those closest to us, as when we recognize and respond to moral emergencies beyond our personal sphere, or that we may have unchosen responsibilities, as we do to much of our family. Perhaps it would be better to say that we have duties to take care of our companion animals simply because *we have made them* our companions. We have, in effect, entered into a contract agreeing to take care of our companion animals, and we must fulfill that contract. There is certainly something correct about this answer. All other things being equal, we do have the responsibility to fulfill our contracts. But this answer is incomplete, given that not all contracts are moral or enforceable. So we need to do more to identify the moral basis of our responsibility to take care of our companion animals.

The utilitarian Robert Goodin (1986) offers another answer, namely that our companion animals are especially *vulnerable* to us. He defines vulnerability as "being under threat of harm," where "harm" is general enough to include both natural threats and those created by humans, both positive actions and omissions (p. 110). For Goodin, vulnerability implies more than susceptibility to certain types of harm; it also implies that the harm is not predetermined. If harm were predetermined, one would be not vulnerable, but condemned (p. 112). Thus, to be vulnerable, there must be some agent capable of "exercising some effective choice over whether to cause or to avert the threatened harm" (p. 112). About companion animals, he writes, "By domesticating them, we have deprived them of much of their capacity (and most of their will) to protect themselves against cruel masters. That renders them peculiarly vulnerable to their owners [giving rise to] peculiarly strong responsibilities on the part of owners to protect them" (pp. 181–182).

Where, then, would this leave free-living animals in terms of our moral responsibilities? On this view, many animals, particularly free-living animals, are primarily vulnerable to our interference, and thus we owe them mainly noninterference.[1] For instance, Goodin (1986) argues that certain laws regulating hunting are based on our recognition of the moral importance of vulnerability: "We are almost universally prohibited from shooting sitting ducks or from using a spotlight at night to blind or 'freeze' our prey. . . . Under these circumstances the prey would be completely helpless, without any chance whatsoever of escaping" (p. 181). Yet Goodin's approach also gives rise to a problem: To say that we have responsibilities to protect those who are vulnerable potentially broadens the scope of the ethic of care without limit. Goodin's account would not allow us to make a distinction between negative duties, the moral requirement not to interfere with or violate others, and positive duties, the moral requirement to promote the good of others. Surely, we have both sorts of duties, and we have certain negative duties to *all* other beings who are due moral consideration. However, positive duties demand much more of us than do negative duties, and there must be some limit to how extensive our positive duties are. Realistically, that is, one cannot be morally required to take care of all beings who are vulnerable to one's actions.

A third account identifies companion animals' *dependence* on us as the moral basis of our responsibility to take care of them. Daniel Engster (2006) writes, "While I argue that human beings do not have any absolute obligation to care for animals, we do at least owe animals moral sympathy and take on moral duties to care for animals when we make them dependent upon us for their survival and well-being" (p. 522). Notice that this account combines the *contractual* focus of the first account with the *vulnerability* focus of the second account, thereby avoiding the problems of focusing on one to the exclusion of the other. Engster's proposal certainly makes sense on the individual level: By taking in an animal, I take responsibility for that particular animal's welfare. But it also applies on a more general level: We, *humans,* have made these animals into companion animals—that is, into the kind of beings who depend on human care, and thus we, as humans, have the responsibility to provide that care. We are, unfortunately, in many ways failing to meet this responsibility as representatives of our species. As Bernard Rollin (2005) puts it, "there is indeed a contract between humans and companion animals, and animals are holding up their part well, but humans [are] significantly failing to do so" through practices such as "mass euthanasia of companion animals for convenience, puppy mills, public ignorance of companion animal needs; perpetuation by breed standards of vast numbers of genetic defects leading to great suffering and premature death" (p. 114). Of course, this leads to difficult questions about how a general human responsibility to take care of domestic animals translates into individual responsibilities. For instance, assuming I have not participated directly in puppy mills, what are my personal responsibilities to the dogs in puppy mills? Although I do not attempt to answer these difficult questions here, I do think it is important to acknowledge that we *all* have some sort of responsibility for the welfare of animals whom humans have made into beings dependent on humans.

Notice, though, that this principle applies not only to companion animals, whether individually or collectively, but also to animals used in farming. This means that we owe more to domestic pigs than to the wild boars from whom they descended. Domestic pigs are much more deeply dependent on us (because we have made them so), and so our relationship to them is more complicated. James Serpell (1996) writes,

> Traditional hunters typically view the animals they hunt as their equals. . . . This essentially egalitarian relationship disappeared with the advent of domestication. The domestic animal is dependent for survival on its human owner. The human becomes the overlord and master, the animals his servants and slaves. By definition, domestic animals are subservient to the will of humanity and, for the majority of species involved, this loss of independence had some fairly devastating long-term consequences. (p. 5)

If we have moral responsibilities to take care of beings we have made dependent on us, then we have responsibilities to take care of animals used in farming.

Notice that this is a departure from the most often expressed moral views of animals used in farming. In much environmental ethics literature, there is a thinly veiled contempt for domestic animals used in farming.[2] The self-sufficiency of free-living animals (with respect to humans) is thought to be natural or normal, and hence "wild" animals are thought to deserve respect in a way that dependent domestic animals do not. Others from an animal rights perspective would argue that domestic animals, despite their dependence, do deserve equal moral consideration as long as they meet the appropriate criteria. But against both of these approaches, I am suggesting that animals' dependency does not count *against* moral consideration but is instead the very reason we owe them special moral attention. As Stephen Clark writes, with regard to our obligations to humans, "secretly . . . we know that we ought to care for the subnormal precisely because they are subnormal; they are weak, defenceless, at our mercy" (Dombrowski, 1997, p. 96). Of course, calling a category of animal (or human) "subnormal" is probably not a good idea in that it is demeaning and hence not conducive to moral treatment. But the important point here is that our responsibilities to domestic animals are not based on the capacities they possess in themselves; rather they are based on our relationships to them.

This hypothesis is supported by considering the most extreme form of animal farming, the intensive factory-farm production of meat. Assuming that factory farming is in fact morally wrong, what makes it wrong? It is no doubt wrong because it fails to respect animals' sentient, intelligent, and social nature; that is, it is unjust. This is the same reason that hunting would be said to be unjust. But I submit that factory farming is *more wrong* than hunting. And what makes factory farming especially wrong, and worse than killing free-living animals to eat, is the fact that it exploits these animals' extreme dependence on us. In fact, many such animals are so vulnerable that they could hardly survive on their own: They depend on us to survive, which makes it that much easier for us to treat them any way we choose. Most fundamentally, factory farming is wrong because it violates our relationship with these animals; it is, as Engster (2006) put it, the *antithesis* of care. This means that we would not fulfill our responsibilities to animals used in factory farming simply by refraining from interfering with them anymore: it would be wrong simply to release millions of chickens, cows, and pigs into "the wild." Thus, although one can find good reasons to criticize factory farming from a justice perspective, an ethic of care, through its attention to the nature of the relationship between human and animals, best captures what is so morally reprehensible about the factory farming of animals.

Now it is certainly true that there are important differences between the ways in which our companion dogs and pigs used in factory farming are dependent on us. Even though both are in some sense dependent on my choices and actions, I have a one-on-one relationship with my dog, such that he relies on me in particular, whereas I do not know the pigs used in factory farming I might eat, and they do not rely on me in particular. It seems that animals used in factory farming are dependent on humans in general, but not on me in particular. In addition, I have *assumed* responsibility for my companion animals, thereby *making* them dependent on me, but I have not done so for animals used in factory farming. It is for this reason that Engster (2006) asserts that one is not obligated to stop and save a drowning (unknown) cat in the same way one is obligated to care for one's own companion animal; only in the latter situation has the responsibility been self-assumed (p. 527). It seems, that is, that the ethic of care is appropriate only in contexts in which we have more personal involvement than we do with animals used in factory farming.

But as we have seen, there are good reasons to think that things are not as they seem. The crucial factor determining the realm of care is *dependency*, rather than having an *experience* of relationship. This is why we are responsible for providing care to abandoned dogs: although we do not have a one-on-one relationship with them, humans have acted in ways that have made their survival and well-being dependent on human care. Likewise, although we do not have personal relationships with animals used in farming, humans have acted in ways that have made their health and well-being dependent on human care. Difficult questions remain, and I do not pretend to have the answers to them here. Treating these animals morally would involve a complex and difficult task of considering the implications of their present dependence on us. It would require attention to the ways in which humans *have altered and continue to alter* the characteristics of animals used in factory farming, progressively increasing their dependence on us. It would require asking whether it would be in these animals' interests to have their dependence on us eventually minimized or eliminated. Collective responsibility is a controversial notion to begin with. It is not clear what this responsibility entails for each of us, and it is certainly debatable what kind or level of care we must provide. But the starting point for such discussions should be that domestic animals, who are by their nature dependent on humans for their survival and well-being, are owed not just noninterference but care.

To summarize, we tend to group animals used in farms and free-living animals together and to distinguish both from companion animals. We do this because animals used in farms are like free-living animals in that we do not know them individually or have feelings of affection toward them. The standard interpretations of both the ethic of justice and the ethic of care regard animals used in farming as part of the impersonal realm of human–animal relations and thus as governed by the ethic of justice and not the ethic of care. But I have made the case that companion animals and animals used in farming should be put in the same moral category and that both should be understood as within the sphere of the ethic of care because of their dependence on us.

ADDITIONAL QUESTIONS

Expanding the scope of the ethic of care so that it includes animals used in farming raises a number of important questions. Although I cannot resolve or even raise all of these here, I do want to briefly address two such questions in order to show some potential implications of my argument.

One question involves the moral relevance of feelings. We have seen that the ethic of care regards feelings as morally significant in a way that the ethic of justice does not. But in expanding the scope of the ethic of care to include animals used in farming, we call into question the moral relevance of feelings. Singer (1999) is correct to say that our feelings are not moral data: the ethic of care cannot rely on our feelings of affection, or lack thereof, to reveal whom we are and are not responsible for (p. 89). However, it is significant that caring feelings do tend to arise when people interact with animals used in farming. Serpell (1996) writes,

> Unless he takes steps to prevent it from happening, the farmer or stockman will get to know individual animals and may become personally attached to them. Once this has happened, slaughter . . . generates feelings of guilt and remorse because, in human terms, it constitutes a gross betrayal of trust. (p. 187)

For this reason, Serpell argues, farmers typically make use of various distancing devices to avoid these feelings of guilt:

> It is not so much that we avoid killing the animals with which we are friendly. It is more the other way around. Unconsciously or deliberately we either avoid befriending the animals we intend to harm, or we fabricate elaborate and often mythological justification for their suffering that absolves us of blame. (pp. 210–211)

Therefore, there remains an important connection between the ethic of care, even the expanded ethic of care proposed here, and our feelings of care. Although we do not typically have a sense of relationship or feelings of affection toward animals used in farming, this is at least in part because we have prevented ourselves from developing these feelings rather than because these feelings would be inappropriate or irrelevant in the relationship we have with them.[3] Hence, our relationships with our companion animals are not morally irrelevant; instead they remind us of what we can experience when we do not shut ourselves off from the feelings that naturally arise toward those we care for.

A second question raised by this argument is *how* we should treat animals used in farming. So far I have considered the immorality of factory farming, arguing that it is most fully understood as a violation of the ethic of care. But what about raising animals humanely and then slaughtering them for meat? Is this also a violation of the ethic of care? Recall that Manning (1992) was reluctant to draw this conclusion, although she was also unwilling to call such treatment caring. Engster (2006) considers this question as well and argues that the ethic of care cannot definitively reach the conclusion that such farming is a violation of the ethic of care: "A plausible case can be made for bringing animals into existence and caring for them right up to the moment of slaughter. . . . Care ethics must admit some room for reasonable disagreement among people about what is the most caring approach to take toward animals" (p. 532). Although it is, for this author, difficult to reconcile the idea of caring for an animal with slaughtering that animal, care ethicists are ambivalent. But whether animals' rights are violated when they are raised (humanely) for meat is certainly an important question, and the ethic of justice undeniably addresses this question, even if different versions of the ethic of justice address it in conflicting ways. And it is important to remember that we owe justice to all beings—that is, a being does not lose his or her rights just because he or she is within the scope of care. This is perhaps an important reminder that both ethics are essential: although the ethic of care is ambivalent about "humane" farming, the ethic of justice draws clear conclusions.

But to return to my main point, despite the need for the ethic of justice, this ethic is not sufficient to account for our moral responsibilities to domestic animals. The important moral questions about domestic animals concern not just the morally relevant capacities of individuals (or species) but in addition the nature of the *relationships* between humans and these animals. And it is the ethic of care that directs its attention to such relationships. To say that we must take care of domestic animals does not mean that we must treat them as companion animals or as "members of the family." But it is not enough to refrain from violating the rights of domestic animals, either. We have a responsibility to care for them.

Notes

1. An exception would be when humans have in the past done such harm to a species that we now have a responsibility to take actions to make corrections and help the species. Although this is certainly an important exception, I will leave it aside here.

2. This is documented and discussed in Karen Davis (1995).

3. See Brian Luke's (1995) discussion of this.

References

Becker, L. (1989). The priority of human interests. In T. Regan & P. Singer (Eds.), *Animal rights and human obligations* (pp. 87–94). Englewood Cliffs, NJ: Prentice Hall.

Davis, K. (1995). Thinking like a chicken: Farm animals and the feminine connection. In C. Adams & J. Donovan (Eds.), *Animals and women: Feminist theoretical explorations* (pp. 192–212). Durham, NC: Duke University Press.

Dombrowski, D. (1997). *Babies and beasts: The argument from marginal cases.* Urbana: University of Illinois Press.

Engster, D. (2006). Care ethics and animal welfare. *Journal of Social Philosophy, 37*(4), 521–536.

Goodin, R. (1986). *Protecting the vulnerable: A re-analysis of our social responsibilities.* Chicago, IL: University of Chicago Press.

Held, V. (2006). *The ethics of care: Personal, political, and global.* New York, NY: Oxford University Press.

Luke, B. (1995). Taming ourselves or going feral? Toward a nonpatriarchal metaethic of animal liberation. In C. Adams & J. Donovan (Eds.), *Animals and women: Feminist theoretical explorations* (pp. 290–319). Durham, NC: Duke University Press.

Manning, R. (1992). *Speaking from the heart: A feminist perspective on ethics.* Lanham, MD: Rowman and Littlefield.

Noddings, N. (2003). *Caring: A feminine approach to ethics and moral education.* Berkeley: University of California.

Rollin, B. (2005). Reasonable partiality and animal ethics. *Ethical Theory and Moral Practice, 8,* 105–121.

Serpell, J. (1996). *In the company of animals: A study of human–animal relationships.* New York, NY: Cambridge University Press.

Singer, P. (1992). *Animal liberation: A new ethic for our treatment of animals.* New York, NY: Avon Books.

Singer, P. (1999). Reflections. In J. M. Coetzee (Ed.), *The lives of animals* (pp. 85–91). Princeton, NJ: Princeton University Press.

Tronto, J. (1993). *Moral boundaries: A political argument for an ethic of care.* New York, NY: Routledge.

9 Varieties of Harm to Animals in Industrial Farming

MATTHEW C. HALTEMAN

Skeptics of the moral case against industrial farming often assert that harm to animals in industrial systems is limited to isolated instances of abuse that do not reflect standard practice and thus do not merit criticism of the industry at large. I argue that even if skeptics are correct that abuse is the exception rather than the rule, they must still answer for two additional varieties of serious harm to animals that are pervasive in industrial systems: procedural harm and institutional oppression. That procedural and institutional harms create conditions under which abuse is virtually inevitable only increases the skeptic's burden.

KEY WORDS: animal abuse, animal agriculture, animal cruelty, concentrated animal feeding operation, CAFO, harm, industrial farming, institutional oppression

In recent years, public debate over the moral standing of animals used in farming has enjoyed a higher profile in part because of the efforts of advocacy organizations to bring the realities of industrial farming systems to the attention of wider audiences. One of the most common strategies employed to this end is the online distribution of video footage taken by undercover investigators of the conditions inside industrial farms and production facilities. Presumably in order to achieve maximum impact on viewers, these videos tend to focus on overt and often egregious instances of animal cruelty or neglect, showing workers beating, kicking, throwing, and even sexually abusing animals and depicting worker indifference to animals wallowing in manure pits, languishing on downer piles, living among the corpses of their former cage mates, and suffering from illnesses and deformities that result from extreme neglect.[1]

Given the shocking nature of such footage, it is not surprising that the first inclination of many viewers is to jump to one of two extremes. On the one hand, there are skeptics who cite suspicion of the motives of "biased" activists or perhaps cite personal experience of their friends' or family members' farms as reasons for believing that the cruelty and neglect depicted in such videos are the rare exception rather than the rule and that the industry as a whole should not be judged on their account. On the other hand, there are true believers who readily assume that the vast majority of workers in the vast majority of industrial facilities perpetrate such acts with equally reckless abandon. Though these two common responses are obviously polarized, they both frame the issue (albeit usually implicitly) as if the central question concerning the morality of industrial farming is whether individual workers, as a general rule, do or do not engage in overtly cruel or neglectful treatment of animals.

As important as this question may be, framing the issue in this way has several regrettable consequences. First and foremost, it shifts attention away from the central moral problem at stake—the harm that animals experience in industrial farming systems—and onto the tangential issue of the reprobate behavior of some of the people who farm them. Second, this shift in focus predictably leads to acrimonious disagreement in which clear-eyed assessment of the moral implications of industrial farming *as a system* takes a back seat to heated efforts on both sides to vindicate or villainize the *individuals* who work within it. Third, when the debate takes this direction, skeptics enjoy a significant strategic advantage, insofar as the animal advocate's case against industrial farming now seems to depend on substantiating the unpopular and frankly unlikely claim that those who work in the industry are, by and large, a cruel and negligent lot. Even if this claim were defensible, it would presumably have very little purchase with skeptics, whose firsthand experience with friends or family in agriculture or whose status quo confidence in the good character of most farmers would leave them feeling perfectly justified both in dismissing the concern and in judging its advocates according to all the standard stereotypes: alarmist, misanthropic, sentimental, and generally out of touch with reality.

My aim in this article is to outline a strategy for shifting the burden of proof back onto skeptics while keeping the interests of animals front and center and defusing the hostility that often prevails when individual farmers (rather than systemic problems with the industry) become the focal point for criticism. I consider three distinguishable but closely related varieties of harm that animals endure in industrial farming systems: "abuse" experienced through their cruel or neglectful treatment by farm workers and other handlers, "procedural harm" experienced through their subjection to standard industry procedures for man-aging their confinement and profiting from their production, and "institutional oppression" endured through the deprivation of their ability to exercise their most basic instincts and interests.

Although abuse is without question the most sensational and thus the most publicized of these harms, procedural and institutional harms are arguably more insidious because—though they typically garner much less attention—they occur pervasively, even when workers treat animals as well as is feasible under the current system, and their pervasive occurrence creates conditions that are ripe for the abuses of cruelty and neglect. But if animals experience serious and pervasive harm as a matter of course within the industrial system even when workers are on their best behavior, then skeptics face an unenviable dilemma. Either they must legitimate the harm in question by demonstrating that it is morally justified, or they must deny the widely held assumption that inflicting or supporting serious harm requires a moral justification (claiming, perhaps, that pragmatic justification is enough). That procedural and institutional harms create conditions under which abuse is virtually inevitable only increases the skeptic's burden.

Before commencing my analysis, I should clarify two brief points regarding my intent. First, my account is intended as a descriptive classification rather than an evaluative hierarchy of harm. In my estimation, each of the varieties of harm under discussion is far enough across the threshold of moral seriousness that there is little to be gained, at least for my purposes here, in attempting to discern which, if any, are more or less objectionable than the others. Second, this descriptive classification is intended as a heuristic tool rather than a comprehensive taxonomy of stringently delimited categories. One could no doubt put a much finer point on things than I am able to here. My hope, however, is that the distinctions I propose are nonetheless useful for their intended purpose of complicating matters for those who suspect that the harm animals experience in industrial systems is confined to comparatively rare instances of abuse that are insufficient to merit serious moral scrutiny of the industry at large.

I should also say a bit more about my usage of the term "harm" and my assumptions regarding its application to animals. The sense of "harm" I have in mind is nontechnical and more or less in accordance with common usage. To say that one has been harmed is just to say that one has been hurt, injured, or damaged in some way, including but not limited to physically or psychologically. Although direct instances of physical and psychological injury are among the most common examples of harm, it is not atypical to say that one is harmed when one's interests in general well-being are curtailed or defeated in some respect even if no direct, easily quantifiable physical or psychological injury is involved. In cases of institutional sexism and racism, for instance, when we say that women are harmed by salary inequities and that persons of color are harmed by the inaccessibility of bank loans, the harms we have in mind are not specific physical or psychological injuries per se but rather the curtailment or defeat of these individuals' interests in realizing various goods pertinent to their well-being (e.g., an interest in receiving fair compensation or in becoming a homeowner).

My assumption here is that animals too have analogous, species-appropriate interests in their own well-being and can thus experience harm. However controversial this assumption might once have been, it is now widely accepted. One can readily infer as much simply by considering our national statistics on companion animals: 62% of U.S. households share their lives with animals and spend almost 50 billion dollars annually seeing to their interests and keeping them from harm ("American Pet Products Association," n.d.). However inconsistent our culture may be in its decisions about which animals' interests matter, there is no basis in common sense or contemporary science for denying that—just like dogs, cats, and cockatiels—animals raised for food such as cows, pigs, chickens, and turkeys have basic interests in avoiding physical and psychological injury as well as in realizing day-to-day well-being in keeping with the unique capabilities of their species.[2]

In what ways, then, are these basic interests curtailed and defeated in industrial farming systems? Abuse might seem the obvious place to start. But insofar as the combined effects of procedural and institutional harm create conditions that both increase the likelihood of abuse and influence the types of abuse that occur, I treat these former two varieties of harm first so as to secure the benefit of the perspective they provide on the abuses of cruelty and neglect.

I have defined procedural harm as harm that animals experience through their subjection to standard industry procedures for managing their confinement and profiting from their production.[3] Some procedural harm is inflicted directly and suffered acutely, as when animals undergo dehorning, branding, tail-docking, beak-trimming, artificial insemination, forced separation from their young, transport handling, slaughter, and other painful, stress-inducing procedures at the hands of workers. Other such harm occurs indirectly and is suffered chronically, as when animals experience the daily traumas of confinement, overcrowding, perpetual exposure to respiratory irritants, digestive unrest from supplemented feed, lethargy from unnaturally rapid weight gain, and the aggressive behavior of other stressed animals. In many cases, furthermore, acute harm engenders chronic harm, as when procedural mutilations are executed unskillfully or heal improperly, leaving animals debilitated in any number of ways (unable to eat, groom, self-defend, etc.) and highly vulnerable to further injury. And speaking of vulnerability to injury, even animals' own bodies have been co-opted into instruments of procedural harm, given that they are now commonly bioengineered to produce a higher ratio of meat to bone than their skeletal and respiratory systems can healthfully support.

For the benefit of skeptics who have visited industrial farms without seeing what they discern to be direct evidence of these procedures, it is important to point out that much procedural harm is unlikely to be witnessed by non-employees for several reasons. First, many of the procedures at issue—including some of the most unpleasant ones—take place in other locations such as hatcheries, transport vehicles, and production facilities that are not supervised by the management of the farm one is visiting. Second, when harmful procedures are performed on site, visitors are not typically permitted to attend, since (among other reasons) the allowance of spectators adds further stress to scenarios that are already taxing and even dangerous for animals and workers alike. Finally, many instances of procedural harm—especially those that involve chronic pain, discomfort, or psychological stress—are not directly discernable to people who are unfamiliar with animal behavior and thus are unable to detect the often subtle signs of disorder.

As such, when friends, family, and media representatives visit a shed or two on a given farm, they typically are neither witness to the most harmful procedures that occur there (much less those carried out elsewhere) nor in a position, as casual observers, to "see" the discomfort of a steer's feed-induced digestive unrest, a sow's crate-induced leg abrasions and depression, or a hen's cage-induced osteoporosis. This realization is an important one, given that the discovery of such missing information about procedural harm could change the game for some skeptics. One might become more favorably disposed to the concerns of animal advocacy, for instance, upon learning that, regardless of how well hens may be said to have it in some of the "better" operations, modern egg production nevertheless depends on the procedure of "chick culling"—the maceration or suffocation of hundreds of millions of live male chicks per year just days after they hatch because they have no economic value to the industry.

One could cite many other examples, but the upshot is that managing and producing large populations of confined animals requires the aggressive and ongoing regulation of these animals' lives from pre-conception to death, and the infliction of serious harm is endemic to the process. A simple Web search of any of the procedures noted here, moreover, will provide ample evidence that the industry is well aware of this reality, as their own publications and instructional materials acknowledge the harms in question, discuss potential ways to address them, and frequently conclude that the financial or procedural challenges associated with their mitigation are too burdensome to meet.[4] The crucial insight to grasp about procedural harm, then, is that its pervasive infliction is an irreducible feature of industrial farming systems even when workers are simply following standard procedures—indeed, even when they go the extra mile to conduct these procedures as humanely as the system permits. I shall leave it to skeptics to defend whatever resemblance there is to discern, if any, between the ordinary meaning of "humane" and the sense of the term at issue when one speaks of conducting these procedures "as humanely as possible."

The wide array of virtually inevitable physical and psychological maladies that animals endure by dint of procedural harm should be sufficient, on its own, to give the inquiring skeptic pause. Nonetheless, a full account of the harm that animals experience in industrial farming systems must go beyond their procedurally inflicted pain and suffering to account for their institutional oppression—for the ways in which the system that dictates their circumstances deprives them of the ability to realize their interests in general well-being even when they are not discernibly in pain or under stress. Like procedural harm, institutional oppression is endemic to the system, insofar as it results inevitably from the standard operating procedures that comprise the system. The distinguishing difference, however, is that, whereas procedural harm is typically experienced in the *infliction of maladies* that degrade animals' well-being, institutional oppression is typically endured through the *deprivation of goods* required for realizing well-being.

To make this distinction more concrete, consider the case of a gestating sow on a particularly well-managed confinement farm who, unlike many of her less fortunate contemporaries, is as fit as is possible under the circumstances. Though she has experienced procedural harm in the past and will no doubt experience it again in the future, at the moment she is abrasion-free, mentally stable, well fed and watered, and protected from the elements. Setting aside the likelihood that she is bored (a condition that some might consider an instance of procedural harm), she is not currently suffering any acute or chronic physical or psychological distress. Even so, it would be difficult to describe her as realizing the kind of well-being for which her interests and capabilities suit her. She cannot turn around, much less move about or go outdoors. She has little to no interaction with other sows. And though her crate is flushed twice daily, she cannot maintain hygiene as she is disposed to by nature. Her inability to obtain these basic goods, moreover, is not the result of any defect of her interest in or capacity for realizing them; had she been born a free-living woodland pig, or raised on a typical farm in 1930, or even sold into a contemporary non-confinement setting, she presumably would have realized them all. As such, though she may be enjoying a temporary respite from procedurally inflicted maladies, she is nonetheless being harmed through institutional oppression.

And she is not alone. At least the following basic goods are among those that are unduly difficult or impossible to realize for most animals living in contemporary confinement settings: free range of movement, regular access to the outdoors, regular physical exercise, and the pursuit of basic interests in grooming, foraging, nesting, caring for offspring, and establishing social relations with other members of their species. Though skeptics sometimes protest that farmed animals in today's confinement systems have had these interests bred out of them, or that in any case they cannot aspire to realize goods they have never experienced, such claims are belied by the thousands of animals who have escaped confinement only to take up the pursuit and realization of these and other goods within days and even hours of beginning their new lives as sanctuary residents or adopted companions.[5]

Admittedly, discerning the extent and limits of animals' institutional oppression is less straightforward than accounting for procedurally inflicted harm that the industry itself acknowledges. Indeed, there is a wide diversity of opinion even among committed animal advocates on the questions of what animals' well-being amounts to, which goods are requisite for it, and whether it is compatible with their domestication and use by human beings.[6] I cannot engage that important debate here. Rather, in keeping with my modest aim of aiding animal advocates in complicating matters for skeptics, I have chosen to highlight examples of institutional oppression that all animal advocates and hopefully many inquiring skeptics can acknowledge as instances of serious harm.

But if I have elected to set aside some of the more contested suggestions regarding animals' institutional oppression—the suggestion, for instance, that the deprivation of freedom entailed by their status as property is the most foundational harm of all (Francione, 2008)—I maintain that even a limited discussion of some of its more obvious examples can serve, upon reflection, to nudge at least some skeptics beyond welfare concerns into serious consideration of the rights position. After all, for those who come to realize that animals are institutionally oppressed in these less controversial respects, it is often just a matter of time before they discover that the central moral question on their minds is no longer "how should we treat the animals we use?" but rather "should we be using animals at all?"

The principal strategic advantage of the foregoing analysis is that it puts skeptics back on the defensive: Even if one assumes for the sake of argument that cases of abuse are relatively isolated instances that do not reflect the practices of the industry as a whole, skeptics must still answer for the industry's infliction of procedural and institutional harms that are serious, pervasive, and systemically inevitable. The two options at their disposal for meeting this burden, moreover, both present daunting obstacles. Either they must provide a moral justification of these harms—a challenge that is increasingly formidable in view of what contemporary science and philosophy tell us, respectively, about the capabilities of animals and the consideration we owe to them as a result,[7] or they must deny that inflicting or supporting serious harm requires a moral justification, arguing perhaps that a pragmatic or economic justification is sufficient and rejecting thereby a basic moral principle that is strongly entrenched in the majority of both secular and religious approaches to moral reasoning. In case the moral fallout associated with this second option is not worrisome enough on its own, I should add that any proposed pragmatic or economic justification would have to contend with competing pragmatic and economic concerns raised by the burgeoning evidence that industrial animal agriculture is among the leading contributors to global environmental and energy crises.[8]

A second key advantage of my analysis is the additional perspective it provides on harm inflicted through abuses of the sort described at the outset. Although there is no excusing such voluntary acts of cruelty and neglect (even skeptics and industry representatives repudiate them), an awareness of how procedural and institutional harms affect the respective living and working conditions of animals and their handlers does render these instances of abuse somewhat easier to understand. The animals, for their part, are not exactly eager or compliant patients: Traumatized and often debilitated by acute injury, worn down from the chronic rigors of confinement, dispirited from deprivation of their natural interests, and understandably wary of human beings, they have every reason to avoid, resist, and even retaliate against their handlers.

Workers too face taxing, frustrating, and often dangerous conditions: They work long hours in the same inhospitable environment as the animals; their labor is difficult, often unfulfilling, and low-paying relative to the risks involved; and the high rate of employee turnover as a result of job dissatisfaction (especially in slaughterhouses) often means that they are poorly trained and inexperienced (Schlosser, 2002). Given that their jobs require them daily to oversee and carry out procedures that repeatedly cause harm to large numbers of unwilling and often resistant animals, it is hardly surprising that many of them come to view animals as objects rather than individuals—indeed, as obstacles and even adversaries to the accomplishment of their work. To take an empathetic view of animals' interests under such conditions would likely compromise one's ability to do the job, and in any case, it can be hard to muster empathy for those who make one's job more difficult.

In view of these considerations, it does not take a great leap of inference to see that abusive acts of cruelty and neglect are not just likely but fully expectable under such conditions; it would be surprising, in other words, were they not to occur from time to time, if not routinely. The important point to distill from this discussion is that the proposed analysis of procedural and institutional harm can exercise two different forms of leverage over the skeptical suspicion that abuse is a rare occurrence: It can *neutralize* this suspicion by showing that industrial farming systems do serious harm to animals even on the assumption that abuse never occurs, but it can also potentially *dispel* this suspicion by showing that the pervasive occurrence of procedural and institutional harm renders the opposite inference more plausible, namely that abuse is routine rather than rare.

A third and final advantage, in conclusion, is the potential of this analysis to diminish some of the rancor that often prevails when animal advocates and skeptics butt heads on the moral implications of industrial animal farming. By shifting the focus of the discussion from the shaming and blaming of uncharitably typecast individuals ("despicable farmers" and "animal extremists") to the more measured consideration of systemic problems in which everyone has a stake, animal advocates stand a much better chance of engaging skeptics in productive conversation, earning their respect, and perhaps even changing their outlook.

Acknowledgments

I am grateful to Andrew Chignell, Terence Cuneo, Brianne Donaldson, and Mark Jensen for helpful conversations on the ideas discussed in this article.

Notes

1. Examples of videos depicting these types of animal cruelty and neglect are in no short supply on the Internet, as a simple key word search reveals. See, for instance, the websites of Mercy For Animals (http://www.mercyforanimals.org/investigations .aspx) and Compassion Over Killing (http://www.cok.net/investigations), two promi-

nent animal advocacy organizations that specialize in undercover investigations of industrial farming facilities.

2. Recent literature in the field of cognitive ethology not only confirms the common sense of most people that animals have basic interests but also strongly suggests that the cognitive and emotional capacities of animals used in farming are considerably richer and more complex than is commonly supposed. See, for example, Balcombe (2007, 2010) and Bekoff (2007). Other helpful sources on the inner lives of animals include Grandin (2005) and Masson (2003).

3. In addressing procedural harm, it is important to note that the procedures discussed here are standard industry practices widely documented in current scholarly and journalistic writing, recent video footage taken by facility employees and undercover investigators, eyewitness interviews, and even the trade publications of the industry itself. Reliable sources on the methods of industrial animal agriculture and its effects on animals used in farming are too numerous to list here, but the following sources are particularly helpful: Grandin (2005); Mason and Singer (2006); Regan (2004a, 2004b); Safran Foer (2009); Scully (2002); and Schlosser (2002). Peter Singer (2002) has compiled an account of the practices of industrial animal farming that is drawn largely from the trade publications of the industry itself.

4. I strongly encourage readers to conduct their own web research on industry descriptions of these and other common procedures. Not only are the results eye opening, but also the fact that these procedures and the harms that result from them are openly documented by the industry itself typically carries more weight with skeptics than the best-researched work by "advocates." The following are just a few examples that resulted from searches of several key terms: On dehorning, see http://www.avma.org/reference/backgrounders/dehorning_cattle_bgnd.asp; on beak trimming, see http://www.poultryhub.org/index.php/Beak_trimming; on stress during animal transport and handling, see http://www.grandin.com/references/handle.stress .html (originally published in Grandin, 1997).

5. Stories about animals' surprising and often inspiring transitions from life in confinement in farms to life on sanctuaries or in adoptive homes are available at the websites for Farm Sanctuary (http://www.farmsanctuary.org) and Animal Place (http://www.animalplace.org). See also Baur (2008).

6. For an overview of the spectrum of positions held on these matters within the philosophical literature, see Sapontzis (2008) and Engel and Jenni (2010). For discussions of the issues involved in what is often called the "rights vs. welfare" or "abolitionism vs. incrementalism" debate within the animal advocacy community, the following sources are helpful: Jones (2008); LaVeck and Stein (2007); and Torres (2007).

7. For an overview of the recent scientific literature, see the extensive notes and bibliographical sources provided in Balcombe (2007 and 2010) and Bekoff (2007). Philosophical resources for defending animals against these and other forms of exploitation can be found in virtually all the major approaches to moral theorizing. For helpful summaries of the philosophical literature, see Sapontzis (2008) and Engel and

Jenni (2010, pp. 21–36). From the utilitarian perspective, see Singer (2002). From the deontological perspective, see Regan (2004). From the perspective of religious ethics, see Linzey (2009). From the care perspective, see Adams and Donovan (2007). For a "consistency argument" that advances from assumptions widely held by members of the general public (rather than from a specific theoretical framework), see Engel (2000). Tzachi Zamir (2007) has argued that the abolition of many human uses of nonhuman animals follows even from "speciesist" assumptions.

8. For an overview of the contributions of industrial animal farming to global environmental, energy, and food security problems, see Halteman (2010).

References

Adams, C., and Donovan, J. (Eds.). (2007). *The feminist care tradition in animal ethics.* New York, NY: Columbia University Press.

American Pet Products Association. (n.d.). http://www.americanpetproducts.org /press_industrytrends.asp.

Balcombe, J. (2007). *Pleasurable kingdom: Animals and the nature of feeling good.* New York, NY: Palgrave Macmillan.

Balcombe, J. (2010). *Second nature: The inner lives of animals.* New York, NY: Palgrave Macmillan.

Baur, G. (2008). *Farm sanctuary: Changing hearts and minds about animals and food.* New York, NY: Touchstone.

Bekoff, M. (2007). *The emotional lives of animals: A leading scientist explores animal joy, sorrow, and empathy—and why they matter.* Novato, CA: New World Library.

Engel, M. (2000). The immorality of eating meat. In L. Pojman (Ed.), *The moral life: An introductory reader in ethics and literature* (pp. 856–890). Oxford, England: Oxford University Press.

Engel, M., and Jenni, K. (2010). *The philosophy of animal rights: A brief introduction for students and teachers.* New York, NY: Lantern.

Francione, G. (2008). *Animals as persons: Essays on the abolition of animal exploitation.* New York, NY: Columbia University Press.

Grandin, T. (1997). Assessment of stress during handling and transport. *Journal of Animal Science, 75,* 249–257.

Grandin, T. (2005). *Animals in translation: Using the mysteries of autism to decode animal behavior.* New York, NY: Scribner.

Halteman, M. (2010). *Compassionate eating as care of creation.* Washington, D.C.: Humane Society of the United States.

Jones, M. (2008, October 24). The barnyard strategist. *New York Times.*

LaVeck, J., and Stein, J. (2007). *Project for the new American carnivore: From Lyman to Niman in ten short years.* http://www.tribeofheart.org/tohhtml/pnac.htm.

Linzey, A. (2009). *Why animal suffering matters: Philosophy, theology, and practical ethics.* Oxford, England: Oxford University Press.

Mason, J., and Singer, P. (2006). *The way we eat: Why our food choices matter.* New York, NY: Rodale.

Masson, J. Moussaieff. (2003). *The pig who sang to the moon: The emotional world of farm animals.* New York, NY: Random House.

Regan, T. (2004a). *The case for animal rights.* Berkeley: University of California Press.

Regan, T. (2004b). *Empty cages: Facing the challenge of animal rights.* New York, NY: Rowman & Littlefield.

Safran Foer, J. (2009). *Eating animals.* New York, NY: Little, Brown.

Sapontzis, S. (Ed.). (2008). *Food for thought: The debate over eating meat.* Amherst, NY: Prometheus Books.

Schlosser, E. (2002). *Fast food nation.* New York, NY: Harper Perennial.

Scully, M. (2002). *Dominion: The power of man, the suffering of animals, and the call to mercy.* New York, NY: St. Martin's Griffin.

Singer, P. (2002). *Animal liberation.* New York, NY: Harper Collins.

Torres, B. (2007). *Making a killing: The political economy of animal rights.* Edinburgh, WV: AK Press.

Zamir, T. (2007). *Ethics and the beast: A speciesist argument for animal liberation.* Princeton, NJ: Princeton University Press.

10 Old McDonald's Had a Farm: The Metaphysics of Factory Farming

DREW LEDER

This article explores the cultural and philosophical foundations of factory farming. Modes of capitalist production play a role: Marx's analysis of the fourfold alienation of labor can be applied to animal-laborers. However, the harshness with which animals are treated exceeds the harshness directed toward human workers. At root is a cultural anthropocentrism that prohibits viewing animals as moral subjects, removing ethical restraints. Ultimately, the modernist ways in which animals are treated as both like and unlike human workers are related to the rise of Cartesian mechanism. The categories of "human" and "animal" are reconfigured by the image of the "machine."

KEY WORDS: factory farm, animal welfare, animal ethics, Marxism, anthropocentrism, mechanism

INTRODUCTION

The phenomenon of factory farming is by now well known and much excoriated. In America's slaughterhouses some 10 billion animals are killed each year. Even more distressing are the unnatural conditions under which most of these animals live. They suffer extreme confinement and the frustration of their most ordinary instincts—for example, that of birds to spread their wings. Family and social systems are disrupted and replaced by overcrowded mass housing, leading to stress, aggression, and a variety of abnormal behaviors. Treated as "vices" that threaten production, these behaviors are often restrained by even more unnatural procedures—for example, cutting off with a hot knife the beaks of chickens living in high-density conditions to stop them from pecking each other. Bred and fed for rapid meat and egg production, animals develop severe anatomical problems and disease patterns that are only partially addressed—and often exacerbated—by a stream of hormones, food additives, and antibiotics (Singer, 2001, 2006).

Not only animals but also humans suffer from factory farms, also known as concentrated animal feeding operations (CAFOs). Such operations are energy-intensive and largely petroleum-based, using up nonrenewable resources. They produce large quantities of environmentally toxic waste that enters ground, air, and water and affects the health of surrounding inhabitants. The fatty animal flesh produced by CAFO farming contributes to an epidemic of obesity among overfed Americans. Animal diseases (e.g., mad cow disease) and the breeding of antibiotic-resistant bacteria, also threaten human health (Pollan, 2006; Kirby, 2010).

In order to effectively challenge the factory farm paradigm, it is important to understand it in depth. This means reflecting on not only the technology, economics, and ethics of factory farming but also their historical and metaphysical underpinnings. How did factory farming become conceivable as an enterprise? What does its existence tell us about the nature of animal, human, and machine and their interrelationships as culturally constructed? How might the theories and practices represented within the factory farm best be transformed?

One way into such issues is to examine the term itself: "factory farm." It contains within it a number of hinges. A hinge is a joint that holds two parts together, while allowing one to swing relative to the other.

First, the word "farm" operates as a conceptual hinge between the human and the natural/animal world. A farm is a human construction designed to meet human needs. Yet to accomplish this, humans must tend to nature, drawing on its intrinsic powers of fertility and growth. Historically, working farms employed animals to assist in labor, to manure the fields, and from whom to take meat, milk, eggs, and other products. As the song goes, "Old MacDonald had a farm . . . and on this farm he had some chicks" and a cow, pigs, a geese, a horse, and so on. The cacophony of sung animal noises reminds us that this farm is a hinge, regulating the interactions of MacDonald and his animal associates.

If a "farm" is a hinge, so too is a "factory." Often defined as buildings used for the manufacturing of goods, factories also embody a complexity of beings and relationships. They include not only the building but also the people—factory workers, on-site supervisors, and more distant executives—who keep it humming, along with the machinery that produces goods.

The term "factory farm" then constitutes a meta-hinge. It operates to join and swing together farm and factory; agrarian and industrial; human, animal, architectural, and mechanical. The open-aired farm, drawing energy from the sun, is reconceived along the lines of closed-in manufacturing plants, most often coal- and petroleum-based. Old MacDonald's cows and pigs are subsumed within a world of workers, corporate owners, machines, and commodity markets. This, of course, is precisely the kind of "farm" utilized by fast-food corporations such as McDonald's. Unlike Old MacDonald's farm, a McDonald's farm is designed to maximize large-scale, efficient, and highly profitable food production.

Admittedly, some such companies have made efforts to improve conditions. McDonald's, for example, working with PETA from 2000 to 2009, animal wel-fare expert Temple Grandin, and others, now contractually specifies animal-treatment standards to be employed by its suppliers (Kaufman, 2002; Barboza, 2003). Though not the focus of this article, such on-the-ground reforms are important. Ultimately, however, they fail to challenge the fundamental paradigm of the factory farm and most of its intrinsic cruelties.

Again, we must ask, how did something as oxymoronic as a "factory farm," this meta-hinge, first become conceivable and constructable? This query will lead us to survey the respective roles and interlockings of three great "isms" in Western culture—capitalism, anthropocentrism, and mechanism. Here too the factory farm serves as a meta-hinge for large-scale cultural movements.

CAPITALISM: ALIENATED ANIMAL LABOR

Karl Marx, an early, influential, and insightful critic of industrial capitalism, pro-vides a point of entry. Famously, the early Marx (1964b) discusses the four-fold "alienation" or "estrangement" (*Entfremdung*) that characterizes wage labor in a capitalist system (pp. 106–119). The worker is alienated from the product of his labor, which does not belong to him or express his creative nature. Rather, it rules over him as something apart, something even hostile and oppressive, condemning him to toil and poverty. This alienation is realized not only in the object of production but also in the act of production. This is forced labor, dic-tated by another, and is often harsh, repetitive, and subhuman, which "mortifies his body and ruins his mind" (Marx, 1964b, p. 110).

Thus, humans are alienated from their species-being (*Gattungswesen*). This notion of Marx, drawn from Feuerbach, is complex, unclearly defined, and much debated, but relates to a number of features that Marx took to be essentially human. Human beings, unlike animals, do not simply labor under the dominion of immediate physical need but produce freely and consciously, taking the whole of nature as a potential field of endeavor, working for goals beyond private self-interest, utilizing a full range of cognitive, aesthetic, and practical powers, such that, ideally, one's work serves as a tool of creative expression and self-expansion. Not so for the wage laborer. "Estranged labor tears him from his species life" (Marx, 1964, p. 114), eradicating from work that which is human and humane.

As such, and finally, wage labor estranges "man from man" (Marx, 1964b, p. 114). Instead of forging genuinely human relationships, based on individual characteristics, free right of consort, shared goals, and affections, human interactions are governed by economic forces, rendering one an owner, another a worker, one coercive, another enslaved.

Marx's analysis of the 19th-century factory worker's plight is applicable to the contemporary factory farm. Many of the human workers in CAFOs suffer such modes of alienation. Perhaps more so do animals, the primary "laborers" in this "factory." A brief sketch will suffice, though it could easily be expanded.

Alienation from the product of one's labor takes extreme form when the product is one's own flesh, built up through confinement and force-feeding and made accessible by one's slaughter. Marx (1964b) writes, "So much does labor's realization appear as loss of realization that the worker loses realization to the point of starving to death" (p. 108). There is a curious inversion for the animal used for meat, who is often deliberately overfed, albeit in ways that induce nutritional deficiencies and incipient disease, before being killed. Other animal products, such as milk and eggs, are made in ways less lethal to the "worker." Nonetheless, these too are usually bound up with slaughter—for example, the killing of young calves and male chickens when the females are preserved for dairy and egg production.

It might be rightly said that since animals do not know their ultimate fate, they suffer less "alienation from the product" than would a human being in comparable circumstances. We can imagine a well-fed, oblivious chicken enjoying her brief life. But of course, this is unlikely on a factory farm. That the product is alienated—not one's own—is intertwined for Marx with alienation from the productive process. Chickens, like most animals in factory farms, suffer conditions that are harsh and unnatural, designed to maximize production, not quality of life. For example, hens used for eggs may spend virtually their entire existence in artificially lit and environmentally manipulated barracks, confined some seven or eight birds to a small cage, feet perched on wire mesh, unable to exercise natural drives, and tended to by perhaps one worker for every 150,000 chickens (Mason & Finelli, 2006).

As with Marx's wage laborer, this alienation from productive activity is also an alienation from one's species-nature. Though Marx reserves the term "species being" to refer to humans' capacity for self-conscious, universalized, free activity, he recognizes that animals have fixed species-characteristics. Creatures have their natural habitats; their instincts for predation, aggression, seeking, playing, mating, and child-rearing; their social rituals and pecking orders; and even their capabilities of high-level cognition, skill development, and emotional response that we are just beginning to appreciate. All these can be systematically frustrated in the unnatural world of the factory farm. Just as workers are "dehumanized" by alienated conditions, so, for example, is a pig, a highly intelligent creature, unable to express his or her pig-nature in a crude confinement facility. Moreover, factory farms manipulate not only the environment but also the genetic animal itself. Breeding for a single trait, as with large-breasted "white meat" chickens, can lead to animals who are deformed, neurologically or cardiologically damaged, and generally unhealthy, alienated from their original species-character (Grandin & Johnson, 2005, pp. 69–81).

Finally, Marx's notion of "man's alienation from man" is applicable to animals used on farms in both inter- and intraspecies form. In traditional agriculture, as represented in "Old MacDonald's Farm," there is often a close and symbiotic relationship between humans and animals. Such relationships are severed by large agribusiness CAFOs. So too are the relationships between fellow animals. The instincts, rituals, hierarchies, and affective ties that organize animal families and societies are thoroughly disrupted.

Thus, as Benton (1988) writes, "the pathological distortions from the properly human mode of life which Marx attempts to capture in his concept of 'estrange-ment,' or 'alienation,' are in important respects paralleled in the modes of life imposed upon animals by precisely the same structures of social action" (p. 11). Marx's analysis, thus extended, clarifies the "hinge" that links the fate of humans and animals who are impressed into factory labor.

However, a hinge is that which both connects and separates. This dialectic of connection and separation is seen in Marx's own portrayal of humans and ani-mals. On the one hand, he seeks to counter Hegelian idealism with a naturalistic conception of man. "*Man* is directly a *natural being*," a "*corporeal,* living, real, sensuous, objective being full of natural vigor" (Marx, 1964a, p. 181). Hence, man and animal are connected. On the other hand, he asserts that humans are distinct from the natural world, including higher animals, by virtue of their freedom and self-consciousness (Benton, 1998). He sees animals as tied to an instinctive fulfillment of pressing needs, whereas "conscious life activity distin-guishes man immediately from animal life activity" (Marx, 1964b, p. 113).

This human/animal hinge is central to Marx's analysis. We can become alienated laborers only insofar as we are both *like* other creatures—caught up in a perilous struggle for corporeal survival—and *not like* other creatures and therefore bound to suffer when reduced to an animalistic existence. The horror of alienated labor is that the worker "only feels himself freely active in his animal functions—eating, drinking, procreating, or at most in his dwelling and in dressing up, etc.; and in his human functions he no longer feels himself to be anything but an animal" (Marx, 1964b, p. 111).

In contrast to the natural hinge that connects/separates the human and animal, capitalism thus creates an *unnatural* hinge. It swings together, even reverses, what should be separate: "What is animal becomes human and what is human becomes animal" (Marx, 1964b, p. 111). The worker is made brutish by labor's brutal conditions.

However, Marx's emphasis on the human/animal separation may limit his utility in any critique of factory farming. Marx envisions communism as taking over, even furthering, the productive powers developed in capitalism. In his words, communism "will be the fully developed domination of man over natural forces, over nature in the strict sense, as well as over his own nature" (Vaillancourt, 1996, p. 53). Marx's focus on human liberation did not extend to a concern with animal liberation.

More generally, there is a large scholarly literature about the relationship between Marx and environmentalism. Some view him as unfortunately Promethean, supportive of the development of productive powers that facilitate human control over nature. Others read him as more ecologically sensitive and valuable. The latter authors, seeking a so-called greening of Marxism, point to Marx's naturalism and his quasi-environmentalist critique of the devastations wrought by capitalism (Benton, 1996). Authors such as O'Connor (1998) and Barry (1999) seek to extend the Marxist paradigm to address contemporary ecological crises. For example, such crises clarify the impossibility of "unlimited growth" as forces of production outrun and exhaust natural conditions.

However, I will sidestep any lengthy discussion of such scholarly developments. Regarding Marx, it seems fair to assert, as he himself did, that his system remained fundamentally a kind of humanism. He is concerned with the quality of *human* life and society. He believes in appropriating the natural world as a setting for *human* expression. In Barry's (1999) words, "unlike radical green theory, eco-Marxism is firmly anthropocentric" (p. 276). Although his critique of capitalism is useful for understanding the modern factory farm, we are thus led to briefly examine the role of this other "ism"—*anthropocentrism*.

ANTHROPOCENTRISM

A predominant element of the Western tradition, broadly conceived, has been a focus on human beings as the pinnacle of nature and/or as having a unique supernatural significance. Nonhuman nature is often consigned to an instrumental role; it is important insofar as it serves human needs. We find this anthropocentric orientation in much ancient, medieval, and modern philosophy and theology (Mason, 1993); in this regard, Marx is no revolutionary.

Aristotle, for example, writes in Book 1 of his *Politics*, "If nature makes nothing incomplete, and nothing in vain, the inference must be that she has made all animals for the sake of man" (McKeon, 1941, p. 1137). St. Thomas Aquinas, in his grand synthesis of Aristotelianism and Christianity, reinterprets such notions theologically. Only rational creatures, insofar as they have dominion over their own actions and are made in the divine likeness, are cared for by God "for their own sake"—not so for animals, created to be "subordinated to others" (Aquinas, 1956, p. 115).

> Through these considerations we refute the error of those who claim that it is a sin for man to kill brute animals. For animals are ordered to man's use in the natural course of things, according to divine providence. Consequently, man uses them without any injustice, either by killing them or by employing them in any way. (Aquinas, 1956, p. 119)

Any biblical passages that seem to forbid cruelty to animals, Aquinas contends, are only meant to prevent the cultivation of mental states or actions that may lead us to harm other men.

Immanuel Kant (1963) famously concurs with such judgments in a modern idiom, defending them through appeal to reason and the categorical imperative: "So far as animals are concerned, we have no direct duties. Animals are not self-conscious and are there merely as a means to an end" (p. 239). He too suggests we should be kind to creatures only to assure we do not become hardened in our dealings with humans.

Such historical examples could be multiplied indefinitely, as has been done elsewhere. Looking at the big picture, Linzey (2009) isolates six reasons that have been used, historically and in contemporary discourse, to minimize the significance of or justify animal suffering. The first four are mainly philosophical and include the notions that animals are (1) naturally subordinate and slave-like; (2) nonrational; (3) linguistically deficient; and (4) not themselves moral agents (pp. 11–29). These constitute arguments—ones that Linzey himself seeks to refute—that animals are incapable of serious suffering and/or not to be included within the community of moral consideration.

In addition, Linzey (2009) discusses two theological arguments that have played an important role in Western culture: namely, that animals are soulless beings, and are not made in the divine image—a scriptural description reserved only for humans (Genesis 1:26–28). Such passages can ground a theological anthropocentrism, as seen in Aquinas, that sanctions the unrestrained use of other creatures (White, 1967).

For Linzey, as for many contemporary theologians, this scriptural interpretation is a misinterpretation (2009, pp. 25–29; 1987, pp. 22–39). The biblical notion of "dominion" need not imply domination, but can refer to the kind of loving stewardship characteristic of God's care for the world. Moreover, whereas some biblical passages are clearly instrumentalist—the human community will prosper if it practices proper husbandry—others point to the natural world, God's creation, as possessing intrinsic value and interests independent of the human agenda.

Just as there has been a "greening of Marxism," there are thus many contemporary thinkers who have sought to draw an environmental ethic from biblical sources (Austin, 1988; Kay, 1988; Clark, 1993; Linzey, 1987, 1995; Berry, 2009). Even the current Pope Benedict XVI, then Cardinal Ratzinger, told a journalist,

> Certainly, a sort of industrial use of creatures, so that geese are fed in such a way as to produce as large a liver as possible, or hens live so packed together that they become just caricatures of birds, this degrading of living creatures to a commodity seems to me in fact to contradict the relationship of mutuality that comes across in the Bible. (Scully, 2004)

Still, this sort of reflection and challenge has been a subsidiary thread in the Western tradition. Religious doctrine and practice has tended to be dominated by an assumption that the good *for human beings* is the focus of God's concern and so should be ours. The Western philosophical tradition has usually agreed, appealing to the uniqueness of human reason and moral choice.

Though seemingly benign in intent, this anthropocentrism provides another conceptual and cultural underpinning for the cruelties of the factory farm. It posits animals as resources for unconstrained human exploitation. Marx details the harshness of human factory work, but we have also seen in the West an evolution of moral concern and legal protection for workers. There have been movements, albeit imperfect, to prohibit child labor, limit the workweek, protect the health and safety of laborers, and so on. Not so, not yet, or not nearly to the same extent has this happened for animals who are factory-farmed. We see a synergy of harshness when capitalism meets anthropocentrism.

Embedded within this synergy is a paradox. Extending Marx's analysis to the factory farm depends on making a connection between humans and animals. Insofar as animals are treated *like* human workers, they fall prey to similar modes of alienation. However, the role of anthropocentrism implies the opposite. It is precisely because animals are treated as *unlike* human beings that we are seen to have no "direct duties" to their welfare; they can be abused without ethical restraint. When Jonathan Swift (1996) suggests in "A Modest Proposal" that we breed, fatten, and slaughter the children of the Irish poor for "a most delicious, nourishing, and wholesome food, whether stewed, roasted, baked, or boiled" (p. 53), we know this must be satire. What cannot be done to human beings, even the underclass, is, however, standard treatment for animals.

Again, we have arrived at something like a hinge, "a joint that holds two parts together." The factory farm depends on animals being treated like human beings (qua alienated laborers) and unlike human beings (qua ethical subjects). Wherein lies the hinge that allows for both this equation and this opposition?

Our answer: It lies in that which is neither human nor animal, yet both links and contrasts them with each other—*the machine.*

MECHANISM

In a much-told story, early modern science ushered in a new world-picture. As developed by experimentalists and theorists such as Galileo and Descartes, the natural world was reconceived according to the physics and mathematics of mechanics (Burtt, 1952; Butterfield, 1997). This effected what Merchant has famously termed "the death of nature" (Merchant, 1980). The natural world was no longer conceived of as ensouled and purposive. Expunged were both the neo-Platonic ascription of occult sympathies and antipathies to matter and the Aristotelian notion of substantial forms with final causes they sought to actualize (Thomas, 1997). What remained was nature viewed as machinelike, its passive matter driven by mechanical forces.

Even living bodies were assimilated to this paradigm based on the inanimate. As Descartes (1911) writes in *The Passions of the Soul,*

> We may judge that the body of a living man differs from that of a dead man just as does a watch or other automaton (i.e., a machine that moves of itself), when it is wound up and contains in itself the corporeal principle of those movements for which it is designed along with all that is requisite for its action, from the same watch or other machine when it is broken and when the principle of its movement ceases to act. (p. 333)

For Descartes, humans are unique in that our machine-bodies are conjoined with an immaterial and immortal soul exercising thought, desire, and will. The difficulties involved in his dualist position are legendary and need not be reviewed here. However, in his own expression of anthropocentrism, Descartes denies any such metaphysical complexity to animals. In the *Discourse on Method* he argues that their lack of language demonstrates that despite manifesting well-organized behavior and what can appear to be feelings and cognition, animals in fact possess no rational soul. Again, he refers to clocks and other automata to show how their behavior can be accounted for mechanically (Descartes, 1911, pp. 116–118).

There is debate within the literature about whether Descartes really meant to argue that animals have no conscious awareness whatsoever, including that of pain. Certain scholars argue that Descartes did ascribe perceptual experience to animals, or was at least agnostic, not precluding that possibility (Cottingham, 1978; Harrison, 1992; Thomas, 2006). On the other hand, there is a dominant tradition of interpreting Descartes in his original writings, subsequent correspondence, and replies to objections to be saying that animals are devoid of both sentient and rational consciousness (Steiner, 1988). However one views Descartes' own stance, this modernist equation of the natural world in general—and animals in particular—with inanimate machines has profoundly influenced our culture.

Equally influential has been the technological project that mechanistic science was meant to subserve for Descartes, as for Bacon before him. Descartes (1911) writes of his scientific breakthroughs,

> They caused me to see that it is possible to attain knowledge which is very useful in life . . . that we may find a practical philosophy by means of which, knowing the force and the action of fire, water, air, the stars, heavens and all other bodies that environ us, as distinctly as we know the different crafts of our artisans, we can in the same way employ them in all those uses to which they are adapted, and thus render ourselves the masters and possessors of nature. (p. 119)

Although Descartes' understanding of the human relation to the natural world is far from univocal (Wee, 2001), we hear the resonances of biblical language and theological anthropocentrism in this quest for technological mastery. Religion and science need not be in opposition: Here they seemingly converge to sanction human power over nature.

Descartes' primary practical goal, as stated in the *Discourse* and personal letters, was the advancement of medicine. He sought to combat disease and the infirmities of age and to elongate the human lifespan. To these ends he viewed study of the animal body as an invaluable resource. During certain periods he made almost daily trips to the butcher shop to obtain animal organs for dissection (Descartes, 1972, pp. vii–ix). He also apparently engaged in vivisection, for example describing in detail the pulsations one feels when slicing off the pointed end of a heart in a living dog and thrusting in a finger (Steiner, 1998, p. 288). Descartes' paradigm and practices were influential. Nicholas Fontaine described the Cartesianists at Port Royal who, believing dogs to be unfeeling machines, beat and vivisected them with indifference, claiming their cries were simply like the noises made by a clock spring when touched (Federici, 2004, p. 159).

Earlier I wrote that the factory farm operates as a conceptual hinge. Its cruel practices arise because animals are treated both *unlike* human beings (qua having no moral status) and *like* human beings (qua alienated factory laborers). Analysis of the mechanistic worldview can help us understand how these opposites can be conjoined.

The farm can become a factory when the animal comes to be viewed as a machine, whether used for meat, milk, or egg production. *Unlike* human beings, these animal-machines are seen as soulless, without intrinsic ends and desires or the capacity to experience pain and suffering. Hence, we are free to become their "masters and possessors" without ethical restraint. No limit is placed on our manipulation of their life and death. Moreover, we can effect this control using the knowledge gained by our study of these animal-machines. This assists us to manipulate and accelerate their growth, alter their genetic stock to favor profitable traits, and maximize yield in artificial CAFOs while minimizing loss through antibiotics, dietary supplements, and mutilations. In an ironic twist on Descartes' dream of improving *human* health and longevity, the results for animals are often quite the opposite.

Yet if the machine-paradigm can serve to differentiate animals from humans, it also has been used to link them together. Historically, Descartes' religiously informed dualism often gave way to materialistic monism, from which references to soul are expunged. The treatise *"L'Homme Machine"* (Man-the-Machine) by La Mettrie (1996), French physician and philosopher, is one famous example. Foucault (1979) comments,

> The great book of Man-the-Machine was written simultaneously in two registers: the anatomico-metaphysical register, of which Descartes wrote the first pages and which the physicians and philosophers continued, and the technico-political register, which was constituted by a whole set of regulations and by empirical and calculated methods relating to the army, the school and the hospital, for controlling or correcting the operations of the body. (p. 136)

So too does the modern factory control the body-machine via the division of labor and its manipulation of time, space, and motion to maximize productivity. The metaphysics of mechanism subserve the practices of industrial capitalism. Marx described how human workers become alienated when treated as adjuncts to machines and as machinelike themselves. This applies as well to animals manipulated on the factory farm.

Many traditional cultures posit a close ontological relationship between humans and animals. We see this in mythology, the performing arts, sacred ceremony, and shamanistic practices. The human–animal worlds are porous and interconnected, allowing shape-shifting back and forth and the magical sharing of perspectives and powers (Abram, 1996). Mechanism also posits a human–animal equation. However, this equation tends toward the constrictive and monological. The inanimate object, the automaton, remakes all in its flattened image.

The more creative possibilities of machines and human-machine cyborgs have been explored by authors such as Haraway (1991) and Mazis (2008). Nonetheless, historically, mechanism has lent itself to reductionist applications; living creatures are remodeled upon the inanimate.

As evidenced by the factory farm, the paradigm of *L'animal machine* has proved even more powerful than that of *L'homme machine*. Whereas our sense of human intelligence, dignity, rights, and even divinity has often played a powerful counter-role to "man-the-machine," animals have been less protected by an alternative metaphysics. There have been elements within the romantic, and subsequently the ecological, movements to recall us to the richness of animal-being. In daily life, many enjoy the song of a bird or the personality of a beloved animal companion. But this has largely failed to counteract the mindset that determines conditions for the billions of animals who dwell on our factory farms.

THE BIG MAC

We have sought the origins not of "Old MacDonald's Farm" celebrated in song, but the new McDonald's farm of high-profit industrial agriculture. (Again, while using this company as an example, I do not mean to single it out for censure; it has adopted certain animal-welfare reforms.) In honor of the company's signature product, we might label what we have discovered as the Big MAC. The paradigmatic structures underlying the factory farm have proven to be materialism, anthropocentrism, and capitalism (hence, the Big MAC). Which, we might ask, is the true heart of the meal, the most important and foundational of these three forces? It depends on one's perspective.

In terms of cultural history, we might grant priority to anthropocentrism, which predates the advent of mechanism and capitalism. But we have seen, through a comparison of animals used on factory farms and Marx's alienated laborers, that anthropocentrism could be removed and animals and humans equated, yet key elements of the factory farm would be left intact.

Perhaps, then, capitalism is the central culprit, particularly if we view, à la Marx, economic structures, processes, and motivations as more significant than airy metaphysics. Yet in a transition to a communist state, again one can imagine the factory farm left fully operative.

Philosophically, one might then view mechanistic metaphysics as the most powerful "engine" powering the factory farm. We have seen that it links together religious and scientific elements of the Western tradition. It helps us better understand how animals and humans can both be treated similarly (qua alienated labor) and differently (qua our unrestrained cruelty to animals who are farmed). As such it serves as a hinge holding together the disparate elements that form the factory farm. This entity seems inconceivable without the philosophy, science, and technology of mechanism.

Finally, though, the three elements of this Big MAC might best be understood as a synergistic sandwich. The cultural tradition of anthropocentrism, the economics of capitalism, and the worldview and practices of mechanism interact in ways that are mutually enhancing—or from another point of view, maximally destructive—for the animals subject to their rule.

CONCLUDING THOUGHTS

Many seek not simply to understand but to significantly modify or dismantle the factory farm. This analysis is meant as a helpful propaedeutic. The direction of one's philosophical or practical challenge to the system might depend on which aspect of this Big MAC one takes to be most important. One can oppose, as many are now doing, the logic of the mass-production-and-consumption food industry; the theo-philosophical presumption of human superiority; and/or limited mechanist/behaviorist understandings of animal psychology.

If our Big MAC is synergistic, perhaps the best counters will be as well, reaching to the heart of what these logics hold in common. I take this to be— using something like Marx's terms—an alienation from, or obscuring of, the true species-nature of animals. From a quasi-Marxist point of view, this alienation derives from the structures of capitalism that make animals into commodities to be produced and consumed. A critic of anthropocentrism might say the species-natures of animals are obscured by human egocentricity: Animals are viewed as our servants or possessions rather than as they are unto themselves. With regard to mechanism, alienation results when the animal is reconceived as that which is non-animal and inanimate, a passive, unfeeling machine.

Yet what these logics all have in common is that they do not allow the animal to be an animal. The animal is not viewed as pursuing his or her own ends, inhabiting his or her own world, and exhibiting the unique powers and propensities characteristic of his or her species and individual personality. Instead, the animal is reduced to something other than him or herself. Any powerful challenge to factory farming would begin here—by genuinely *recognizing* the animals with whom we inhabit the earth.

This has scientific ramifications. Much of animal psychology still remains veiled in mystery, our research limited by behaviorist assumptions, artificial laboratory conditions, and industrial agendas. There is a need for fuller study and appreciation of the richness of animal consciousness and behavior.

This goes hand in hand with ethical ramifications. Whether animals are thought of as God's own creatures (as developed in ecotheology), ends in themselves (to use a Kantian logic), beings capable of suffering (invoking a utilitarian calculus), or embodied creatures coinhabiting the earth (as explored in phenomenology, ecofeminism, and deep ecology), animals have their own experience of the world, one that demands our attention and concern. To *recognize* animals is to take seriously the moral and existential claims imposed by their subjectivity.

This is more than viewing animals as *others* whose violation is prohibited. They are also *partners* with whom we share a world. For untold centuries humans and animals have coevolved through symbiotic relationships. One of the ironies of factory farming is that in rendering animals totally subservient to human constructs, CAFOs also exclude most animals from the human community. We never meet the cow until he arrives as our Big Mac.

It is not only animals who suffer from the CAFO. Factory farms do not create good landscapes, ecosystems, communities, health, and food for human beings. Grandin and Johnson's recent book is titled *Animals Make Us Human* (2009). When animals are alienated from their species-nature and our shared world, we too lose something essential. The counter to factory farming is not simply to negate a negative. Rather it is to reintroduce elements of diversity, creativity, and "humanity" into our human–animal relations.

This article has asked how it is that factory farms became *conceivable*. As important is the question of how—remembering backward or thinking forward—we can reach a place where they again become *inconceivable*.

References

Abram, D. (1996). *The spell of the sensuous: Perception and language in a more than human world.* New York, NY: Pantheon Books.

Aquinas, St. T. (1956). *On the truth of the Catholic faith: Summa contra gentiles. Book three: Providence, part II.* New York, NY: Image Books.

Austin, R. C. (1988). *Hope for the land: Nature in the Bible.* Atlanta, GA: John Knox Press.

Barboza, D. (2003, June 25). Animal welfare's unexpected allies. *New York Times,* p. C1.

Barry, J. (1999). Marxism and ecology. In A. Gamble, D. Marsh, & T. Tant (Eds.), *Marxism and social science* (pp. 259–279). Urbana: University of Illinois Press.

Benton, T. (Ed.). (1996). *The greening of Marxism.* New York, NY: Guilford Press.

Benton, T. (1998). Humanism equals speciesism: Marx on humans and animals. *Radical Philosophy, 50,* 4–18.

Berry, W. (2009). *The gift of good land: Further essays cultural and agricultural.* Berkeley, CA: Counterpoint.

Burtt, E. A. (1952). *The metaphysical foundations of modern science.* Atlantic Highlands, NJ: Humanities Press.

Butterfield, H. (1997). *The origins of modern science.* New York, NY: Free Press.

Clark, S. R. L. (1993). *How to think about the earth: Philosophical and theological models for ecology.* New York, NY: Mowbray.

Cottingham, J. (1978). A brute to the brutes? Descartes' treatment of animals. *Philosophy, 53,* 551–559.

Descartes, R. (1911). *The philosophical works of Descartes: Vol. 1* (E. Haldane & G. R. T. Ross, Eds.). Cambridge, England: Cambridge University Press.

Descartes, R. (1972). *Treatise of man.* Cambridge, MA: Harvard University Press.

Federici, S. (2004). *Caliban and the witch: Women, the body, and primitive accumulation.* New York, NY: Autonomedia.

Foucault, M. (1979). *Discipline and punish: The birth of the prison.* New York, NY: Vintage Books.

Grandin, T., & Johnson, C. (2005). *Animals in translation.* New York, NY: Harcourt.

Grandin, T., & Johnson, C. (2009). *Animals make us human: Creating the best life for animals.* Boston, MA: Houghton Mifflin Harcourt.

Haraway, D. (1991). *Simians, cyborgs, and women: The reinvention of nature.* New York, NY: Routledge.

Harrison, P. (1992). Descartes on animals. *Philosophical Quarterly, 42,* 219–227.

Kant, I. (1963). *Lectures on ethics.* London, England: Methuen.

Kaufman, M. (2002, June 28). Guidelines for treatment of food animals released; retailers urge improved conditions on farms. *Washington Post,* p. A3.

Kay, J. (1988). Concepts of nature in the Hebrew Bible. *Environmental Ethics, 10,* 309–327.

Kirby, D. (2010). *Animal factory: The looming threat of industrial pig, dairy, and poultry farms to humans and the environment.* New York, NY: St. Martin's Press.

La Mettrie, J. O. D. (1996). *Machine man and other writings.* Cambridge, England: Cambridge University Press.

Linzey, A. (1987). *Christianity and the rights of animals.* New York, NY: Crossroad.

Linzey, A. (1995). *Animal theology.* Urbana: University of Illinois Press.

Linzey, A. (2009). *Why animal suffering matters: Philosophy, theology, and practical ethics.* Oxford, England: Oxford University Press.

Marx, K. (1964a). Critique of the Hegelian dialectic and philosophy as a whole. In *The economic and philosophic manuscripts of 1844* (pp. 170–193). New York, NY: International Publishers.

Marx, K. (1964b). Estranged labor. In *The economic and philosophic manuscripts of 1844* (pp. 106–119). New York, NY: International Publishers.

Mason, J. (1993). *An unnatural order: Uncovering the roots of our domination of nature and each other.* New York, NY: Simon & Schuster.

Mason, J., & Finelli, M. (2006). Brave new farm. In P. Singer (Ed.), *In defense of animals: The second wave* (pp. 104–122). Malden, MA: Blackwell.

Mazis, G. (2008). *Humans, animals, machines: Blurring boundaries.* Albany: State University of New York Press.

McKeon, R. (Ed.) (1941). *The basic works of Aristotle.* New York, NY: Random House.

Merchant, C. (1980). *The death of nature.* San Francisco, CA: Harper and Row.

O'Connor, J. (1998). *Natural causes: Essays in ecological Marxism.* New York, NY: Guilford Press.

Pollan, M. (2006). *The omnivore's dilemma: A natural history of four meals.* New York, NY: Penguin.

Scully, M. (2004, October 4). Factory farm meat not on menu for feast of St. Francis. *Dallas Morning News.* Retrieved from http://www.matthewscully.com/factory_farm_meat.htm

Singer, P. (2001). *Animal liberation.* New York, NY: Harper Perennial. (Original work published 1975)

Singer, P. (Ed.). (2006). *In defense of animals: The second wave.* Malden, MA: Blackwell.

Steiner, G. (1988). Descartes on the moral status of animals. *Archiv für Geschichte der Philosophie, 80,* 268–291.

Swift, J. (1996). *A modest proposal and other satirical works.* Mineola, NY: Dover.

Thomas, J. (2006). Does Descartes deny consciousness to animals? *Ratio, 19,* 336–363.

Thomas, K. (1997). *Religion and the decline of magic: Studies in popular beliefs in sixteenth and seventeenth century England.* New York, NY: Oxford University Press.

Vaillancourt, J.-G. (1996). Marxism and ecology: More Benedictine than Franciscan. In T. Benton (Ed.), *The greening of Marxism* (pp. 50–63). New York, NY: Guilford Press.

Wee, C. (2001). Cartesian environmental ethics. *Environmental Ethics, 23,* 276–285.

White, L., Jr. (1967). The historical roots of our ecological crisis. *Science, 155,* 1203–1207.

11 Australia and Live Animal Export: Wronging Nonhuman Animals

SIMON COGHLAN

The decades-old trade of exporting nonhuman mammals by ship from Australia became a major political issue in 2011, when video taken by animal rights group Animals Australia was broadcast on television, showing Australian cattle being appallingly abused in Indonesian abattoirs. Taking its cue from the unprecedented response from Australians to the 2011 footage, many of whom were haunted by the video images, this article argues that the live export trade may be seen to wrong nonhuman animals according to several key ethical frameworks.

KEY WORDS: live animal export, animal welfare, Australian government, normative theory, theory-independent ethics

INTRODUCTION

Australia is the world's largest exporter of live nonhuman animals, and its export market is growing (Phillips & Santurtun, 2013). In 2012, 617,301 cattle were exported for slaughter, mainly to Indonesia, and over 2 million sheep went to the Middle East (LiveCorp, 2014). It is thought that the transport of sheep from Australia to the Middle East is the "largest, planned mass movement of animals by sea in the history of the world" (Georges, Evans, Cooney, & Siddons, 1985, p. 9). In terms of technological and commercial ingenuity, live export is a triumph.

Australia has stronger nonhuman animal protection laws than many other countries. It has energetic nonhuman animal (hereafter, animal) protection organizations and its citizenry and media are increasingly concerned about animal welfare. The government's Department of Agriculture, Fisheries, and Forestry (DAFF; 2013) claims that "Australia leads the world in animal welfare practices."

Journal of Animal Ethics 4(2): 45–60

In 2011, live export became a major political event after Lyn White from the animal rights group Animals Australia took footage of cattle being eye-gouged, tail-twisted, beaten, and repeatedly slashed with knives by indifferent Indonesian slaughtermen (Animals Australia, 2013). Horrified viewers watched as Australian cattle were forced to fall heavily to the ground, slapping their heads on hard floors, sometimes chipping the concrete (Jones, 2011, p. 21). A sense of shock and outrage spread around the country, as rallies were organized and petitions were signed by thousands. White, the central figure in the expose, was applauded for her courage and compassion in shooting the footage. Even government and industry leaders professed a moral concern for the animals themselves, with the CEO of LiveCorp, Cameron Hall, claiming to be "shocked . . . and appalled by the cruel actions" (Hall, 2011). To this day, LiveCorp (2014) insists it is "strongly committed to the health and wellbeing of animals" and that the "welfare of Australian livestock are of the utmost importance." The Australian agriculture minister swore that the "health and wellbeing of exported livestock is a priority for the Australian Government" (Ludwig, 2012). Facing accusations of complacency and ignorance, both industry and government entities conceded self-regulation had failed and promised that new measures would ensure the future welfare of exported animals.

Not everyone believes that animals have noninstrumental moral value. Nonetheless, the main players in the live export debate—industry, government, concerned politicians and citizens, animal protection groups—at least *profess* a belief that animals, even to some minimal degree, matter morally in their own right, over and above their connection with human interests. Unlike the Indonesian authorities, perhaps, the Australian export industry proclaims a commitment to welfare improvements, however small and gradual, for the animals traded for food. Apparent agreement thus exists among the trade's supporters and opponents that animals have some minimal intrinsic moral value that is not entirely derivative or instrumental in nature.

To further clarify the ground held in common between the supporters and the opponents of live animal export, recall Kant's well-known notion that it can be wrong to treat an animal "cruelly," but only because it can harm human beings or harden human hearts against them. This article takes at face value avowals of live export supporters that animals do not matter merely in this derivative fashion, but rather they matter because they can be directly wronged, as when they are used cruelly in food production. It is in this sense that supporters and opponents agree that animals have some minimal intrinsic moral value, despite the great disagreement on the nature and extent of that value.

The article goes on to interpret how several normative ethical theories, and one nontheoretical moral framework, could assess the live export trade. This philosophical exploration is organized around the 2011 Indonesian revelations, especially White's video footage and the profound moral responses it drew. Emerging from the discussion are several important ways of appreciating what it may be to wrong these animals.

BACKGROUND

Georges et al. (1985) found the first consignments of sheep to be shipped by sea sailed in the 1830s between the Australian states of Victoria and Tasmania, with an average mortality rate of 15% (p. 3). Commonwealth regulations on animal welfare were not introduced for sea voyages until 1926 (Georges et al., 1985, p. 3). Following the 1973 oil crisis, tankers were refitted for the trade, and 15,000 kilometres of Indian Ocean (Georges et al., 1985, pp. 4, 10).

Animal rights groups opposed live export from the late 1970s. Opposition intensified after the *Farid Fares* sank in 1980, drowning the 40,605 sheep on board, and again in 1983, when cold weather killed around 15,000 sheep in a Victorian feedlot prior to boarding (Georges et al., 1985, p. 5). The entire journey, or "export supply chain" as it is called, is a long one:

> It begins with the mustering of the stock, often on remote properties, and it ends with animal slaughter in the country of destination. In between, the stock will be handled at least a further five or six times and the whole process is likely to last between one and two months. Little is known about the cumulative effects of these combined stresses on the welfare of the animals. (Phillips, 2008, p. 139)

Animals in the export supply chain are largely hidden from the direct gaze of ordinary citizens and independent welfare scientists (Phillips, 2011). Nevertheless, knowledge of some of the conditions can be gleaned by other means.

PROBLEMS AT SEA

In 2003, the *Cormo Express*, with 57,937 sheep on board, set sail from Australia for the Red Sea, only to be rejected by Saudi Arabia on the dubious grounds of "scabby mouth" (Keniry, Bond, Caple, Gosse, & Rogers, 2003, p. 29). As sheep began to weaken and die in extreme heat, a media storm erupted. After 80 days at sea, 5,691 sheep, or nearly 10% of the total, had perished (Keniry et al., 2003, p. 29). Australia suspended live export to Saudi Arabia—a suspension that lasted until 2005. Although the government's review of Australia's animal export trade accepted that steps had been taken to improve animal welfare, it complained that the industry's approach was reactive and incremental (Keniry et al., 2003, pp. 32–33). Unless community concerns were rapidly addressed, it argued, opposition to this "uniquely and inherently risky" (Keniry et al., 2003, p. 34) trade would grow. This proved prophetic.

Live animal export has survived many spectacular disasters, but routine conditions have also been criticized. Australian Standards for the Export of Livestock specifies a "reportable mortality event"—2% for sheep and goats and 1% for long haul cattle voyages—that triggers an investigation. According to DAFF, average mortality rates have fallen significantly over the last decade, down to 0.28% for long haul cattle and 0.91% for sheep (DAFF, 2013). However, the improved mortality rates still exceed those for land transport (Phillips & Santurtun, 2013) and there are many individual deaths for journeys of just a few weeks. Many more sheep suffer from starvation and salmonellosis, often due to the change to pelleted food, and from extreme weather (Norris, Richards, Creeper, Jubb, Madin, & Kerr, 2003).

A veterinarian in the live trade industry recently revealed that the "voyages are not all short and clean as depicted by industry and their public relations machine" (Simpson, 2012). Dr. Lynn Simpson criticized the use of mortalities as the sole benchmark of welfare and claimed that many of the conditions violate the OIE Terrestrial Animal Health Code of which Australia is a signatory. She claimed: "Animals are regularly injured while trying to rest in crowded pens. They are stepped on with leg, muscle, tail, and pizzle damage. . . . Newborns have been trampled to death. Animals have been smothered when trying to rest" (Simpson, 2013).

Animals routinely suffer from noxious ammonia (Phillips & Santurtun, 2013), "fecal waterfalls," severe foot damage, and deliberate water deprivation in high heat (Simpson, 2013). There are "only one or two stock people on each shipment and possibly one veterinarian, supported by crew, to observe and care for up to 100,000 animals" (Phillips & Santurtun, 2013, p. 310). The veterinarian is employed by the exporter.

PROBLEMS IN DESTINATION COUNTRIES

About three quarters of sheep mortalities occur on ships; the remainder occur mainly at the discharge port (Norris, 2005), perhaps from undernutrition and acute stress (Phillips & Santurtun, 2013). Cattle sent to Indonesia are feed-lotted for several months. Importantly, the cultural and legal standards in these destination countries are typically very different from those in Australia. Even recently, animals at Kuwaiti and other markets have been observed with their legs bound together, crammed into stifling car boots, and dragged over concrete slabs. Halal slaughter standards are often breached (Animals Australia, 2013; DAFF, 2013) and are inconsistent with Australian halal standards that require the stunning (Cranley, 2011) of animals before slaughter.

In 2003, veterinarian Dr. P. H. Sidhom (2003b) described how the larger Australian breeds were sometimes treated in Egyptian abattoirs:

> About four to five cattle are herded there [the killing place] and surrounded by slaughtermen. And they then strike out with long knives and they cut further tendons and they smash the joints. And finally the animal breaks down and the eyes are stabbed. So when the eyes are stabbed out, and the cattle breaks down, sometimes they can't get up again and it's very severe how the cattle are dealed (sic) with then.

Although similar acts were observed in 2013 (Johnson & Tovey, 2013), Australia's agriculture minister continued to claim that regulations were working and that the trade had a bright future (Hawke, 2013).

The Indonesian slaughter practice is to cast animals onto their sides with ropes (Jones, 2011, p. 5). In an attempt to improve welfare, Australia introduced the infamous and now obsolete Mark 1 slaughter boxes, which made cattle fall over sideways onto a concrete "plinth," a method Temple Grandin (2012) called "absolutely atrocious" (p. 31). Recently, an industry-commissioned report rated the welfare of Australian cattle in Indonesia "generally good" (Caple, Neville, Cusack, & McGown, 2009–2010), despite observing that cattle had been badly mistreated. By 2011, some 6.4 million Australian cattle had entered Indonesia (LiveCorp, 2014). How many of them experienced a similar fate can only be guessed.

REGULATIONS AND PROTECTIONS

Regulations clearly have not prevented breaches of animal welfare protections and, even when followed, they may not prevent prolonged suffering. Significantly, Australian anticruelty law does not extend to foreign jurisdictions. An Egyptian veterinarian said recently:

> Egyptians don't care—and our government doesn't care about animal welfare. We only care about meat inspection. Before the animal is killed, we don't

care. So no-one orders the workers to stop these bad actions and there is no punishment. So, it continues. (Abdelwhahab, 2013)

The political legitimacy of the industry's "progressive and incremental change" policy was destroyed in 2011 (Sterle, 2011, pp. 30, 56–57). Belatedly, the Australian government strengthened its Memoranda of Understanding with other countries and introduced the heralded Export Supply Chain Assurance System.

However, there was a loss of public confidence in exporters and government (Sterle, 2011, p. 46, 90) and perhaps even in the new regulations themselves. In 2012, for example, after Bahrain rejected a consignment of sheep on dubious disease grounds, the Australian government authorised a diversion to Pakistan, which, until then, lacked regulatory approval. Seemingly offended by Australia's lack of transparency on the animals' disease status, Pakistani authorities ordered a mass cull, in which apparently untrained personnel hurriedly stabbed and beat 20,000 sheep. The sheep were thrown, many still alive, into a "hole that filled [with sheep] within a matter of minutes" (Alam, 2012). The exporter was found by DAFF to have acted in line with the new regulations (DAFF, 2013).

THE 2011 INDONESIAN REVELATIONS

Although proponents of the live trade industry deny suffering and cruelty is widespread in live export (Animals Australia, 2013), the evidence (typically from animal protection groups) suggests otherwise. In fact, many of the problems in this "uniquely and inherently risky" trade have been reported in the media for decades. Why then did the Australian public only begin to show real concern after the Indonesian incident? Part of the answer is that they could finally see with their own eyes the brutal, violent, and callous treatment of cattle. White's 2011 video elicited strong feelings of compassion for the cattle, as well as disgust, anger, and powerlessness (Tiplady, 2012, p. 4). Some observers suggested counselling contacts be made publically available to viewers of the film to "acknowledge the disturbing effect animal cruelty exposes can have on the public" (Tiplady, 2013, p. 1).

ETHICAL CONSIDERATIONS: A CASE STUDY

One important scene in White's (2011) video footage from the Indonesian abattoirs stood out for the gravity of its effect on viewers. This scene, which shall be a focus in the ensuing discussion, involved a particular individual called

"Steer 3." In the absence of the actual footage, I have selected parts of Dr. Bidda Jones's report on the fate of Steer 3:

> Case Study 4: Slaughter of Australian Steer 3 in one of 4 copy boxes, Location 8, 22 March 2011.
> Time 0m:09s. Camera moves to reveal 3 more steers, one in each copy box. Three have their leg ropes tied, one steer (Steer 3) has no leg ropes tied yet.
> 0:54. Steer 1 walks out, trips, then falls head first down the plinth. Steer 3 looks around at what is happening and is visibly trembling.
> 3:44. Man cuts throat of Steer 1. Snorting and vocalising can be heard throughout the room.
> 4:13. Steer 3 has backed up into the railing behind him. He has his head down looking under the railing away from the other 3 steers.
> 5:23. Steer 4 has had his throat cut in full view of Steer 3.
> 7:29. Still visibly trembling, Steer 3 looks behind him at Steer 2 which is being hosed and continues to bleed out. Steer 3 vocalises.
> 9:30. Steer 3 is trembling and watching Steer 4 being skinned. Men are whistling.
> 10:04. Steer 3 is still standing in the box watching—trembling, ears twitching.
> 10:44. Man is chopping up Steer 4 with an axe. Steer 3 is watching.
> 12:12. Steer 3 kicks out as the man ties his back leg to the pole and tightens.
> 12:27. Still struggling violently, the steer slips over then gets back up.
> 13:06. Door opens, steer stands there momentarily, then his back leg slips.
> 13:21. Steer 3 struggles to get up and slaps his head down onto the concrete twice.
> 13:26. Steer 3 is breathing heavily. Knives can be heard being sharpened.
> 14:01. Man puts rope around Steer 3's neck and kicks him in the head to move his head into position [for throat cutting]. (Jones, 2011, pp. 42–44)

How are we to understand the moral import of this scene and the circumstances surrounding it? Veterinary professor Ivan Caple appeared to describe some of the slaughtermen's actions as "a little bit exuberant" (Hall, 2011). Although most Australians would not share his attitude, some arguments for live export do have traction in Australia because the trade has become enmeshed with the interests and activities of many people.

SUBSTANTIAL MORAL FRAMEWORKS

In this discussion, I assume that a full moral analysis of live export must ultimately make reference to a philosophically substantial moral framework—a framework that is normatively detailed and philosophically serious. Although normative ethics is a highly contentious field, there are a number of well-known moral frameworks that have a philosophical pedigree. Most substantial moral frameworks are established "ethical theories"; and the subsequent analysis will explore the contributions to this debate of utilitarianism, virtue ethics, and animal rights theory.[1]

The justification of these theories—and of one theory-independent view—as "substantial moral frameworks" will not be explored here. Some may find this a particular problem for the "nontheory" framework presented below—a view that may seem to entail a "subjectivist" account of moral belief. However, this framework, like the others, now has a philosophical pedigree (e.g., Diamond, 1995; Gaita, 2005; Mulhall, 2009). But a further reason for including it is that it foregrounds and clarifies the nature of the unprecedented moral responses to the footage in Australia—not the least of which was the way people became haunted by one particular traumatized animal. But let us first turn to the better-known ethical theories.

LIVE EXPORT AND UTILITARIAN THEORY

The consequences of this trade frequently form the substance of debates about its morality. Could utilitarianism be used to defend the live export business? If live export has a utilitarian justification, its supporters will have a significant moral weapon in their armory—all the more so because the concession of "equality of consideration" between human and animal interests (Singer, 1993) mitigates the suspicion of speciesism and of arbitrary bias against nonhuman beings. The utilitarian argument for live export runs as follows.

The livestock export industry earns about a billion dollars annually and creates employment for more than 10,000 people in rural and regional Australia (DAFF, 2013), including for Indigenous Australians who are victims of historical injustices (Sterle, 2011, p. 67). In northern and western states, the cattle industry has restructured itself around the live trade so that the type and location of its cattle make them suitable only for overseas markets (Sterle, 2011, pp. 69, 81). Although some claim the loss of this export market would not seriously harm the Australian economy (Sterle, 2011, p. 65), others argue the opposite. Notwithstanding government aid, a temporary reduction in the Indonesian trade would cause hardship in many rural communities (Sterle, 2011, p. 73) and put at risk of starvation the cattle who would otherwise have been exported.

Some opponents of live export allege that switching to a chilled meat export market would advantage jobs and industry (Sterle, 2011, p. 83). Yet, it is difficult to evaluate the relative commercial value of live export versus local meat processing. For example, proponents say that stopping live trade would dampen meat prices in Australia, thereby damaging employment and the economy (Sterle, 2011, p. 70). The 2011 Senate committee concluded that although the cattle industry is overly reliant on live export, it is better off with a combination of live export and local slaughter (Sterle 2011, p. 87). In contrast, the World Society for the Protection of Animals (WSPA) argues that a report by ACIL Tasman (2012) presents evidence that ending live export is economically viable.

Suppose it is accepted, pending further evidence, that ending live trade will be worse for the economy (though not disastrously), that it will cause hardship in rural communities, and that animals bred for live export may be at immediate risk of poor welfare. Although these factors are clearly relevant to the utilitarian calculus, utilitarianism does remind us to take a longer perspective. If the harms to animal interests are immense, manifold, and ongoing, as the history and nature of the trade suggests is likely, the greater good may be served by painful but temporary industry restructuring or replacement. The market that encouraged this lucrative use of animals can usually furnish at least some employment opportunities and the government can try to ameliorate the harm.

The other main argument in favor of live export is that if Australia stops exporting livestock, other countries with less exemplary ethical positions will step in, causing greater animal suffering. Therefore, non-Australian animals benefit from Australia's involvement: "Australia is the only country that requires specific animal welfare outcomes for livestock exports. Our ongoing involvement in this trade provides an opportunity to influence animal welfare conditions in importing countries" (DAFF, 2013).

Clearly, this could be an important utilitarian consideration—but is it decisive? Utilitarianism insists upon weighing equally in decision-making the like interests of non-Australian and Australian animals. It also insists that the probability of predicted consequences be factored. In this case, it is not clear that supporters of the trade have provided, or even could provide, sufficiently strong evidence that other countries would ship animals in similar numbers, over similar distances, and in worse land and sea conditions than those endured by Australian animals. It might even be the case that importing nations would be forced to turn increasingly to packaged meat and that Australian companies will successfully market this option. Arguably, the only certainty is that maintaining live export indefinitely will perpetuate suffering for millions of Australian animals.

The case that Australian involvement significantly and reliably improves conditions for local animals over the long term is not a strong one. There are historical precedents like the Mark 1 cattle boxes where Australian input has preserved or exacerbated welfare problems (Sterle, 2011, p. 60) in other countries, and evidence continues to emerge of animals being brutalized in some of the very abattoirs Australian exporters have deemed first rate. Moreover, it is widely acknowledged how tremendously difficult it is to change ingrained moral standards in destination countries. Thus, there is reason to conclude that either Australian animals will be treated better than their local counterparts (Vets Against Live Export, 2012), or that poor welfare standards will often apply to both groups of cattle. Jones (2011), of the Royal Society for the Prevention of Cruelty to Animals, says,

> Unless the slaughter of Australian cattle could be restricted to locations where a skilled and permanent workforce was employed, pre-slaughter stunning was effectively used, training and auditing programs were in place, and enforceable animal welfare legislation was introduced, it is difficult to see how their treatment could be reliably and sustainably improved. (p. 32)

A final utilitarian argument in favor of live export is that the trade provides valuable protein in third-world countries. On utilitarian grounds, this argument is weak for at least two reasons. First, it is not typically the destitute who receive this protein—they cannot afford it and would, in any case, be better served by foreign assistance and cheaper protein sources. And second, compared to undernourishment, a mere interest in eating meat among a burgeoning middle class is not morally compelling. As many utilitarians have also argued, meat-eating exacerbates environmental problems. These considerations are sufficient to cast doubt on this pro-trade argument.

In summary, utilitarianism insists that the short- and long-term consequences, their relative weight, and their likelihood of occurring must be measured impartially in the utility calculus that determines what we ought to do. Correctly understood, then, this moral theory not only falls short of justifying the trade, it also provides serious grounds for condemning it. Indeed, utilitarians might suggest that, in terms of animal welfare standards and the greater good, the best moral example Australia could set would be to end the trade as New Zealand did and work more diligently for the implementation of much stronger global animal welfare standards.

LIVE EXPORT AND VIRTUE THEORY

In search of a substantial moral framework to defend their position, live trade supporters may appeal to virtue theory. Virtue ethics asks how a clear-headed, impartial, informed, and sensitive person—a virtuous exemplar—would respond to his or her nation's treatment of its animals (e.g., Hursthouse, 1999, 2000). This theory may appear more promising for those supporters of live export who reject the principle of equality of consideration, embrace what may be regarded as speciesism, and claim that human beings have far greater intrinsic value than animals. However, it is far from obvious that a thoughtful person who shows appropriate compassion for both human beings and animals could support the export trade.

For a start, virtue ethics has another way of approaching this issue: It may claim that Australians have, or should have, a greater moral responsibility for their own country's animals. The idea that we may have special duties toward "our" animals, roughly analogous to duties we may have to our fellow citizens, may strike some people as odd. Can we really have special duties to cattle and sheep over and above the general duties we have of not treating animals badly irrespective of their geographical location? Is there really nonutilitarian moral significance in the fact that certain animals are bred by us for our nation's benefit and happen to fall under our protective laws?

Such a reaction overlooks the kind of perspective that virtue theory invites us to adopt. In contrast to utilitarianism, the virtue ethics invitation is one that *requires* us to look from a perspective that is not exhausted by concern for the consequences. (This is also a feature of the two moral frameworks below.) In general, live trade supporters who appeal to Australian moral sensibilities, and who cite alleged welfare benefits to distant animals, have not recognized the possibility of a morally thoughtful Australian feeling a special duty of care for the particular animals sent abroad in their name. The Australian people have a general belief that sheep and cattle may be killed for the sake of economics, food, and employment. Equally, Australians are intolerant of gross abuse and suffering—even, it is important to stress, when it is for the sake of genuine human goods. Interestingly, a WSPA-commissioned survey found that 7 out of 10 Australians believe live export should be ended (Lonergan Research, 2012). We may not know whether these Australians feel animals have been betrayed by a nation owing them special duties of care and protection, but we cannot assume that it plays no role at all in their thinking.

The broader point here is that virtue ethics opens up further interesting avenues of moral response. So, let us now apply the basic virtue ethics test, that of the virtuous exemplar. To apply this test, the following questions must be posed. First, could a morally sensitive and thoughtful person consent to placing thousands or millions of their country's animals at risk of barbaric treatment for the sake of human employment and economics? Second, would such a person approve of exposing, for the same reasons, animals under their nation's care to the danger of severe suffering aboard ships and on foreign land?

People will judge differently. However, what should be stressed here is the entirely obvious point that virtue ethics places, at the very forefront of our moral thinking, "the virtues"—not least of which are the virtues of compassion and care. From this perspective, it is surely doubtful that virtue ethics will assist the proponent of live export, for it is quite doubtful that consent to live export could be given by a seriously compassionate exemplar, even when that individual is aware of the threat of nontrivial (if shorter-term) harm to human communities from the trade ending. Perhaps, the virtue ethicist may continue, this story has already revealed moral exemplars from whom we can learn about animals and their moral value: For many people, this edifying exemplar was White, the woman whose courage and compassion brought us the Indonesian slaughterhouse film and the spoken words which moved the Australian people with a force that few other exposes of animal suffering have matched.

LIVE EXPORT AND ANIMAL RIGHTS THEORY

The general moral assessment of live animal export provided by the animal rights theory of Tom Regan (1985) is relatively easy to discern. Unlike utilitarian theory but like virtue ethics, this theory regards the harmful consequences arising from the end of live export as playing no *decisive* moral role. Moreover, such consequences are simply irrelevant to the fundamental wrongness of the trade when there is a question of violating basic rights, such as the right not to be killed or seriously harmed. The point holds regardless of the identity of the bearer of those rights. It would clearly violate the moral rights of human beings to expose them to serious harm, let alone to kill them, for the sake of food, employment, or economic opportunity. All these forms of treatment are instances of using rights-bearers as a means to someone else's ends, and in these circumstances the magnitude of the expected gains (e.g., employment, pleasure, financial, etc.) makes no difference to the fact that it is an injustice to invade an individual's rights. But this applies also to nonhuman animals, assuming they are bearers of rights.

Some nonhuman animals, this theory says, are bearers of rights. To deny this is to rely upon the arbitrary biological criterion of species to morally distinguish between, for example, a young or brain-damaged human being and a nonhuman being with comparable cognitive and affective abilities. For what is there apart from mere biology to ground a moral difference in status between these two individuals? It is here that the force of the classic criticism of speciesism is evident.

Furthermore, an individual has rights if it has inherent value and, according to Regan's (1985) theory, it is a sufficient condition of possessing inherent value that an individual is a *subject-of-a-life*. A subject-of-a-life has certain cognitive/affective capacities, including beliefs, desires, and memory. For Regan, these capacities are certainly present in all normal mammals over 1 year old. It follows that the goats, cattle, sheep, camelids, and buffalo used in live export are subjects-of-a-life. Consequently, it is a violation of respect for their inherent value, and an infringement of their rights, to use them as means to promote the ends of human beings or, for that matter, the ends of other animals, such as those foreign animals who are the alleged beneficiaries of Australia's participation in live export. The apparent beneficiaries, human and nonhuman, have no right to expect or receive the sacrifice of the lives and basic welfare of other rights-bearers for the furtherance of their own good. Nor are any of their rights overridden by the abolition of the live export trade.

Furthermore, the nonhuman, rights-bearing victims of this trade are not responsible for the predicament they find themselves in; the trade, rather, exists as a result of willing human participants who have chosen to engage in it. Animal rights supporters, therefore, argue that termination of the live trade must proceed as a matter of strict justice. For Regan (1985) and others, the anger and pain felt by witnesses to the 2011 revelations are thoroughly justified, precisely because theoretical considerations about rights show what a serious moral injustice this use of animals represents.

LIVE EXPORT AND THE AUSTRALIAN
RESPONSE: A NONTHEORY VIEW

The feelings of horror, anger, and compassion that many viewers of the Animals Australia video experienced were deeply associated with a developing moral opposition to both the cruel suffering they witnessed and to the system that allowed it. Now, each of the moral theories considered before have their methods of evaluating the moral significance of these responses. Utilitarians may stress the fact that, because of their strong emotions, Australians could no longer ignore something otherwise obvious but all too easily dismissed or overlooked: The trade's propensity to cause harm to large numbers of sentient beings. After all, utilitarians may say, if it is easy to ignore human suffering, how much more disposed are we to ignore the suffering of beings who are routinely exploited? Agreeing with this, animal rights theorists may further highlight the opportunity viewers had to appreciate that the exported animals are cognitively and affectively complex beings possessing a welfare that matters to them. In Regan's terms they are, undeniably, subjects-of-a-life. Recall the importance of the images that impressed upon viewers Steer 3's vivid responses to his pitiful circumstances. Few viewers who watched these scenes would be able to deny that animals like Steer 3 are living subjects in something like Regan's sense.

Still, according to utilitarianism and animal rights theory, such affectively laden human responses, even if they sometimes facilitate the correct application of moral principles and are "justified" or underwritten by those principles, are strictly irrelevant to the determination of fundamental ethical values. Virtue theory, by contrast, maintains that human feelings and dispositions are constitutive of the basic ethical test that determines moral matters such as what it is to wrong a nonhuman animal. Like the other ethical theories, however, virtue ethics seeks to ground the search for correct ethical values in theoretical considerations (e.g., Hursthouse, 1999).

However, there are substantial moral frameworks that do not in any significant way rely upon the construction of ethical theories. One of these, an approach inspired by the thought of Wittgenstein, seems particularly useful for clarifying the nature of the response in Australia to the revelations we have been considering. The Wittgensteinian framework I will concentrate on marks the centrality and the theory-independent status of *critical human responses* in moral judgement (e.g., Diamond, 1995; Gaita, 2005; Mulhall, 2009). This approach holds that speaking of "emotional" reactions to (say) the treatment of animals can obscure its claim that human responses may play a structural role in forming the *constituents* of both the moral understanding and the objects of a critical mode of moral thought. These responses are constituent elements of moral understanding in that they are conceptually necessary for its possession. In addition, the relevant responses are themselves a structural part of the objects of that understanding and, in that way, they help determine what it is to wrong a person or an animal.

To illustrate this approach, let us apply it to the central case we are examining and consider how a person may critically reflect upon the example of Steer 3 from White's film and the responses to it that this person shares with White. Such a critically reflective person may ask whether the compassion and outrage felt and shown by oneself and White is really an unsentimental and serious moral response to the images of the brutalized steers. In addition, the person may ask oneself whether such responses are essential to the question of what it means to treat Steer 3 and the other cattle in the way the Indonesians and Australians did. The present framework of critical moral reflection raises the possibility that if we do without certain human responses to the treatment of the animals, we will not have an adequate moral understanding of their treatment. For, if we neglect to accord to these responses the intimate role they have in the understanding, we will necessarily have failed to grasp the meaning or moral shape of any wrong and will be left with a distorted comprehension, or with no comprehension at all, of the kinds of wrong that can be done to animals. This means that if we eliminate from basic moral thought certain critical human responses, we undermine the possibility of understanding and illuminating the morality of live export. In a nutshell, this is the basis of this approach.

Whether or not we are sympathetic to this view, or indeed to any view that eschews "theory," let us deploy it as we try to deepen our examination of the Australian reception of White's footage. We know, of course, that viewers were moved by the fact that the animals in the 2011 footage were sentient beings, subjected to terrible suffering, treated with violence and callousness, and abandoned by their country. This is important. But it is also important to see that Australians were not jolted by these facts alone. In my view, the impressive effect of White's footage also lay in the image these viewers saw of a single, stricken individual (or of a number of such individuals). Viewers could not miss the nature of the strickenness of the individual steer, for his sensitive responsiveness as a living subject was there unmistakably on the screen—in his trembling skin, in his fast breathing and twitching ears, in the way he looked at his fellows being butchered or looked away from them, and in his frantic attempts to elude the men. White herself singled out this individual and his fate as being particularly important; she even gave him a name.

We may safely assume that during Steer 3's fatiguing journey through the "export supply chain" he was sometimes confused, frightened, and unwilling as well as reassured by his fellows. Here was a creature who was, as viewers could see, a cognitively and affectively complex subject-of-a-life. Yet what many viewers were also confronted with was the fact that they were *haunted* by him as he appeared in the images, by his fear and suffering, and by his callous treatment and abandonment by their country. Such a response, we can note, is also applicable to other aspects of his treatment, like the conditions he or others like him endured on the boats. Recognizing this sort of response is important, on the present view, because it gives rise to a descriptive elaboration that can change our sense of the moral shape of what it is to wrong an animal of this type. The response of a person who is haunted by this single individual and who, at the same time, finds that possibility entirely morally fitting and necessary is fundamentally on a view that assigns a structural role to such possibilities as our capacity to be haunted, as that kind of possibility can be constitutive of our understanding of the value of animal life and, therefore, of our sense of the morality of live export. With this view, the nature of a wrong can only be appreciated in connection with descriptions of certain and relevant critical responses. Again, this sort of understanding eludes us if we do not have responses of the right kind.

Of course, some supporters of live export were also troubled by those scenes. Yet not everyone was haunted by them; or if they were, not everyone was haunted by an individual animal and his fate in the way others were. Furthermore, some people who were haunted by Steer 3 may have tried to shrug it off or they may instead have turned to moral theory to justify it. But for others, their immediate and nontheoretical response was essential to their reflective moral assessment of the wrong done to this animal: They continued to see the steer and his life, rendered pitiful by those who had control over it, as the fitting object of the haunted response.

So, in the present view, the difference between being upset and even traumatized by the suffering, violence, and indifference on the one hand and being haunted by Steer 3 as the sensitive and responsive subject of this fate and treatment on the other is the sort of difference that may be invested with great ethical significance. The ethical understanding of those who occupied the latter position is thus markedly distinguished from those who merely occupied the former. A great many Australian viewers seem to have been moved in what they might well affirm as the more profound of these two ways.

Our descriptive elaboration of this particular Australian response can be completed by raising a final question. Could someone who was haunted by Steer 3 (or one of the other animals) in the ways that have been described give their moral consent to live export? A person who was upset or traumatized by the cruelty and suffering might claim that, notwithstanding the undesirability of those elements of the trade, live export can be justified by its benefits. Of course, they would not necessarily be right to make that claim but, if they are right, that is consistent with the fact that they were upset or traumatized and consistent with them continuing to be affected by the frequent and continuing reports of serious abuse and suffering emerging from live export. However, those many Australians who remained haunted by the individuals they saw on the screen, and whose perspective on live export was shaped by this fact, were not like this.

Rather, their inability to justify the benefits so loudly championed by government
and industry appeared to be internal to the way they were moved. The internal
way these Australians were haunted by the cattle created a sense of disbelief
and anger that those benefits, as impressive as they may be, were being used to
defend a trade that allows unspeakable things to happen to sensitive animals. No
one, then, whose moral perspective on the industry was shaped by being moved
in this manner, could conceivably give moral consent to the live export industry.

CONCLUSION

This article has sought to analyze the ethics of live export by examining how a
range of frameworks might treat the facts of the trade, including the politically
charged revelations of 2011 and the responses it created. It has argued that live
export cannot be justified by those substantial moral frameworks which grant,
in line with the professed views of the main parties to the debate over the trade,
that nonhuman animals have some noninstrumental moral value. In particular,
three major ethical theories, and one theory-independent moral framework,
were seen to contain the resources for strong moral condemnation of live animal
export. Finally, the article's discussion of the extraordinary *Animals Australia*
footage and its aftermath suggests that support for live animal export cannot be
morally reconciled with the unprecedented response that it generated in 2011
from many horrified Australians.

Acknowledgment
I thank Peter Coghlan for his helpful comments.

Note
1. Although Kantianism and contract theory are major ethical theories, my analysis will focus on moral frameworks that normally and clearly conclude, as even the
live export industry and government apparently do, that animals have at least some
intrinsic or noninstrumental value. Although Kantians and contract theorists *may*
make this claim, many of them do not and, on the terms provided by their theories,
probably need not.

References
Abdelwhahab, M. (2013). *Animals Australia*. Retrieved from http://www.animals.
    australia.org/media/press_releases.php?release=189
ACIL Tasman. (2012). *An economic analysis of the live exportation of cattle from
    northern Australia*. Retrieved from http://www.wspa.org.au/Images/Transition
    ReportSummary_tcm30–31304.pdf#false

Alam, K. (2012, 21 September). Death-row: Culling aside, sheep dying a slow death [Web log post]. Retrieved from http://kazimalam.wordpress.com/category /australian-sheep/

Animals Australia. (2013). Exposing live export cruelty. Retrieved from http://www .animalsaustralia.org/issues/

Caple, I., Neville, G. G., Cusack, P., & McGown, P. (2009–2010). *Final report—Public Release. Indonesian Point of Slaughter Improvements.* Retrieved from http://www .beefcentral.com/u/lib/cms/indonesia-live-trade-point-of-slaughter-.pdf

Cranley, J. (2011). Sensibility during slaughter without stunning in cattle. *Veterinary Record, 168 (16),* 437–438.

Department of Agriculture, Fisheries, and Forestry (DAFF). (2013). *Live animal export trade.* Retrieved from http://www.daff.gov.au/animal-plant-health/welfare /export-trade

Diamond, C. (1995). *The realistic spirit: Wittgenstein, philosophy and the mind.* Cambridge, MA: MIT Press.

Gaita, R. (2005). *The Philosophers Dog.* New York, NY: Random House.

Georges, G., Evans, J., Cooney, B., & Siddons, J. R. (1985). *Export of live sheep from Australia. Senate Select Committee on Animal Welfare* (Senate Report). Canberra, Australia: Australian Government Publishing Service.

Grandin, T. (2012). *Welfare during slaughter without stunning (kosher or halal) differences between sheep and cattle.* Retrieved from http://www.grandin.com/ritual /welfare.diffs.sheep.cattle.html

Hall, C. (2011, 30 May). A bloody business [Television series episode]. In M. Doyle (Producer), *ABC Four Corners.* Sydney: Australian Broadcasting Commission.

Hawke, B. (Producer). (2013, June 5). *The 7.30 Report.* [Television broadcast]. Sydney: Australian Broadcasting Commission TV.

Hursthouse, R. (1999). *On virtue ethics.* Oxford, England: Oxford University Press.

Hursthouse, R. (2000). *Ethics, humans and other animals: An introduction with readings.* London, England: Routledge.

Johnson, C., & Tovey, J. (2013, May 5). 'Cruelty' stops live exports to Egypt. *The Age.* Retrieved from http://www.theage.com.au/national/cruelty-stops-live-exports-to -egypt-20130504-2j07k.html

Jones, B. (2011). *The slaughter of Australian cattle in Indonesia—An observational study.* Retrieved from RSPCA website: http://www.banliveexport.com/documents /RSPCA-Australia-2011-Slaughter-of-Australian-Cattle-in-Indonesia.pdf

Keniry, J. Bond, M., Caple, I., Gosse, L., & Rogers, M. (2003). *Livestock export review* (Report to the Minister for Agriculture, Fisheries and Forestry). Retrieved from http://www.daff.gov.au/__data/assets/pdf_file/0008/146708/keniry_review_jan_04 .pdf

LiveCorp. (2014). *Programs.* Retrieved from https://www.livecorp.com.au/programs

Lonergan Research. (2012). *WSPA live export study* (Report 4–6). Retrieved from http://www.wspa.org.au/latestnews/2012/Almost_7_in_10_Australians_against _live_animal_export.aspx

Ludwig, J. (2012, October 17). *Minister Ludwig's letter to Animals Australia.* Retrieved from http://www.daff.gov.au/animal-plant-health/welfare/export-trade/letter-to-animals-australia

Mulhall, S. (2009). *The wounded animal: J. M. Coetzee & the difficulty of reality in literature and philosophy.* Princeton, NJ: Princeton University Press.

Norris, R. T., Richards, R. B., Creeper, J. H., Jubb, T. F., Madin, B., & Kerr, J. W. (2003). Cattle deaths during sea transport from Australia. *Australian Veterinary Journal, 81*(3), 156–161.

Norris, R. T. (2005). Transport of animals by sea. *Revue Scientifique et Technique—Office International Des Epizooties, 24*(2), 673–681.

Phillips, C. J. C. (2008). "The welfare of livestock during sea transport." In Appleby, M. C., Cussen, V., & Garces, L. (Eds.), *Long distance transport and welfare of farm animals (pp. 137–156).* Wallingford, England: CABI Publishing.

Phillips, C. J. C. (2011, July 9). Animal exports: how the industry controls research to shut down debate. *The Conversation.* Retrieved from http://theconversation.com/animal-exports-how-the-industry-controls-research-to-shut-down-debate-1750

Phillips, C. J. C. & Santurtun, E. (2013). The welfare of livestock transported by ship. *The Veterinary Journal, 196*(3), 309–314.

Regan, T. (1985). *The case for animal rights.* Berkeley: University of California Press.

Sidhom, P. H. (2003a). Letter. *Australian Veterinary Journal, 81*(6), 364–365.

Sidhom, P. H. (2003b, July 27). Making a killing. [Television broadcast]. In H. Sacre (Producer), *60 Minutes.* Willoughby: Channel Nine, Australian TV. Retrieved from http://sixtyminutes.ninemsn.com.au/article/259069/making-a-killing

Simpson, L. (2012). *Submission to DAFF review.* Retrieved from http://www.daff.gov.au/animal-plant-health/welfare/export-trade/submissions-export-livestock

Singer, P. (1993). *Practical ethics* (2nd ed.). New York, NY: Cambridge University Press.

Sterle, G. (2011). *Animal welfare standards in Australia's live export markets.* (Senate Report). Canberra, Australia: Senate Printing Unit.

Tiplady, C. M., Walsh, D. B., & Phillips, C. J. C. (2013). Public response to media coverage of animal cruelty. *Journal of Agricultural and Environmental Ethics, 26*(4), 869–885.

Vets Against Live Export. (2012). *"Inevitable cruelty" in live export—but is it acceptable cruelty?* Retrieved from http://www.vale.org.au/uploads/1/0/4/3/10438895/press_release_121228.pdf

White, L. (2011, 30 May). *Tommy's story—Indonesia 2011.* Retrieved from http://www.banliveexport.com/videos/tommy.php

12 The Morality of the Reptile "Pet" Trade

CLIFFORD WARWICK

The trade in, and private keeping of, reptiles as "pets" raises several ethi-cal concerns regarding animal welfare (associated with handling, storage, transportation, intensive captive breeding, captivity stress, injury, disease, and high premature mortality); public health and safety (associated with zoonotic disease and animal-linked injuries); species conservation and envi-ronmental degradation (associated with wild capture); and ecological altera-tion (associated with invasive alien species). Also, many captive reptiles are fed other animals, raising broader ethical questions. Misperceptions about reptiles by proponents of their captivity mean that these animals are subject to conditions that would likely be considered unacceptable for dogs or cats.

KEY WORDS: reptile, pet, trade, ethics, premature mortality, welfare, stress, disease, environment, zoonoses

INTRODUCTION

Reptile trading and keeping has undergone several cyclic phases in popularity, with regard to the species and types that are marketed and the way in which they are sourced, sold, and maintained. Unknown tens of millions of individual animals and thousands of species are "wild-caught" or captive-bred annually to supply the exotic "pet" trade. According to Karesh, Cook, Gilbert, and New-comb (2007), global "wildlife" trade for pets involves 350 million live animals a year, many of which are for "pets."

About 25% of the "wildlife" trade is thought to be illegal (Karesh et al., 2007). Although some regulations are being increasingly adopted, these are mostly trade-permissive, with illegal and legal trade often sharing routes. Reptiles are a major component of this global trade. Data on the volume of the global rep-tile "pet" trade are unknown, and regional or country-based figures are also incomplete because few countries compile reliable data on reptile trade and

Journal of Animal Ethics 4(1): 74–94

keeping. However, annually perhaps 2 million live reptiles are imported into the United States, and 9 million are exported (HSUS, 2001, 2009). The United States is known to produce 3–4 million baby "pet" turtles annually, mostly for export (Warwick, 1997). In Rosenthal's (2012) study, over 85% of individuals and over 90% of shipments were recorded as "wild-caught." UNEP/WCMC (2009) indicated that between 1997 and 2007, 12.3 million live reptiles (which largely involves "pet" animals) on CITES Appendix II were imported into the European Union—which represents only part of overall trade. The European Union is a very large market for "pet" reptiles. According to trade statistics, between 2005 and 2007 the European Union imported 6.7 million live reptiles (ENDCAP, 2012). In many countries locally caught reptiles are also kept. For example, in the United States historical estimates indicate that between 3 million and 5 million reptiles were "wild-caught" from Louisiana alone for the domestic market in the 1990s (Reaser, Clarke, & Meyers, 2008), and many believe that the trade has increased significantly since then. Reasonable estimates suggest that in the United States approximately 13 million reptiles are kept in homes (American Pet Products Association, 2011), and in the United Kingdom 700,000–800,000 (PFMA, 2012). These figures exclude the substantial numbers of reptiles who are either "wild-caught" or captive-bred for trade and who do not survive to reach private homes.

Reptile "sourcing" for the "pet" trade raises serious concern because whether they are "wild-caught" or captive-bred, securing these animals results in harm. For example, "wild capture" frequently involves injurious and stressful physical handling (resulting in broken limbs and tails and, where tortoises and turtles are concerned, crushed shells); local transport is often conducted using sacks or boxes on motorcycles over long distances (incurring more stress and damage); and storage frequently incurs insanitary holding sites with poor husbandry—all of which frequently leads to significant stress, suffering, and death (Warwick, 1997; 2001; Altherr & Freyer, 2001; Auliya, 2003; Laidlaw, 2005). Captive-bred individuals avoid some of these traumas but face intensive rearing conditions. Regardless of sourcing, reptiles are next subjected to packaging and transport in cramped, often insanitary, and undoubtedly fear-inducing conditions for long periods (Warwick, 1997; 2001; Altherr & Freyer, 2001; Auliya, 2003; Laidlaw, 2005). Arrival in recipient countries commences a new chain of challenges for reptiles, where typically poor husbandry, stress, and disease will culminate in the death of nondomesticated animals who have been transposed from their natural ecological niches to the unnatural world of the living curio.

In the reptile-keeping world, although the terms "pet," "specimen," and (to a lesser extent) "companion" are variously interchanged, here the term "pet" is of choice because it is the simplest way to describe a nonagricultural animal who is arguably not a genuine companion—reptiles have little to no normal behavioral interaction with humans and thus are not true "sharers" of our lives. A historical and, in particular, recent raft of peer-reviewed articles and reports reveals that practices involving both the trade and the private keeping of reptiles as "pets" are laden with issues that raise ethical concerns. In brief these are as follows:

> *Animal welfare*—stress, morbidity, and premature mortality accompany many if not most animals at all points in the trade and keeping chain (see, e.g., Franke & Telecky, 2001; Warwick, 1997, 2001; Laidlaw, 2005; ENDCAP, 2012; Toland, Warwick, & Arena, 2012).
>
> *Public health and safety*—zoonotic disease is now recognized as an emerging problem and a significant and major public health hazard. Injuries from exotic "pets" are a related concern (see, e.g., Brown, 2004; Chomel, Belotto, & Meslin, 2007; Karesh, Cook, Bennett, & Newcomb, 2005; Jones et al., 2008; Praud & Moutou, 2010; Abbott, Ni, & Janda, 2012; Hale et al., 2012; Warwick, Arena, Steedman, & Jessop, 2012).
>
> *Species conservation and ecological alteration*—species conservation threats arise as a result of taking animals from natural populations, and ecological alteration arises from incidental releases of unwanted invasive animals into novel habitats (see, e.g., Auliya, 2003; Krauss et al., 2003; Bomford, Kraus, Barry, & Lawrence, 2009; Kark, Solarz, Chiron, Clergeau, & Shirley, 2009; Shine et al., 2010; Vilà et al., 2010; Henderson & Bomford, 2011; Langton, Atkins, & Herbert, 2011).

Also, offering live foods is a frequent component of the business of selling and keeping many reptiles, and this raises additional questions.

Reptile traders and keepers maintain that there are important side benefits to their activities, including species conservation, arising from financial incentives for local animal collectors to preserve indigenous species; economic value from wholesale and retail commerce; personal satisfaction; formative propagation of professional biologists; and the encouragement of public interest in nature.

HUMAN PERCEPTIONS OF REPTILES

Modern-day reptiles have a long history that, according to group, can be measured at least in the tens of millions of years. Part of that success is attributable to their innate (unlearned) behavioral and psychological profiles. Highly precocious, they are born ready and able to pursue prey, avoid predators, find shelter, and so on. Innateness does not imply an inability to learn or to think. Rather, it means that reptiles are strongly hard-wired to their evolved lives in the natural world.

Some claim that certain species of reptile have become domesticated through multiple generations of captive breeding and artificial selection. However, there is no evidence of true domestication in reptiles. Many desensitize to novel threats as they do to a swaying branch in nature and thus may seem "tame." This kind of behavioral quiescence, though, is not an indicator of adaptation to captivity (Warwick, 1990; Warwick, 1995). Certain individuals of certain species—for example, bearded dragons (*Pogona vitticeps*) and royal pythons (*Python regius*)—have been selected and bred to enhance their natural tendency toward docility. Species that adapt well to domestication possess particular "pre-adaptive traits," such as affiliative behavior toward people (Price, 1984; Cameron-Beaumont, Lowe, & Bradshaw, 2001), and reptiles generally do not possess these traits (Warwick, 1995; Warwick, Arena, Jessop, Lindley, & Steedman, 2013). The evidence demonstrating the lack of adaptability (and domestication) of even the most selectively bred species (including bearded dragons) is freely observable in their behaviors in artificial conditions (Warwick, 1995; Warwick et al., 2013). Basically, captive-bred lizards show the same captivity stress–related signs as their free-living counterparts when those conspecifics are also caged (Warwick, 1995).

Reptiles need nature, and their evolved constitution frequently conflicts with artificial conditions, of which a minimalist vivarium in a bedroom is a common example. So although in the natural world innateness is a strategic advantage, in captivity it becomes a disadvantage. However, largely because of their relatively slow metabolism, reptiles often tolerate poor captive conditions and disease for long periods, giving a false perception that they are "thriving" while actually they may be languishing under stress (Warwick, 1995; Laidlaw, 2005).

Being ectothermic means reptiles are particularly dependent on environmental temperatures to regulate their thermal needs. Popular terminology describes this feature as "cold-blooded," which is actually a somewhat neutral designation, but one that also gets used to convey stoicism or insensitivity. In addition, reptiles are often seen as belonging to the category of "non-cute," and thus gaining sympathy or empathy for them is relatively difficult (Estren, 2012).

One might presume that false perceptions of reptiles reside entirely with those who sport dislike or disinterest and that the "fans" of the so-called cold-blooded animals might be universally able to set themselves apart from those who are reptile-naïve. However, if one considers a few of the common justifications by reptile traders and keepers for confining reptiles in minimalist (or in some cases possibly "naturalistic") cages, the following supposed facts emerge to underpin the claims: Reptiles are "not social, and therefore have reduced needs"; they are "unintelligent, and do not notice their environment"; they are "agoraphobic, and do not need space"; and they "need only food, water, 'proper' temperature, lighting and humidity to lead healthy lives" (Warwick, 1997; 2001). In addition, reptiles who are "good feeders," "good growers," and "good breeders" are viewed as showing all the necessary hallmarks of good well-being.

Notwithstanding that even these very basic goals for "good well-being" are often not achieved, all of these, along with other perceptions, are either weak at best or quite simply wrong. Many reptiles are social and rival mammals for measurable intelligence; all those studied are highly aware of their environments; agoraphobia is a human anxiety disorder and not known in reptiles; range studies reveal both large and small reptiles to be highly active and to need plenty of space; and environmental, physiological, and behavioral needs are often poorly understood (even for "common" species), meaning that "proper" feeding is not a valid concept (Warwick, 1995; Warwick & Steedman, 1995; Arena & Warwick, 1995).

A result of these erroneous perceptions and presumptions is that most captive reptiles will suffer drawn-out stress, morbidity, and premature mortality because they are nondomesticated animals confined to diminutive enclosures wherein many (particularly snakes) will not even be able to extend their bodies to full length. Although false perceptions by the general public may cause reptiles to be shunned or ignored, it may be the misperceptions of their admirers that result in some of the greatest harm.

ANIMAL WELFARE

The best evidence confirms that reptilian sentience and sensitivity are comparable with that of other animals, including humans (Warwick, 1990; Gillingham, 1995; Warwick, Frye, & Murphy, 1995; Warwick, 1995; Warwick et al., 2013). Whether one examines pain and aspects of anatomy and physiology for neurological structure, reception, and transmission; emotion through physiology and behavior; or psychological factors relating to stress, physiology, arousal, quiescence, and comfort, one can quickly recognize the commonalities of consciousness. In fact, early evidence of these characteristics has existed for at least three decades.

Important differences exist between domesticated companion animals and reptiles in that whereas domesticated animals—for example, dogs and cats—generally experience relatively liberal home- and life-sharing associations with humans, reptiles are typically caged for life. This not only takes evolved life management—survival programming—out of the control of reptiles, but also places it firmly in the hands of human beings who, with very little actual knowledge, take on a highly selective role as god and gatekeeper.

If this does not make the point strongly enough, then perhaps consider the responsibilities, demands, and knowledge involved in having and bringing up a child. Modern life provides us with ready access to more or less everything we need to bring a child into the world and send the child on his or her way. Doctors, nurses, surgeons, midwives, psychologists, pharmacists, schoolteachers, ambulance drivers, nutritionists, family, and others are on tap to advise on topics from getting pregnant to how to deal with a departing daughter and everything in between. All these professionals are well qualified, welfare-directed, and readily accessible. But despite the wealth of expert assistance available on "child-keeping," perhaps the most important factor not on this list is that having a child is the result of "what comes naturally." Nature provided us with a suite of physiological, anatomical, psychological, and behavioral attributes that would probably equip us to handle the child-care job on our own from start to finish. Yet despite both nature and nurture seeing us through the raising of our offspring, would we describe the process as easy? Probably not!

Compare all that with keeping a reptile. Not only is the reptile not human, but it also is not even a mammal. It belongs to a distant biological class and has significantly different physiological, anatomical, psychological, and behavioral attributes. It is usually from a different part of the world and inhabits an ecosystem about which we know very little. Similarly, we know very little about the natural biological needs of reptiles, and what we do know appears to indicate that we do not, and probably cannot, provide for them. Finally, lay all these problems in the control of the reptile trade and keeping fraternity, which frequently harbors misperceptions about reptile needs, and the result is nature denatured at the very least or catastrophic failure of welfare, which is the typical consequence.

Stress, Morbidity, and Premature Mortality

At least 30 captivity stress–related behaviors and many more diseases and injuries are regularly observable in most kept reptiles (Frye, 1991; Warwick, 1995;

Warwick et al., 2013). Many diseases and injuries are identifiable from reptile behavior in the same way that a limping dog conveys leg damage. However, some behaviors are signs of captivity stress, such as hyperactivity and interaction with transparent boundaries, both of which involve persistent attempts at escape, and hypoactivity, which involves efforts to biologically "shut down" from a poor environment. What is more, these problematic behaviors are extremely common and can themselves become self-compounding and physically injurious. Despite being regularly observed, many of these signs are simply ignored by keepers as irrelevant, a disregard that marks a failure in understanding of important behaviors.

Stress, morbidity, and mortality linked to reptile trading and keeping occurs at a variety of hubs. Mortality associated with "wild capture" is unclear, but observations range from 5% to 100% according to species, and captive breeding frequently involves a mortality rate of 5–25% (Toland, Warwick, Arena, & Steedman, n.d.). At wholesalers, premature mortality has been found to be approximately 70% during a six-week period, which is also the reported industry standard (Toland et al., 2012). Shipping or transport mortalities can be measured within the margins of 1–100% according to species and situation (Toland et al., unpublished).

It should be borne in mind that although most shipments may be in the 1% mortality range, those deaths occur in relatively short (e.g., 12- to 24-hour) periods and thus represent a large number of animals given that globally numerous millions of animals are involved. A 1% transport mortality rate applied to human travel would represent approximately four people dying on a single long-haul flight from London, England, to Perth, Australia. Losses at retailers are thought to be approximately 12% per week (Toland et al., n.d.).

A study of reptiles (turtles, tortoises, lizards, and snakes) in the United Kingdom found that the premature mortality rate was 75% in their first year in the home and 81% annually if one includes wholesale and retail losses (Toland et al., 2012). By comparison, a study of life span for domesticated dogs in the United Kingdom indicated an average of over 11 years (Mitchell, 1999). These studies used different assessments (average longevity versus premature mortality), but the net result is that most dogs achieve natural longevity whereas most reptiles do not.

Survival and Mortality in Nature Versus Captivity

A commonly presented counter argument to trade and keeping mortality is that captive reptiles live longer than those in nature and that high mortality in captivity is no worse than natural attrition in the "wild"—that is, the attitude is that a loss is a loss. So if nature itself could not better the attrition rate, then should humans, as animal managers, be held to higher standards?

First, it is by no means clear whether animals in nature generally live shorter lives than captive animals, or indeed what proportion do and do not achieve their natural potential longevity. There is some evidence to show that some individual reptiles do live long captive lives. However, it is untenable to claim that these examples are unique to captivity, when there are few or no compa- rable opportunities to examine longevity of individuals in the "wild"—which may also reveal long individual life spans. There is a general paucity of data on animal life spans in nature, and thus the argument is not evidence-based. Even where the argument may be true, for a few animals anyway, the issue of quality of life requires consideration. An animal in nature is doing (or even dying while doing) what he or she has evolved and is adapted to do, whereas, by contrast, a captive animal cannot achieve this fundamental prerequisite of life.

Second, once in our care, causes of natural attrition are largely altered or omitted, and animal well-being is transferred to our responsibility. Even in captivity, longevity remains a natural goal. Also, when early-life mortality in nature is high, these losses typically occur within an ecological context and assist in the survival of other animals, which is unlike captive animal attrition, where there are few or no relevant direct beneficiaries of death. Nature can no longer be blamed for an animal's health, welfare, morbidity, or mortality—the animals' suffering and premature death are essentially in *our* hands. Therefore, it is plainly arguable that comparing morbidity and mortality in nature versus captivity is a mismatch.

Third, as humans we regard *potential* longevity as a measure of normality and premature mortality as a tragic event that should have been averted wherever possible. In most parts of the world, we do not measure acceptable human life spans by what may be considered typical in global regions of high premature mortality. Similarly, if at least three out of four domestic dogs died within their first year in the home due to maladaptation and human negligence (as do reptiles), then this would very likely be considered unacceptable. Indeed, many people might regard longevities of even several years among domestic dogs to constitute tragic deaths. Whether it is a human who dies at 40 years or a dog who dies at 4 years, both are considered lamentable deaths that should not have happened.

However, is it being selective to rule out natural attrition as a comparison for captive attrition while at the same time accepting that potential long life spans, as experienced by many animals in nature, should form the basis of what are acceptable life spans in captivity? No, it is not. Longevity is a biological potential and a marker of success, indicating, for example, an organism's ability to overcome adversity—its fitness. In nature a short life span may not indicate any sort of failure because a brief, productive life within a natural context may be highly beneficial for the individual, the individual's species, and his or her environment. By comparison, there are no benefits for either a long or short stressful life in captivity.

Ethical consistency requires that the view of successful longevity we use for ourselves and for dogs should also be the marker for captive reptiles. Unfortunately, the evidence suggests that reptile traders and keepers, along with legislators and regulators, are currently prepared to apply altered and inferior standards for reptiles.

Live Food and Feeding

Sacrificing one live animal to a preferred species is very much part of reptile keeping, with animals who might to another person be a favored companion ending up as prey. Fishes, frogs, and birds are fed to snakes; snakes are fed to cannibalistic snakes; lizards are fed to snakes; and rodents (rats, mice, and their babies) and many invertebrates are fed to just about any reptile. So even species (such as gecko lizards) that one might intuitively think are "safe" in the appreciative hands of a reptile keeper are sometimes freely immolated as a meal for a more "interesting" animal such as a tree snake.

Although certain preferences are also made for other species, such as giving cats canned food made from fishes, this is probably some way from routinely feeding a cat live trout—let alone feeding a cat another live cat! Also, cats are already domesticated—it is a human responsibility to care for existing cats, whereas reptiles remain nondomesticated animals who do not need us, and thus we have no obligation to keep them.

Indeed, there exists a substantial allied industry of intensively produced live food (typically invertebrates and rodents) to keep captive reptiles nourished. The treatment of these so-called "food animals" is often concerning because during their short captive lives they are regarded as—and manifestly become—fodder. Lee et al. (2007) described conditions of rodent suppliers in Texas where stocking density was 1,800 rats and mice per 4.6 m x 4.6 m room, at 12 rodents per (45 cm x 41 cm x 20 cm) tray and 154 trays per room. The scale of the global trade in rodents as food animals is unknown. However, Lee et al.'s (2007) study of just four Texas-based suppliers found that between them they produced about 4.2 million rats and mice annually.

Approximately 1–2% of these rodents die, largely as a result of difficult births, overgrown teeth, and drowning in overfilled water trays during production. Lee et al. (2007) also noted that the rodent feeder industry has not been well regulated throughout the United States and recommended greater scrutiny.

Globally, rodents (typically rats and mice) for reptile food who are killed individually are commonly terminated by cranial percussion (striking the head of the animal or striking the animal against a hard object), which may cause rapid concussion and death or result in convulsions and death. Similarly, whole-body impacts involve placing a small rodent in a bag or sack and striking the sack against a table or other hard object. Cervical dislocation is also used on the smaller animals. Large numbers are often killed using carbon dioxide (Conlee, Stephens, Rowan, & King, 2005). However, CO_2 is an irritant gas, which induces desperate and painful suffocating sensations (Close et al., 1996a, 1996b; Conlee et al., 2005). When supplied live, and aside from the handling, packaging, and transport processes, the fate of a rodent will depend on what predator awaits. These issues make the point that both reptiles held for their keepers' pleasure and those animals who will become those reptiles' artificial food may all be subjected to unnecessary suffering as a result of a spurious hobby.

Large lizards are brutal attackers, using powerful jaws, strong curved teeth, and strong curved claws to damage and dismember prey. Snakes may attack by biting, constricting (causing death by asphyxiation and/or circulatory strangulation), or using poison. It is particularly difficult to estimate the extent to which fear might impact on the general traumas experienced by prey animals, but it is likely not insignificant. For smaller predators (certain snakes and lizards), prey will frequently consist of invertebrates such as crickets, larvae, fishes, or frogs, and these are either chewed slightly or swallowed whole—and alive. There is now good evidence to suggest that invertebrates (including crustaceans, insects, arachnids, and others) are sensitive to pain and other aversive stimuli; thus, the welfare of these animals used as food correctly warrants concern (Smith, 1991; Elwood, 2011; Crook, 2013; Horvath, Angeletti, Nascetti, and Carere, 2013). Under natural conditions the act of a reptile or other predator subduing and consuming prey may be very different from what occurs when a living animal is merely cast into the domain of a hungry captive individual. In nature, long-evolved biological strategies probably exist that ameliorate the predator–prey relationship. For example, in free-living animals, antipredator behavior and physiology include exceedingly powerful stress- and pain-reducing responses such as endorphin release mechanisms that likely assist to minimize the trauma of attack (Warwick, 1995). In captivity, these normally involved or incidental mechanisms of nature may be circumvented by the artificiality of husbandry, to leave prey animals both behaviorally and physiologically deprived of essential strategic protections that make life and death more humane.

Reptiles are no less humane killers than other animals, and their evolved dietary needs and prey apprehension strategies, whether entirely humane or not, are nevertheless part of nature. In captivity, however, any inhumanities arise because of the human practice of choosing to keep animals in an unnatural situation where people become the middlemen between those who live and those who die, in this case not as part of natural survival, but as part of a hobby.

PUBLIC HEALTH

Around 200 zoonotic (animal-to-human) diseases exist, and at least 40 are associated with reptiles (Warwick, Arena, Steedman, & Jessop, 2012). Most notable among these is reptile-related salmonellosis, which accounts for between 1% and 5% of all salmonella infections or about 70,000 cases in the United States and 5,600 in the United Kingdom annually (Toland et al., 2012). It is estimated that 61% of human diseases may have a zoonotic origin (Karesh et al., 2005) and that 75% of global emerging human diseases are of animal origin (Brown, 2004). The selling and keeping of reptiles and other exotic animals has been likened to a Trojan horse of infection and infestation because people acquiring these animals are commonly unaware of the risks of introducing stealthy and infiltrative diseases right into the home (Warwick, 2006; Smith et al., 2012).

Although domesticated animals—for example, dogs and cats—are frequent carriers of zoonotic agents, most veterinarians and doctors are aware of the more common zoonoses and may quickly recognize many risks and advise accordingly. However, veterinarians encounter exotic "pets" (which harbor more diverse and novel pathogens) less frequently, so zoonotic disease may go unrecognized or misdiagnosed, and exotic agents are frequently more persistent and severe than domestic ones. Combined, both the relatively low veterinary and medical awareness and the more diverse, and in some cases more robust reservoir of potential pathogenic agents, make reptiles a particularly worrisome risk around the house.

A notorious source of poor animal treatment and selling practices is reptile expos, breeders' meetings, and shows—all of which are essentially rummage sale or car boot–like "pet" markets. A study of such European markets found that public health risks at markets were significant and "appear unresolvable given the format of the market environment" (Arena, Steedman, & Warwick, 2012; Warwick, Arena, & Steedman, 2012). Another recent academic assessment of 56 breeders and sellers at a reptile expo in the United States found that 17.4% of people stated they either had been ill with reptile-related salmonellosis or had known someone who had been ill (Rosenthal, 2012).

In the United States, in the 1960s and 1970s, an estimated 280,000 cases of "pet" turtle–related salmonellosis occurred annually, despite governmental efforts at educating people on prevention and control (Mermin et al., 2004). No measures worked until the trade in baby slider turtles was banned in 1975, and the following year saw a 77% reduction in cases of the disease (Mermin et al., 2004). Currently in the United States it is estimated that around 70,000 cases of reptile-related salmonellosis occur annually (Mermin et al., 2004).

Decades of formal and informal intervention and guidance on preventing reptile-related human salmonellosis have merely toyed with the problem. Abbott et al. (2012) conclude,

> Unfortunately, despite recommendations to the US public beginning in the mid-1990s, regarding the potential risk for acquisition of salmonellae infections from exotic pets, the number of infections in the US caused by subspecies associated with these sources does not appear to be abating. (p. 638)

Much guidance has centered on hand-washing to reduce human infection risk after touching a reptile. However, this somewhat naïve caution overlooks the incidental transference and transmission of bacteria from hands to nearby surfaces, which then recontaminate hands, mouth, and gut (Warwick, Arena, Steedman, & Jessop, 2012). The only way for an individual to be safe and—to not present a risk to others—is to not handle reptiles at all nor touch those who handle them.

Modern science and politics have embraced the somewhat holistic philosophy that the fates of environment, animals, and peoples are all entwined—popularly labeled as the "one health" or "healthy animals, healthy people" message. Captured, caged, mishandled, and misunderstood reptiles get stressed. It is bad for them, but stressed animals also are more likely to shed infectious agents to others and to us. It is a sound message—stress in any link of this chain adversely affects the next.

There is no cure for "pet" reptile and other animal zoonoses so long as the capturing, breeding, selling, and keeping of these animals continues. Major commercial "producers" have tried and failed to eradicate even regular bacteria from, for example, turtles, and in fact this (as with other animals, such as ornamental fishes) has led to the development of antibiotic-resistant bug strains (Diaz, Cooper, Cloeckaert, & Siebeling, 2006; Rose, Hill, Bermudez, & Miller-Morgan, 2013). As Akhtar (2012) explains, a "considerable amount of human suffering may be avoided if rather than asking ourselves how to thwart an epidemic once it has begun, we ask whether we can prevent an epidemic by treating animals differently."

Diseases, including zoonotic forms, among reptiles and other nondomesticated animals are now fully established as significant and major threats to both human health and the health of animals who are farmed, and potentially major pandemics such as severe acute respiratory syndrome (SARS) and avian influenza have already risen in association with the exotic "pet" trade. It cannot be ignored and should not be downplayed that within the trade and keeping of reptiles and other nondomesticated animals, there likely exists a global reservoir of novel, durable, and invasive pathogens. The emergent strategies of these bugs may be latent, dormant, or insidious or spontaneous and aggressive. So many human and animal health problems relate directly to the way in which animals are sourced, transported, stored, treated, and kept. Some improvements consistent with commerce may be possible, but resolutions are not. As the nonchalance of exotic "pet" selling and keeping increases, and the trade-favoring laxity of government lumbers forward, so too do the risks of unleashing the next major AIDS-like pandemic or other biological catastrophe.

Many commentators focus on the joy or comfort people derive from "owning" an animal, be the animal reptilian or other. But when animals suffer and die as a result of such "ownership," a perceptive mind would recognize exotic "pet" keeping as an indulgent and confounded pleasure. Overlooked, too, can be the stress, rumination, and depression that, for the sensitive caregiver, inevitably accompanies the bereavement of any animal. So significant can be the loss of an animal companion that today psychologists and special animal grief counselors are relatively common and often busy (Akhtar, 2012).

SPECIES AND ECOLOGICAL CONSERVATION

As mentioned elsewhere, the global market for reptiles is virtually unknown, which is in itself a disturbing fact. It is known that the reptile "pet" trade is very large indeed and probably expanding. Although captive breeding is significantly more common today, the trade continues to involve a major "wild-caught" component (Marano, Arguin, & Pappaionou, 2007). The effects of trade on

species and ecologies are becoming increasingly known. For example, Schlaepfer, Hoover, & Dodd (2005) point out that the "wild-caught" amphibian and
reptile trade is largely unregulated and occurs in a void of knowledge about
the ability of species to tolerate that collection. They comment,

> The management and monitoring of amphibians and reptiles may have been
> historically overlooked because of a perception that the level of take was
> insignificant relative to natural rates of replenishment. Now, however, am-
> phibians and reptiles are experiencing global declines, and the commercial
> trade is a global force that has the potential to contribute to these declines.
> (Schlaepfer et al., 2005, p. 263)

Parry-Jones and Englar (2007) report that the trade in free-living animals
(including for "pets") is "huge and escalating" and includes rare and endangered species with potentially "devastating" effects. Laidlaw (2005) warns that
the exotic "pet" trade (including reptiles) is "driving species toward extinction
and disrupting ecosystems" (p. 5).

Collection of "wild" reptiles also frequently involves practices that are ecologically damaging—for example, targeting mature and thus reproductively
important individuals and the incidental take of particularly vulnerable and
protected species (Warwick, 1997; Laidlaw, 2005). A 2013 study by 200 scientists led by the Zoological Society of London found that 19% of the world's
reptiles face the threat of extinction, with deforestation and biological harvesting—including for the meat and "pet" trades—cited as relevant causes (Bohm
et al., 2013).

Contrary to some beliefs, captive breeding is often not a solution to species
conservation and ecological problems, and the perception that captive breeding
is curative of the problems associated with "wild-caught" reptiles may actually
increase some "wild-caught" animal trade (Warwick, 1997; Akhtar, 2012). To
begin with, many claims that animals are captive-bred are actually unverifi-
able or false. TRAFFIC (2012) has reported that tortoises, turtles, birds, frogs,
lizards, snakes, and mammals are notable components of false "captive-bred"
declarations and has commented, "Most people would never imagine their
pet might have been sourced illegally, that they have inadvertently supported
wildlife crime, or that their purchase could have contributed to the threatened
status of species in the wild." Next, it is often difficult to distinguish between
"wild-caught" and captive-bred animals (Akhtar, 2012), and many so-called
captive-breeding operations supplement both their breeding stock and their
sales stock with "wild-caught" animals (Akhtar, 2012; TRAFFIC, 2012). In
addition, even where genuine, captive breeding frequently presents a groove

through which "wild-caught" animals are concomitantly traded (Warwick, 1997; Akhtar, 2012). Accordingly, "wild-caught," captive-bred, legal, and illegal animals are all traded under the façade of "captive-bred."

Human population has increased from 1 billion in 1900 to 6.5 billion today (Chomel et al., 2007), and it is predicted that by 2032 more than 70% of the land surface globally will have been damaged or disturbed (UNEP, 2002). Habitat loss has been identified as a major threat to 85% of all species described in the International Union for Conservation of Nature (IUCN) Red List (those species classified as threatened or endangered; WWF, 2011). In short, there are simply fewer free-living animals out there, making the human impacts on free-living animals now greater than ever. It is not difficult to argue that the exotic "pet" industry is one unnecessary burden the world does not need.

Invasive Alien Species

Escaped or unwanted and released "pet" reptiles have become a significant concern in numerous countries because of the actual and potential consequences of these animals forming introduced or "invasive alien" species (Arena, Steedman, & Warwick, 2012; ENDCAP, 2012; Toland et al., 2012). Invasive alien species are those animals and plants that once in foreign habitat essentially become a "pest" by altering indigenous ecology—for example, through competing with less hardy local "wildlife." Along with climate change, overexploitation, pollution, and habitat alteration, invasive alien species (IAS) are regarded as one of the major threats to the natural biodiversity of Europe (Shine et al., 2010). Unnatural competition and predation of indigenous animals by introduced species, contamination from novel pathogens, and alteration of ecosystems are all major concerns. IAS can also impact on human health—for example, through injuries and poisonings from lizard and snakebites (NISC, 2013). IAS-related problems cost hundreds of billions of dollars in economic damage and ecosystem management programs around the world (Strayer, Eviner, Jeschke, & Pace, 2006).

Although the proportion of IAS damage attributable to released reptile "pets" is unknown, the effects are believed to be significant (ENDCAP, 2012) and probably increasing along with wildlife trade. Of the 174 European species listed as critically endangered by the IUCN Red List, 65 are in danger as a result of invasive species (EEA, 2010). Fifty amphibian and reptile species have become established in Europe (Kark et al., 2009), and a recent survey indicated that approximately 51 types of nonnative amphibians and reptiles live "wild" in the London, England, area alone (Langton et al., 2011). Taking reptiles from where they do belong, or breeding them, and putting them where they do not belong appears to be a double-edged sword with no blunt end.

Do Trade and Keeping Generate Conservationists?

Both the pro-reptile "pet" community and some well-regarded biologists believe that reptile keeping often engenders respect for free-living animals and constitutes a formative period in the development of future conservationists. Here, the implication is that regardless of the fate of any animals, the ends justify the means for how and why some conservationists do what they do. This perspective might be modestly persuasive if there existed the evidential gravitas to support it. For that to be the case, several things (at least) would need to be established.

Reptile trading and keeping would have to produce either many active, dedicated, and—above all—effective conservationists or a few extraordinary individuals whose endeavors outweigh the indisputable harm surrounding practices involving captive reptiles. It is worth recapping just a few sample areas of concern. In the United Kingdom alone, annually at least 700,000 (Toland et al., 2012) "wild-caught" and captive-bred reptiles enter the reptile trade and keeping "system," and four out of five die prematurely in their first year (Toland et al., 2012). Invasive alien species continue to dominate many world conservation headlines, with released "pet" reptiles being an important component of that threat. Claims that the selling and keeping of reptiles aids species conservation reside between speculation and falsehood. What is well established is that trading and keeping reptiles (both "wild-caught" and captive-bred) can directly and indirectly harm species populations, whole species, and entire ecologies (Akhtar, 2012). Incidentally, even where some effective conservationists emerge who attribute their role to earlier reptile keeping, can it truly be said that they would not have chosen that path anyway?

Regardless, even if the argument that the ends justify the means was considered to be ethically acceptable, the reality is that the collateral damage from reptile trading and keeping is expanding, not receding. Accordingly, there does not exist a genuinely significant impact from ambassadorial conservationists who were once reptile keepers, and the "philosophy," if it ever possessed a sound rationale, has catastrophically failed.

COMMERCE AND ECONOMICS

Industrial Freedoms or Liberties?

The commercial and economic dynamics of reptile trading share many commonalities with other industries, but also several significant differences. Many if not most of the things we engage with have been rigorously and independently tested prior to being made publically available and are subsequently controlled by stringent regulation. They are typically "pre-checked" regarding their safety for people and the environment rather than being openly marketed and retrospectively investigated or controlled. The trade in reptiles and "wildlife" in general is one of few industries anywhere in the world that escapes entirely these protection norms. In fact, in almost all countries the monitoring process for the entire trade operates in reverse of this precautionary approach.

Essentially, there are two systems used to "control" such trade in animals. The standard and almost universal system is the "negative list." This is the fundamental structure of the Convention on International Trade in Endangered Species (CITES) and involves placing species on monitored, restricted, or banned lists. Species are added only following an inertia-laden and trade-favoring process that applies to a minority of species, and the system is poorly regulated (Warwick, 1997; Laidlaw, 2005). The alternative system used by a few countries is the "positive list" and was historically also known as the "green list" or "reverse list." The positive list turns the standard negative list on its head and implies that no species can be traded unless it is first proven safe for commerce under independent scientific evidence-based criteria. A "positive" listing does not automatically suggest that something is good for people, animals, or environment, but merely indicates that it has been checked to establish that it is not people- and environment-unsafe. Where the system is used, it is significantly superior to the negative-list principle of CITES. The positive-list system uses the same principle as virtually all other industries. Trains, planes, cars, buildings, electrical goods, drugs, and even people—dentists, doctors, pilots, almost anyone whom the public may rely on for their well-being—are subject to a list of verified and approved (effectively "positive-listed") things or professionals.

Unlike most producers, there are no requirements for reptile traders to prove that their "merchandise" is safe for the public, safe for the environment, or even safe for the so-called product (a live animal) itself. In fact, unlike other industries, "wildlife" trading is systematically given the benefit of the doubt—meaning that trade continues in any direction and with any implication until others, in their own time and at their own cost, gather all salient evidence and gain protective legislation. Even where successful, all this amounts to is certain species being included on negative lists (i.e., animals who are restricted or banned), and traders and keepers then commonly either flout the regulations or move on to another species, starting the entire cycle again. So while the "wildlife" industry steams ahead almost unencumbered, animal welfare, species conservation, environmental, and public health organizations and campaigners labor against governmental regulatory inertia wherein the "control" of practices amounts to little more than a fluctuating smokescreen.

If the normal protections required of responsible industries were directed at the trade of reptiles (and other animals), then the business would comprehensively fail on all counts. For example, in terms of animal welfare, the "products"—sensitive, sentient creatures—will probably die (fail) within a year, making neither "manufacturer's" nor statutory guarantees possible. Regarding public health and safety, all reptiles would fail hygiene tests at the very least. In terms of environmental impact, between damaging collection methods and release of invasive (arguably even toxic) species into nature, reptiles would also fail a number of these precautions.

A simple example of how the reptile trade fails its customers where other industries at least aspire to succeed can be represented using a child's toy—for convenience we can make that example a soft fabric turtle. To be sold, the toy turtle will typically require eyes that cannot be pulled from the product, so that the child cannot ingest or choke on them. There will be no sharp edges that could cause any incidental harm. The materials will be environment- and child-safe, in case the child puts the toy to his or her mouth. Also, the whole thing will be machine-washable so that it does not become an infection hazard. There is a reasonable chance the toy will also be fire-resistant as an extra safeguard. And finally, a few stitched-in labels will demonstrate the hoops that had to be jumped through to get that toy turtle onto the market and who behind it is fully accountable for any failures.

Compare that with the reptile trade, where anyone can stroll into their local animal store, demand a live turtle, and deliver that animal right into the hands of a child. Unlike the soft toy, surface contaminants, skin detritus, feces, and bacteria likely reside on and in the turtle. Sharp jaw plates and claws can easily cause injuries and result in infections. Turtles cannot be cleaned of their "contaminants"—typically these are as normal to the turtle as our own bacteria are to us. In brief, there can be no genuine guarantees whatsoever about either the safety of the "product" or the turtle's own health, and a purchaser is unlikely to know where the animal came from, how the animal got here, and what to do with him or her. All this raises serious questions about people's capacity to practice informed consent when purchasing a reptile. Worse, in contrast to the dearth of information about any aspect of live turtle safety, there exists a veritable library of independent, scientific, and medical material that unequivocally demonstrates that "pet" turtles, like all reptiles, are distinctly unsafe for children, as well as for many normal healthy adults (Mermin et al., 2004; Chomel et al., 2007; Brugere-Picoux & Chomel, 2009; Smith et al., 2012; Warwick, Arena, Steedman, & Jessop, 2012).

The notion of having to conform to the normal requirements of the positive list system strikes fear deep into the hearts of reptile traders and keepers because it would mean an end to the multi-decade-long free ride that they have enjoyed while animals, many people, and the environment have not.

Balancing the Books?

Why the reptile trade and other trades in nondomesticated animals have enjoyed this red-tape free ride for decades remains a mystery. Big business is often perceived as getting away with things simply because of its basic economic importance and the financial feedback to the state. The trade in animals is certainly big business. For example, a 2009 TRAFFIC report estimated that all legal trade in "wildlife products" was worth approximately €100 billion for the European Union in 2009 (ENDCAP, 2012). However, this would include skins and furs as well as some live animals for "pets." A 2007 report cited a value of €7 million for live reptiles, and €100 million for skin-based products (Engler & Parry-Jones, 2007). Generally, captive-bred animals within the European Union and United Kingdom will not show in these data, so these figures understate the scale. But do these numbers add up to justify the incidental exemption of reptile trade from commercial norms? Representative data specifically for reptiles are lacking. However, taking "wildlife" trade as a whole, the €100 billion figure sounds impressive until one considers at least some of the covert costs and destructive disbursements.

In the European Union the annual cost of damage from IAS is estimated at approximately €12.5 billion—many of these invasives are released "pet" reptiles (European Commission, 2011). That is only part of the picture. There are over 10,000 animal and plant species alien to Europe on the continent now, yet ecological impacts are documented for only 11% of the total and economic impacts for only 13% of species (Vilà et al., 2010). The costs in global biodiversity loss from reptile capture for "pets" are not known. However, a recent report concluded that protecting even the world's most endangered species from extinction would cost over $76 billion a year (McCarthy et al., 2012). There are also public health costs and costs of health care for treating reptile-borne human disease: a single doctor's consultation can be €50, a single hospital consultation €250, and a single day in the hospital €2,500. To this one can add days off work and lost productivity.

What broader costs are associated with ecological damage from reptile "pet" trading? One can add a variety of costs, including public money donated to charitable causes (animal welfare, species conservation, and public health) that work on relevant problems; costs of managing the array of largely ineffective but expensive "regulatory" organizations; and local, national, and international governmental and parliamentary time spent on reviews and legislation, however ineffective. Across a nation, these costs will be high—across the European Union, very high. It is highly questionable whether, even on economic grounds, the reptile trade can balance its own books.

CONCLUSION

Reptiles are not afforded all the same considerations as traditionally "cute" animals. At least three reasons probably account for this. First, the anthropomorphic bond is dramatically weaker with reptiles than with many other animals. This non-communication may be associated with or result from certain typical reptilian anatomical features, such as minimal facial expression and vocalization. Second, reptile behavior is often not socially centered, making reptiles less "interactive." Third, awareness within both the scientific and lay communities regarding indicators of stress and disease in reptiles is poor, and thus signs (and suffering) that may be obvious to experienced observers can typically go unrecognized by others.

Would dog caregivers put their loved companion in a vivarium and observe him or her clawing at the glass for hours each day? Would society accept the vast majority of dogs dying within one year from mistreatment, maladaptation, and stress-related disease? The answer, one hopes, in all these cases has to be a resounding no! A major result of this reptilian–mammalian mismatch is that reptiles are routinely subject to abuses by people who probably would not direct the same treatment at familiar and intrinsically valued animals.

It is difficult to avoid the conclusion that reptile trading and keeping operates largely on a mis-evolved and maladapted belief system based on outdated biological understanding and cumulative erroneous presumptions. The harm and failures endemically caused by those who sell and keep reptiles are compounded by regulatory inertia among those with whom resides the formal responsibility to prevent and control the negative consequences of the entire "business." There are no valid reasons that reptile trading and keeping should avoid the normal precautionary investigation and control (e.g., the "positive list") required of other industries and, arguably, no good reason that reptiles should be sold or kept as "pets" at all.

One inarguable fact is that people benefit financially or derive other satisfaction from trading and keeping reptiles. Another inarguable fact is that countless individual animals, species, environments, ecologies, and people suffer to produce those benefits.

Reptiles are physically, emotionally, and psychologically sensitive. They possess complex biological needs, and their sensitivity and sentience is clear to anyone who chooses to be mindful of these animals. Few people who hold them captive seem to appreciate those needs or look beyond the mundane practicalities of how one can obtain and "keep" a reptile to whether it is right to do so. Perhaps ironically, although reptiles possess the cold-blooded reputation, it is humans themselves who are emotionally insensitive—to the detriment of reptiles, humans, and the world in which they live.

References

Abbott, S. L., Ni, F. C. Y., & Janda, M. J. (2012). Increase in extraintestinal infections caused by *Salmonella enterica* subspecies II–IV. *Emerging Infectious Diseases, 18*(4), 637–639.

Akhtar, A. (2012). *Animals and public health.* London, England: Palgrave MacMillan.

Altherr, F., & Freyer, D. (2001). *Morbidity and mortality in private husbandry of reptiles.* A report by Pro Wildlife to the RSPCA.

American Pet Products Association. (2011). New survey reveals pet ownership at its highest level in two decades and pet owners are willing to pay when it comes to pet's health [Press release]. Retrieved from http://media.americanpetproducts .org/press.php?include=142818

Arena, P. C., Steedman, C., & Warwick, C. (2012). *Amphibian and reptile pet markets in the EU: An investigation and assessment.* Animal Protection Agency, Animal Public, International Animal Rescue, Eurogroup for Wildlife and Laboratory Animals, Fundación para la Adopción, el Apadrinamiento y la Defensa de los Animales.

Arena, P. C., & Warwick, C. (1995). Miscellaneous factors affecting health and welfare. In C. Warwick, F. L. Frye, & J. Murphy (Eds.), *Health and welfare of captive reptiles* (pp. 263–283). London, England: Chapman & Hall/Kluwer.

Auliya, M. (2003). *Hot trade in cool creatures: A review of the live reptile trade in the European Union in the 1990s with a focus on Germany.* Brussels, Belgium: TRAFFIC Europe.

Bohm, M., Collen, B., Baillie, J. E. M., Bowles, P., Chanson, J., Cox, N., et al. (2013). The conservation status of the world's reptiles. *Biological Conservation, 157*, 372–385.

Bomford, M., Kraus, F., Barry, S. C., & Lawrence, E. (2009). Predicting establishment success for alien reptiles and amphibians: A role for climate matching. *Biological Invasions, 11*, 713–724.

Brown, C. (2004). Emerging zoonoses and pathogens of public health significance: An overview. *OIE Scientific and Technical Review, 23*, 435–442.

Brugere-Picoux, L., & Chomel, B. (2009). Importation of tropical diseases to Europe via animals and animal products: Risks and pathways. *Bulletin de l'Academie Nationale de Medecine, 193*, 1805–1819.

Cameron-Beaumont, C., Lowe, S. E., & Bradshaw, J. W. S. (2001). Evidence suggesting preadaptation to domestication throughout the small Felidae. *Biological Journal of the Linnean Society, 75*, 361–366.

Chomel, B. B., Belotto, A., & Meslin, F.-X. (2007). Wildlife, exotic pets and emerging zoonoses. *CDC Emerging Infectious Diseases, 13*, 6–11.

Close, B., Bannister, K., Baumans, V., Bernoth, E. M., Bromage, N., Bunyan, J., Warwick, C. (1996a). Recommendations for euthanasia of experimental animals. Part 1. *Laboratory Animals, 30*, 293–316.

Close, B., Bannister, K., Baumans, V., Bernoth, E. M., Bromage, N., Bunyan, J., Warwick, C. (1996b). Recommendations for euthanasia of experimental animals. Part 2. *Laboratory Animals, 31*, 1–32.

Conlee, K. M., Stephens, M. L., Rowan, A. N., & King, L. A. (2005). Carbon dioxide for euthanasia: Concerns regarding pain and distress, with special reference to mice and rats. *Laboratory Animals, 39*, 137–161.

Crook, R. A. (2013). The welfare of invertebrate animals in research: Can science's next generation improve their lot? *Journal of Postdoctoral Research, 1*(2), 1–20.

Diaz, M. A., Cooper, R. K., Cloeckaert, A., & Siebeling, R. J. (2006). Plasmid-mediated high-level gentamicin resistance among enteric bacteria isolated from pet turtles in Louisiana. *Appl Environ Microbiol., 72*, 306–12.

Elwood, R. W. (2011). Pain and suffering in invertebrates? *ILAR Journal, 52*, 175–184.

ENDCAP. (2012). *Wild pets in the European Union*. Author.

Engler, M., & Parry-Jones, R. (2007). *Opportunity or threat: The role of the European Union in global wildlife trade*. Brussels, Belgium: TRAFFIC Europe.

Estren, M. (2012). The neoteny barrier: Seeking respect for the non-cute. *Journal of Animal Ethics, 2*, 6–11.

European Commission. (2011). *Our life insurance, our natural capital: An EU biodiversity strategy to 2020*. Communication from the Commission to the European Parliament, the Council, the Economic and Social Committee and the Committee of the Regions. Retrieved from http://www.europarl.europa.eu/sides/getDoc .do?type=TA&language=EN&reference=P7-TA-2012-146

European Environment Agency. (2010). *EU 2010 biodiversity baseline*.

Franke, J., & Telecky, T. (2001). *Reptiles as pets: An examination of the trade in live reptiles in the United States*. Humane Society of the United States.

Frye, F. L. (1991). *Biomedical and surgical aspects of captive reptile husbandry*. Malabar, FL: Krieger.

Gillingham, J. C. (1995). Normal behaviour. In C. Warwick, F. L. Frye, & J. Murphy (Eds.), *Health and welfare of captive reptiles* (pp. 131–174). London, England: Chapman & Hall/Kluwer.

Hale, C. R., Scallan, E., Cronquist, A. B., Dunn, J., Smith, K., Robinson, T., . . . Clogher, P. (2012). Estimates of enteric illness attributable to contact with animals and their environments in the United States. *Clinical Infectious Disease, 54*(S5), S472–479.

Henderson, W., & Bomford, M. (2011). *Detecting and preventing new incursions of exotic animals in Australia.* Report prepared for the Detection and Prevention Project in Australia. Canberra, Australia: Invasive Animals Cooperative Research Centre.

Horvath, K., Angeletti, D., Nascetti, G., & Carere, C. (2013). Invertebrate welfare: An overlooked issue. *Ann Ist Super Sanità, 49*(1), 9–17. doi:10.4415/ANN_13 _01_04

HSUS. (2001). The trade in live reptiles: Imports to the United States. The Humane Society of the United States.

HSUS. (2009). *The trade in live reptiles: Imports to the United States.* Retrieved from http://www.humanesociety.org/issues/wildlife_trade/facts/trade_live _reptiles_imports_us.html

Jones, K. E., Patel, N. G., Levy, M. A., Storeygard, A., Balk, D., Gittleman, J. L., & Daszak, P. (2008). Global trends in emerging infectious disease. *Nature, 451,* 990–993.

Karesh, W. B., Cook, R. A., Bennett, E. L., & Newcomb, J. (2005). Wildlife trade and global disease emergence. *Emerging Infectious Disease, 11,* 1000–1002.

Karesh, W. B., Cook, R. A., Gilbert, M., & Newcomb, J. (2007). Implications of wildlife trade on the movement of avian influenza and other infectious diseases. *Journal of Wildlife Diseases, 43*(S3), 55–59.

Kark, S., Solarz, W., Chiron, F., Clergeau, P., & Shirley, S. (2009). Alien birds, amphibians and reptiles of Europe. In DAISIE (Ed.), *Handbook of alien species in Europe* (pp. 105–118). Dordrecht, Netherlands: Springer.

Krauss, H., Weber, A., Appel, M., Enders, B., Graevenitz, A. V., Isenberg, H. D., Zahner, H. (2003). Zoonoses. *Infectious diseases transmissible from animals to humans* (3rd ed.). Washington, DC: ASM Press.

Laidlaw, R. (2005). *Scales and tails: The welfare and trade of reptiles kept as pets in Canada.* World Society for the Protection of Animals.

Langton, T. E. S., Atkins, W., & Herbert, C. (2011). On the distribution, ecology and management of non-native reptiles and amphibians in the London area. Part 1. Distribution and predator/prey impacts. *London Naturalist, 90,* 83–156.

Lee, K. M., McReynolds, J. L., Fuller, C. C., Jones, B., Herrman, T. J., Byrd, J. A., & Runyon, M. (2007). Investigation and characterization of the frozen feeder rodent industry in Texas following a multi-state *Salmonella typhimurium* outbreak associated with frozen vacuum-packed rodents. *Zoonoses and Public Health, 55,* 488–496. doi:10.1111/j.1863–2378.2008.01165.x

Marano, N., Arguin, P. M., & Pappaionou, M. (2007). Impact of globalization and animal trade on infectious disease ecology. *Emerging Infectious Disease, 13*(12), 1807–1809.

McCarthy, D. P., Donald, P. F., Scharlemann, J. P. W., Buchanan, G. M., Balmford, A., Green, J. M. H., Butchart, S. H. M. (2012). Financial costs of meeting global biodiversity conservation targets: Current spending and unmet needs. *Science, 338*(6109), 946–949. Retrieved from http://dx.doi.org/10.1126/science.1229803

Mermin, J., Hutwagner, L., Vugia, D., Shallow, S., Daily, P., Bender, J., Angulo, F. J. (2004). Reptiles, amphibians, and human Salmonella infection: A population-based, case-control study. *Clin. Infect. Dis., 38*, 253–261.

Mitchell, A. R. (1999). Longevity of British breeds of dog and its relationships with sex, size, cardiovascular variables and disease. *Veterinary Record, 27*, 625–629.

NISC. (2013). National Invasive Species Council. Retrieved from http://www .invasivespecies.gov/main_nav/mn_faq.html#harm_humans

Parry-Jones, R., & Englar, M. (2007). *Opportunity or threat: The role of the European Union in the global wildlife trade*. Brussels, Belgium: TRAFFIC Europe.

PFMA. (2012). 2011 pet population figures. Retrieved from http://www.pfma.org.uk/pet -population/

Praud, A., & Moutou, F. (2010). *Health risks from new companion animals*. Brussels, Belgium: Eurogroup.

Price, E. O. (1984). Behavioral aspects of animal domestication. *Quarterly Review of Biology, 59*, 1–32.

Reaser, J. K., Clarke, E. E., Jr., & Meyers, N. M. (2008). All creatures great and minute: A public policy primer for companion animal zoonoses. *Zoonoses Public Health, 55*, 385–401. doi:10.1111/j.1863–2378.2008.01123.x

Rose, S., Hill, R., Bermudez, L. E., & Miller-Morgan, T. (2013). Imported ornamental fish are colonized with antibiotic-resistant bacteria. *Journal of Fish Diseases, 36*(6), 533–542. Retrieved from http://www.ncbi.nlm.nih.gov/pubmed/23294440

Rosenthal, H. (2012). *The global wildlife trade and its implications for public health: A case study on reptiles and salmonella*. Center for Environmental Studies, Brown University.

Schlaepfer, M. A., Hoover, C., & Dodd, C. K., Jr. (2005). Challenges in evaluating the impact of the trade in amphibians and reptiles on wild populations. *BioScience, 55*(3), 256–264.

Shine, C., Kettunen, M., Genovesi, P., Essl, F., Gollasch, S., Rabitsch, W., ten Brink, P. (2010). *Assessment to support continued development of the EU strategy to combat invasive alien species*. Final Report for the European Commission. Brussels, Belgium: Institute for European Environmental Policy.

Smith, J. A. (1991). A question of pain in invertebrates. *ILAR Journal, 33*, 25–31.

Smith, K. M., Anthony, S. J., Switzer, W. M., Epstein, J. H., Seimon, T., et al. (2012). Zoonotic viruses associated with illegally imported wildlife products. *PLoS ONE 7*(1), e29505. doi:10.1371/journal.pone.0029505

Strayer, D. L., Eviner, V. T., Jeschke, J. M., & Pace, M. L. (2006). *Trends in ecology and evolution, 21*(11), 645–651. doi:10.1016/j.tree.2006.07.007

Toland, E., Warwick, C., & Arena, P. C. (2012). The exotic pet trade: Pet hate. *Biologist 59*(3), 14–18.

Toland, E., Warwick, C., Arena, P. C., & Steedman, C. (n.d.). *Premature mortality rates in exotic pet fishes, amphibians and reptiles in the UK*. Unpublished manuscript.

TRAFFIC. (2012). *Captive-bred or wild-taken? Examples of possible illegal trade in wild animals through fraudulent claims of captive-breeding.* TRAFFIC/WWF.

UNEP. (2002). *Global environment outlook 3: Past, present and future perspectives.* Earthscan.

UNEP/WCMC. (2009). *Review of non-CITES reptiles that are known or likely to be in international trade: A report to the European Commission Directorate General Environment.* United Nations Environment Programme/World Conservation Monitoring Centre.

Vilà, M., Basnou, C., Pyšek, P., Josefsson, M., Genovesi, P., Gollasch, S., DAISIE partners. (2010). How well do we understand the impacts of alien species on ecosystem services? A pan-European, cross-taxa assessment. *Frontiers in Ecology and the Environment, 8*(3), 135–144. doi:10.1890/080083

Warwick, C. (1990). Reptilian ethology in captivity: Observations of some problems and an evaluation of their aetiology. *Applied Animal Behaviour Science, 26*, 1–13.

Warwick, C. (1995). Psychological and behavioural principles and problems. In C. Warwick, F. L. Frye, & J. Murphy (Eds.), *Health and welfare of captive reptiles* (pp. 205–238). London, England: Chapman & Hall/Kluwer.

Warwick, C. (1997). The shelf life of reptiles. In M. E. Drayer (Ed.), *The animal dealers: Evidence of abuse of animals in the commercial trade 1952–1997.* Washington, DC: Animal Welfare Institute.

Warwick, C. (2001, March 19). Cold-blooded conspiracy. *BBC Wildlife Magazine*, pp. 58–62.

Warwick, C. (2006). Zoonoses: Drawing the battle lines. *Veterinary Times, 36*, 26–28.

Warwick, C., Arena, P. C., Jessop, M., Lindley, S., & Steedman, C. (2013). Assessing reptile welfare using behavioural criteria. *In Practice, 35*(3), 123–131. doi:10.1136/inp.f1197

Warwick, C., Arena, P. C., & Steedman, C. (2012). Visitor behaviour and public health implications associated with exotic pet markets: An observational study. *J R Soc Med Sh Rep, 3*(63), 1–9. doi:10.1258/shorts.2012.012012

Warwick, C., Arena, P. C., Steedman, C., & Jessop, M. (2012). A review of captive exotic animal-linked zoonoses. *Journal of Environmental Health Research, 12*, 9–24. Retrieved from http://www.cieh.org/jehr/default.aspx?id=41594

Warwick, C., Frye, F. L., & Murphy, J. B. (1995). Introduction. In C. Warwick, F. L. Frye, & J. Murphy (Eds.), *Health and welfare of captive reptiles* (pp. 1–4). London, England: Chapman & Hall/Kluwer.

Warwick, C., & Steedman, C. (1995). Naturalistic versus unnaturalistic environments in husbandry and research. In C. Warwick, F. L. Frye, & J. Murphy (Eds.), *Health and welfare of captive reptiles* (pp. 113–129). London, England: Chapman & Hall/Kluwer.

WWF. (2011). *Impact of habitat loss on species.* Retrieved from http://wwf.panda.org/about_our_earth/species/problems/habitat_loss_degradation/

13 Transgenic Animals, Biomedical Experiments, and "Progress"

KAY PEGGS

By conducting a critical discourse analysis of a scientific research article that claims additional potential for using transgenic marmosets in biomedical experiments, this article critiques instrumental approaches to scientific progress as they are expressed in scientific research that uses nonhuman animal experiments. Following an analysis that focuses on issues associated with access to publication, assertions about scientific breakthrough and scientific facts, and the construction of science as impartial, the article concludes that manipulating the genetics of nonhuman animals to engineer a predisposition to the development of feared human health hazards represents moral deterioration rather than progress.

KEY WORDS: nonhuman animals, ethics, experiments, progress, transgenic

INTRODUCTION

This article explores ethical issues associated with the development of transgenic nonhuman animals for use[1] in biomedical science.[2] Because I aim to explore ethical issues, my focus on biomedical experiments, which are seen as *most* ethical (if we can apply a continuum of ethics), is apposite. Although experiments that use nonhuman animals have a long and controversial history (Tester, 1991), and public concerns about nonhuman animal experiments have increased recently (see, for example, Commission of the European Communities, 2008), there is more public acceptance of such experiments if they have biomedical objectives. This is because biomedical experiments are more likely to be perceived as crucial to human health (Garner, 2005; Henry and Pulcino, 2009). Such experiments increasingly rely on the use of genetically modified nonhuman animals (Brown and Michael, 2001), which perhaps increases the controversy associated with nonhuman animal experiments because although scientific reports suggest that the public is open generally to biomedical research

Journal of Animal Ethics 3(1): 41–56

that uses genetically modified nonhuman animals (e.g., see Holmes, 2010, p. 35), social research points to some public aversion to the genetic modification of nonhuman animals (e.g., see Macnaghten, 2004). Nevertheless, because genetic modification is becoming easier, we are likely to see the development of increasing numbers of transgenic nonhuman animals from a growing range of species for increasingly diverse purposes (e.g., see Holmes, 2010). This is the context in which Erika Sasaki and her colleagues (2009) undertook their research, and it is their published article that I focus on in my discussion here.

In their article published in May 2009 in the science journal *Nature,* Sasaki et al. claim extra potential for using nonhuman primates in biomedical experiments based on the possibility that transgenically modified marmosets could give birth to young who could develop human diseases. Sasaki et al. (2009) write in the language of biomedical progress, a language that heralds scientific and technological advancement (e.g., see Gray, 2003) based on the potential for a healthier future for many humans. Their claim to progress on previous research is primarily based on the development of transgenic marmosets who could be more useful in biomedical research due to their "size, availability, and unique biological characteristics" (Sasaki et al., 2009, p. 523). Of course, the history of progress cannot be seen as a smooth walk up a hill to benefits. For example, Walter Benjamin offers a critique of the standard history of progress by presenting a dialectical conceptualization in which "progress is adjoined to catastrophe" (e.g., see Leslie, 2007, p. 196). In this regard "progress" is seen as a wavering and jagged process of discontinuities that involves ups and downs, starts and stops, advancement and retreat, devastation and success, and calamity and fortune (e.g., see Wolfe, 2010). For this reason, Norbert Elias (2000) observes "diminishing confidence in progress" (p. 462) associated with nuclear and other manifestations of technical and scientific developments. Such observations point to problems inherent in science's account of itself as a story of progress (for discussion see Wolfe, 2010). Nevertheless, biomedical scientific discourse often proclaims benefits rather than catastrophe, and nonhuman animals are time and again used by humans in this story of human health progression, which neglects sincere moral considerations for the nonhuman animals themselves.

This idea of progress, as it relates to *scientific development,* is distinct from *moral development,* which can be associated with equal consideration of others, in this case nonhuman animals. To be sure, philosophers such as Bernard Williams (2006) argue that moral progress is best served by affirming the distinct and separate moral status of the human. This is the principle of much bio-medical research; even though some moral consideration might be accorded to the living beings used in biomedical experiments, these beings are clearly viewed in terms of their use-value to humans. In this regard, Phil Macnaghten's (2004) observation is helpful; he detects a "clear tension between 'moral' and 'instrumental' approaches to animals" (p. 533)—that is, between our treatment of nonhuman animals in terms of what is right for them and our treatment of them as means to our ends. This "clear tension" is evident in Sasaki et al.'s (2009) article, yet it is a tension they appear to ignore. Even though I center on Sasaki et al.'s article, this is not to single out their research. I could have focused my attention on a range of articles that attribute biomedical "progress" to the development of genetically modified nonhuman animals for biomedical research. I have chosen to focus on Sasaki et al.'s work here and elsewhere (Peggs, 2011) because their research was hailed as a major breakthrough by many scientists (e.g., see Schatten and Mitalipov, 2009) and by the news media (e.g., see Sample, 2009) and thus can be seen as an important marker in the use of nonhuman animals in biomedical science. In focusing on the notions, assumptions, and claims of Sasaki et al. about the advancements that their research is designed to achieve, my overall aim is to comment more generally on the human values associated with nonhuman animal experimentation.

My aims are reflected in the structure of this current article. Norms and values associated with the fundamental importance of (biomedical) scientific research are deeply entrenched in Western societies (Gray, 2003; Haraway, 1997); in the opening section I explore the ways in which humans have sought to increase the biomedical utility of nonhuman animals by developing transgenic nonhuman animals who have a predisposition to develop human diseases. This section is followed by consideration of the analytical approach I use. This leads me to Sasaki et al.'s (2009) article. Following a brief synopsis of their article, I use a critical discourse analytical approach to extracts of the article to reflect on notions, assumptions, and claims about progress. My analysis centers on four main areas: access to and the setting for publication; assertions about scientific breakthroughs; assumptions about scientific "facts"; and the construction of science as impartial. I conclude that genetically modifying nonhuman animals so that they are predisposed to develop feared human health hazards cannot be regarded as progress if a moral approach to nonhuman animals is taken; rather, such developments represent moral deterioration based in instrumental human values that drive an already morally degraded history of experiments that use nonhuman animals.

TRANSGENIC NONHUMAN ANIMALS
IN BIOMEDICINE

Among the many applications of genetic modification is the attempt to enhance the utility of nonhuman animals for human health–related experiments (Frese and Tuveson, 2007; Knight, 2008; Fuller, 2008). As a result genomic science has led to an increase in the numbers of transgenic nonhuman animals used for biomedical purposes (see Brown and Michael, 2001). In 2010 in the United Kingdom alone, just over 3.7 million new procedures on nonhuman animals were started, a rise of 3% from the previous year, which "was largely due to an increase to 1.6 million procedures (+87,000, +6%) in breeding to produce genetically modified (GM) animals and harmful mutants (HM), mainly mice (+77,000)" (Home Office, 2011, p. 7).

A transgenic nonhuman animal is one who has had a foreign gene introduced into his or her body (Knight, 2008, p. 94). Two examples show the different ways in which transgenic nonhuman animals are used in the field of biomedicine. Transgenic goats are "genetically engineered to produce human insulin in their milk" (Thacker, 2006, p. 2), and in an effort to develop treatments for cancer, the mouse who is patented as "Oncomouse" has "foreign DNA" inserted into her genome (Schatten and Mitalipov, 2009, p. 515), resulting in a transgenic mouse who has "a predisposition to develop cancer" (Patent Watch, 2004). It is obvious why many humans view the increasing use of transgenic nonhuman animals as a positive development—such research is purported to provide clear human health benefits. For example, the pharmaceutical company GlaxoSmith-Kline (2007) states,

> Transgenic (or genetically modified) animals are proving ever more vital in the discovery and development of new treatments and cures for many serious diseases by helping scientists to characterise the newly-sequenced human genome. Without them, the pharmaceutical industry's ability to discover new treatments would be significantly reduced.

Bob Holmes (2010), a consultant to the journal *New Scientist*, agrees and predicts, "The ability to easily and precisely modify animals will undoubtedly lead to huge pay-offs in research and medicine" (p. 33).[3] There is by no means a scientific consensus about this. For example, Andrew Knight (2008) is unconvinced by such claims and argues that the results of biomedical experiments using transgenic nonhuman animals can be very misleading or wrong. Moreover, he advises that "faulty" human genes can be studied without resorting to experiments on nonhuman animals. These divergent opinions reflect disagreements about the human health benefits of biomedical experiments using nonhuman animals; although some scientists argue that such experiments are essential for biomedical progress (e.g., Research Defence Society, 2007), others argue that such experiments are detrimental to human health (e.g., Greek and Greek, 2002, 2004). Sasaki et al. (2009) are clearly in no doubt about the utility of nonhuman animals in biomedical research and about the usefulness of transgenic nonhuman animals in particular.

Sasaki et al.'s (2009) research can be situated within what Macnaghten (2004) calls a "consequentialist approach" to the history of technological developments, which, he explains, "reinforces the judgement that new techniques of genetic modification should be properly understood as continuous with older patterns of selective breeding" (p. 536). These developments persist in encouraging humans to manipulate nonhuman animals for human use; human manipulation, utilization, and commodification of nonhuman animals have endured for centuries. Because such manipulation has a long history, current public concerns about genetic modification are often disparaged on the grounds that the public is wrong to view all non–genetically modified nonhuman animals as "natural" (for discussion see Macnaghten, 2004, p. 536). For example, the modification of nonhuman animals for use in experiments is not new (Birke, 2003; Rader, 2004). To take a case in point, Karen Rader (2004) observes that "standardized" mice who had been "re-engineered by humans" (in that they were inbred to control their genetic makeup so that experiments on them were reproducible) had become "laboratory fixtures" by the 1960s. Thus, genetic modification should be seen as an additional way of modifying and thus increasing the utility of nonhuman animals for biomedical (and other) research (see Knight, 2008, p. 94).

The first transgenic mice were developed in 1982, and currently millions of genetically modified mice are used in laboratory experiments devoted to cancers and other feared human diseases every year around the globe (Holmes, 2010, p. 33).[4] This is claimed as a triumph because transgenic mice are held to have "produced a wealth of new knowledge, become topics of intellectual property, and spawned a vibrant field of cancer research that is revealing mechanisms of tumorigenesis and suggesting new therapeutic strategies for treating the human disease" (Hanahan, Wagner, and Palmiter, 2007). Sasaki et al.'s research is grounded in this canon of work, and in keeping with this canon, the focus is on the results of the experiments undertaken rather than on the ethical issues involved in using nonhuman animals (e.g., see Birke and Smith, 1995). Yet moral considerations are tremendously important, and Joel Marks (2011) calls for science authors to properly acknowledge the ethical implications of using nonhuman animals (p. 6). Let us look at one example. The essential principle of contemporary biomedical research that requires informed consent from humans is not offered to nonhuman animals (Henry and Pulcino, 2009, p. 305). Gareth Williams and Jennie Popay (1993) note examples of human participants who have used their right to contest the results of a clinical trial on the grounds of "methodological rationale, its results, and ethical justifications" (qtd. in Brown and Michael, 2001, p. 7); nonhuman animals used in biomedical experiments are not granted such a right to contest. This is, of course, an issue of power because the nonhuman animals who are used are so used because they *can* be so used (e.g., see Peggs, 2009), and the moral consensus allows this power to be wielded. Other "moral patients," to use Tom Regan's (1983/2004) terminology, such as children, are owed moral duties and rightly must not be so used. Regan (1983/2004) contends that we should give similar moral consideration to nonhuman animals; however, this is not what happens. For example, Robert Garner (2005) explains that the "moral orthodoxy" in the United Kingdom expects that the interest that nonhuman animals have in not suffering can be overridden for what is considered the greater good of humans (p. 15). The moral orthodoxy is entrenched, and in the biomedical community, Jane Welchman (2003) observes, "it is widely held that partiality to human interests is not only defensible, but obligatory" (p. 245). This required partiality extends beyond the United Kingdom to biomedical research across the globe, and it is this required partiality that enables researchers who use nonhuman animals to claim instrumental progress for their research.

SCIENCE, NONHUMAN ANIMALS, AND SCIENTIFIC DISCOURSE

In order to explore the discourses used by Sasaki et al. (2009) and to critically reflect on the ways in which all nonhuman animals (including transgenic) are used as a resource in biomedical science, I apply critical discourse analysis (CDA) to "focus on the ways in which discourse sustains and legitimizes social inequalities" (Wooffitt, 2005, p. 138). Discourse is an important aspect of knowledge because, as Andrew Linzey and Priscilla Cohn (2011) note, "language is the means by which we understand and conceptualize the world around us, even the means by which we *think* about the world" (p. vii). In the following analysis I center on the language used in scientific discourse in a piece of published research. I examine constructions and assumptions about the utility of developing transgenic nonhuman animals for scientific "innovations" designed to reduce risks to human health, constructions and assumptions that are used to justify the continued—and indeed augmented—subjugation of nonhuman animals.

By applying a CDA approach to extracts from Sasaki et al.'s (2009) article, what I aim to do is explore how unequal power relations are fundamental to the claims of "progress." Of course, I do not claim impartiality in my discussion given that, in common with CDA used in relation to issues associated with, for example, class, gender, "race," and sexual orientation, my analysis begins with clear interests (Wooffitt, 2005, p. 138). To quote Norman Fairclough and Ruth Wodak (1997), "what is distinctive about CDA is both that it intervenes on the side of dominated and oppressed groups and against dominating groups, and that it openly declares the emancipator interests that motivate it" (p. 259). My interests here lie in trying to bring the taken-for-granted to the fore and, in doing so, to challenge human oppression of nonhuman animals.

In order to examine the discourses used by Sasaki et al. (2009), I follow broadly Teun van Dijk's (1993) analytical approach. I center attention on various properties of the context in which the article is published (such as access to journal publication and setting), and then I move on to examine the properties of the article (such as meanings and style). Of course, there are many possible properties of the text and possible contexts of a published article. I focus on some of those that most clearly exhibit the discursive properties of the exploitation of nonhuman animals in biomedical research. However, as William Lynn (2010) makes clear, there are no perfect or indisputable analyses of discourse (p. 80), and all readings are partial. Consequently, my purpose, to refer to Lynn (2010) again, is to "reveal the discursive dynamic that constitutes, at least in part, our individual and collective stance" (p. 77) toward the use of nonhuman animals in biomedical experiments. In order to do this, I begin by summarizing Sasaki et al.'s (2009) claims.

Sasaki et al. (2009) declare that their work advances previous research that has used genetically modified nonhuman animals for biomedical purposes. They claim two innovations. First, whereas previous developments in transgenic nonhuman animals have centered on mammals such as mice, Sasaki et al. used marmosets, who, as primates, are considered particularly beneficial in biomedical research because of their "close genetic relations with humans" (p. 523). Second, the transgene used in this research (in the form of a green fluorescent protein) was passed from parents to young, which points to the potential for transgenic marmosets to pass on, for example, a human cancer gene, by means of natural reproduction (Sasaki et al., 2009, p. 526). This second innovation is declared to be particularly beneficial because it signals the possible establishment of colonies of marmosets born with the potential to develop a range of human diseases. Hence, the authors make the plausible claim that their experiments point the way to advances in biomedical research (Sasaki et al., 2009, p. 523). It is not possible for me to assess the veracity of this claim; indeed, that is not my purpose here. Rather, I aim to explore assumptions about the justifications for such experiments (whether human benefits are possible or not), justifications that are latent in the discourses used in the article and the setting in which it is published.

ACCESS AND SETTING—PUBLICATION AND THE ACKNOWLEDGMENT OF "PROGRESS"

Work chosen for publication in science (and other academic) journals is chosen because it conforms to that which scientists and journal editors feel is important to publicize (Birke and Smith, 1995). Sasaki et al.'s article was published in the distinguished science journal *Nature*. This is a clear indication that Sasaki and her colleagues are recognized as scientists whose work *can* be included in such a journal. Publication in *Nature* requires that articles "report original scientific research," "be of outstanding scientific importance," and "reach a conclusion of interest to an interdisciplinary readership" (Nature, 2010). Competition for publication is fierce, given that only around 10% of the 170 papers received each week are published (Nature, 2010). In 2009, the year of publication of Sasaki et al.'s article, of the 11,769 submissions of original research submitted to *Nature*, 803 were published, representing 6.8% of those submitted (Nature, 2010).

This academic formal setting[5] adorns Sasaki et al.'s article with authority, importance, and acknowledgement of scientific progress and, in the process, the claimed weight of their research is recognized and underscored. The power of this academic setting is enhanced by the news media coverage that followed publication in *Nature* (e.g., see Sample, 2009). Although the research was newsworthy for a range of reasons (among them the strong opposition that such research engenders in public arenas), such news coverage transfers "expert" recognition of the scientific import of the study to a more broad-based public recognition. This gives Sasaki et al.'s research a scientific credibility and identification with progress that spans well beyond the audience of *Nature*.

PROGRESS IN SCIENCE: THE ROLE OF "BREAKTHROUGH"

Sasaki et al.'s (2009) research conforms to a historical tradition in which the use of nonhuman animals provides the experimental method with an identity established in "science" rather than in the arts (Rupke, 1987). Being published in *Nature* demonstrates that nonhuman animal experiments are permissible avenues through which scientific progress *can* be achieved. Indeed, as Nicolaas Rupke (1987) indicates, the very use of nonhuman animals in experiments provides (biomedical) research with a scientific identity. In this way nonhuman animals are constructed as necessary to biomedical research and thus as necessary for medical advances (Birke, 2003; Birke, Arluke, and Michael, 2007). The idea of progress is central to the claims made by Sasaki et al. throughout their article. For example, they claim, "To our knowledge, this is the first report of transgenic non-human primates showing not only the transgene expression in somatic tissues, but also germline transmission of the transgene with the full, normal development of the embryo" (Sasaki et al., 2009, pp. 525–526).

The "germline transmission" refers to the possibility that a faulty foreign gene could be passed on via natural reproduction, through the sperm or egg (Ingham, 2009); thus, the manipulation of these transgenic nonhuman animals so that they can give birth to additional transgenic marmosets is one element of Sasaki et al.'s claim to breakthrough. Indeed, other scientists in the same issue of *Nature* describe the birth of transgenic marmosets as "undoubtedly a milestone" (Schatten and Mitalipov, 2009, p. 515). This "milestone" is purported to be especially significant because Sasaki et al.'s experiments center on the development of transgenic nonhuman *primates.* Although experiments using nonhuman primates are often most controversial because nonhuman primates are regarded as "species with highly developed social skills and behavioural manners that are to some extent similar to those of human behaviour" (Commission of the European Communities, 2008, p. 21), it is their closeness to humans that, Sasaki et al. claim, makes marmosets especially useful. This augments their declaration of progress. Thus they state, "The successful creation of transgenic marmosets provides a new animal model for human disease that has the great advantage of a close genetic relationship with humans" (Sasaki et al., 2009, p. 523).

This claim to progress is endorsed by Richard Ingham (2009) in his declaration that "medical researchers have hankered for an animal model that is closer to the human anatomy than rodents" because, he continues, disorders such as Alzheimer's and Parkinson's disease are too complex to be reproduced in transgenic mice and rats, who are "the mainstay of pre-clinical lab work." So the ethical concern that problematizes experiments using nonhuman primates because of their closeness to humans is overcome by an instrumental commitment to progress that stresses their proximity to humans, thus making their use highly beneficial to humans. Certainly, Sasaki et al. were not the first to develop transgenic nonhuman primates; the first was a transgenic rhesus macaque, who was developed in 2001 (Chan, Chong, Martinovich, Simerly, & Schatten, 2001). What signals a breakthrough in Sasaki et al.'s view is the possibility of "germline transmission" in nonhuman primates who have an instrumentally favorable reproductive rate, given that marmosets have "a relatively short gestation period (about 144 days) [and] reach sexual maturity at 12–18 months, and females have 40–50 offspring in their life" (Sasaki et al., 2009, p. 523). So, like rats and mice, whose high reproductive rates make them nonhuman animals of choice for use in many experiments (Birke, 2003, p. 210), transgenic marmosets are relatively quick and prolific breeders and thus can supply an anticipated high demand. Consequently, standardization and supply of transgenic marmosets could be perpetuated because, as Sasaki et al. (2009) put it, "it should be possible to establish transgenic non-human primate colonies" (p. 526). The potential utility of the marmosets is simultaneous with, and indeed is grounded in, their commodification; this comes as no surprise because for hundreds of years nonhuman animals have been treated as resources for human progress (Franklin, 1999).[6] Thus, the transgenic marmosets, like the cloned sheep Dolly, embody, to use Sarah Franklin's (2007) words, a kind of "genetic capital" and become a "commodity species." So "progress" in this sense is associated not with advancements in how humans treat nonhuman animals but with an expansion of how we can use them.

PROGRESS AND SCIENTIFIC FACTS

To explore further the discourses used in the article, I move on to the "interpretive repertoires" used by Sasaki et al. to present their case. Because interpretive repertoires are "recurrently used systems of terms used for characterizing and evaluating actions, events and other phenomena" (Potter and Wetherell, 1987, p. 149), such an analysis points to distinctive figures of speech, vocabulary, expressions, and metaphors (Wooffitt, 2005, p. 35). A common characteristic in scientific research articles is the use of discourses that allude to unattributed scientific activities that accentuate the sense of factual scientific detachment (Wooffitt, 2005, p. 36). Thus, in the opening sentence of the abstract, Sasaki et al. (2009) claim that "the common marmoset (*Callithrix jacchus*) is increasingly attractive for use as a non-human primate animal model in biomedical research" (p. 523). The language "is increasingly attractive for use" portrays the value of using marmosets in biomedical research as somehow objectively true and not as an outcome of decisions made by these scientists (decisions that are, of course, made within discourses, politics, and economies that construct and constrain possible action by the scientists). No reference is made to the origins of this idea, and there is no querying of its veracity or its objectivity. The seemingly objective and scholarly character of the research is stressed further with the use of the Latin binomial *Callithrix jacchus*, which constructs these nonhuman animals as being in a "natural" rather than "constructed" ontological category (see Wooffitt, 2005) but at the same time, to use Michael Lynch's (1988) terms, transforms the "naturalistic animal" with whom we are familiar into an "analytic animal" for use as data. The construction of transgenic nonhuman marmosets as not only analytical nonhuman animals but *useful* analytic nonhuman animals is reinforced by Sasaki et al.'s (2009) declaration that "the use of transgenic mice has contributed to biomedical science," but the development of genetically modified nonhuman primates "would accelerate the advance of biomedical research" (p. 523). As we have seen, there is some scientific opposition to this notion of biomedical advancement (e.g., see Dr Hadwen Trust, 2006; Greek and Greek, 2004; Knight, 2008). For example, Greek and Greek (2004) argue that "transgenic animals . . . have failed to shed light on human diseases. Why? Because changing one or two genes out of 30,000 will not make a human out of a mouse" (p. 44). There is no reference to such misgivings in Sasaki et al.'s article. In this way the reader is presented with the scientific "fact" of the value of using transgenic nonhuman animals in biomedical experiments, a value that bears the possibility of being enhanced by the research reported in the article.

SCIENTIFIC PROGRESS AS IMPARTIAL

Scientific identity is reinforced through the use of "empiricist repertoires," which, Robin Wooffitt (2005) explains, champion the notion "that the scientist is impartial to the results of scientific work" and that a scientist's "feelings, attitude, personality, and so on, are irrelevant to the outcome of research" (pp. 35–36). Thus, the use of nonhuman animals is part of a scientific practice that lays claim to the generation of value-free "facts" obtained by the scientist, who is depicted as a "disinterested human observer" (Adams, 1995, p. 138). Any feelings that the scientists might have about experimenting on nonhuman animals are not reported; Sasaki and her colleagues are portrayed as free of feeling. Such freedom from feeling is equated with the roles of the scientists and technicians who participate in such research because "scientific objectivity necessitates the rejection of feelings in favor of intellect" (Halpin, 1989, p. 285). Of course, scientists do have feelings, but genre conventions (to use one example) usually prevent those feelings from being discussed in published scientific reports (Birke and Smith, 1995).[7] This distancing promotes scientists as humans who are outside of the realm of the everyday.

Laypeople are not permitted to treat nonhuman animals in the ways that biomedical scientists do. Indeed, if they did, they could be liable to criminal prosecution (see Beirne, 1999). So, as Steve Woolgar maintains, the empiricist repertoire has the function of depicting the "out-there-ness" of scientific phenomena (qtd. in Wooffitt, 2005, p. 36). This encourages the reader to regard the scientific declarations made as expressions of objective characteristics that are independent of the wants, needs, and motivations both of the scientists who have conducted the research (Wooffitt, 2005, p. 36) and of the world in which they are conducted.

Scientific endeavor has many motivations. Self-promotion and ultimately recognition in an expert field are prominent motivators, and the value of scientific research is often found in claims about progress (Augoustinos, Russin, and LeCouteur, 2009). As demonstrated previously, Sasaki et al. are enthusiastic in their claim of breakthrough, and we might see peer recognition as an additional motivator, supplementary to their wish to promote human health benefits. More fundamentally, scientists are also humans, and their motivations are inextricably linked to their being human. Humans understandably want to reduce or eliminate human health risks, and as Garner (2005) comments, advocates of nonhuman animal experiments claim that "using animals in scientific procedures does, in a way that no alternative could, contribute to the longevity of human life" (p. 131). So humans who advocate experiments on nonhuman animals have a vested interest in biomedical experiments, whether they are scientists or not. Consequently, "scientific objectivity" is actually grounded in a set of values and priority systems (Midgley, 2004), and in biomedical research (Sasaki et al.'s included), human values ensure that it is the human who is prioritized (Peggs, 2011). As a result, disinterested scientific experts are out in the open as humans who, like other humans, could gain from any health benefits that their scientific research might provide. This brings me back to my own partiality. Scientists (Sasaki et al. among them) are partial, just as I am. For scientists who use nonhuman animals in experiments, the fundamental subjective partiality associated with human gain is ignored and indeed seems not to be seen as partiality at all. Because this partiality is so ubiquitous, embedded, and taken for granted in human life, this partiality is, paradoxically, invisible. However, once the partiality is visible, it is hard to view claims such as "the development of non-human primate models that mimic various human systems would accelerate the advance of biomedical research" (Sasaki et al., 2009, p. 523) as impartial observations.

The partial and instrumental needs of humans in biomedical research that uses nonhuman animal experiments are often endorsed rather than challenged by the ethical guidelines. Sasaki et al. (2009) state that "all animal experiments were approved by the institutional animal care and use committee, and were performed in accordance with Central Institution for Experimental Animal (CIEA) guidelines" (p. 527). As Lynda Birke and Jane Smith (1995) observe, this "line of defence" (p. 34) against possible criticism is often included, though details are not usually given. Sasaki et al. do not refer to the details of the ethical issues or of the guidelines, but the CEIA guidelines seem to focus on the "reproducibility of animal experiments" and the "quality standards of laboratory animals" (Nomura, 2008). This focus is based on the conviction that bad conditions for nonhuman animals hamper scientific results; the "mutual figure" of "happy" nonhuman animals and "good science" is a recurrent theme in the guidelines of ethics committees and in scientific research publications (Holmberg, 2008).

Thus, the ethics are human-centered and partial; we have seen that some (e.g., Williams, 2006) would suggest that this is appropriate partiality. If we accept this "conventional assumption that we are, simply because we are human, justified in overriding the interests of nonhuman animals when they conflict with our own" (Singer, 2002, p. 3), then it seems that we could unequivocally accept the claims to progress made by Sasaki et al. Of course, a human (whether a scientist or not) would not generally want to endure what nonhuman animals endure in biomedical experiments, so alternatively, we might conclude that such research is speciesist (Singer, 2002, p. 3; for discussion of speciesism, see, e.g., Peggs, 2012) because such research allows the interests of the human species to override the interests of other species. Since the ethical guidelines support these oppressive arrangements, we might go on to conclude that the ethical guidelines themselves are morally wrong and that the instrumental claims to progress are human-centered and thus partial.

CONCLUSIONS: SCIENCE AND MORAL PROGRESS

I have argued that assertions of progressive developments in biomedical research in Sasaki et al.'s (2009) article are based on an instrumental conceptualization of progress that centers on the notion that human needs override those of nonhuman animals (in this case transgenic marmosets). I have used critical discourse analysis to explore some of the ways in which biomedical progress is assumed, claimed, and acknowledged. Claims to progress are important in scientific research, and publication in a respected scientific journal highlights the acceptability and acceptance of such research. This constitutes acceptance of the methodological practices of such biomedical research (that is, it indicates that experiments using nonhuman animals are permissible—indeed some would say obligatory—in biomedical science) along with accord with the claimed import of such research. Any reference to divergent views (e.g., to scientists who argue that it is ethically wrong and/or ineffective to use nonhuman animals in biomedical experiments for human gain) is not included. However, on a practical level, the factual basis of the utility of biomedical experiments using "established" transgenic nonhuman animals (usually mice) is contentious; the use of this assumption as a springboard to a claim to "progress" based on the further use of other transgenic nonhuman animals is, in consequence, problematic. Nevertheless, the utility of nonhuman animal biomedical experimentation is presented as a scientific "fact."

But to focus solely on the practical development that this research might or might not embody is problematic for my argument, given that such a position would constitute agreement with the instrumental notion of progress that I am seeking to challenge. If the research could show, in principle, that transgenic marmosets could be utilized in the future for human benefit, would this be enough to signify progress? We would certainly accept that it would if we concurred with the views of those who have described the research results as a breakthrough in the quest for the ultimate goal of human health benefits. Indeed, in this regard it might be argued that an instrumental position on progress is indeed *the* moral position, because such research is based on a moral obligation to the human. As we have seen, this moral obligation to the human is the mainstay of biomedical ethics, and Williams (2006) assures us that humans can be expected to stress the interests of humans over nonhuman animals because humans are more important to *us*. But is this enough? This partiality to human interests is certainly ubiquitous and is often taken for granted inside and outside of the scientific laboratory (though these values are often not discussed, commented on, or challenged in arenas that presume "scientific objectivity"), but as Dale Jamieson (2008) comments, "explaining our attitudes is not the same as defending them" because this leaves the question of whether "our common humanity" is sufficient moral justification for dividing the world "along the lines of species membership."

My concern here about the development of transgenic nonhuman primates should not be taken to mean that I feel it is morally legitimate to use other nonhuman animals—for example, mice and rats (whether transgenic or not)—in biomedical, or any other, experiments. Moral consideration for all animals (human and nonhuman) confronts the hierarchical moral club that confers, at best, second-class "in" status to nonhuman animals (Rowlands, 2002, p. 27). Moral consideration for all animals indicates that biomedical experiments on nonhuman animals (whether they are mice or marmosets) are a manifestation of the instrumental moral scope of anthropocentrism that harms nonhuman animals. Moral advancement requires us, to use Lynn's (1998) words, "to live morally in concert with a diversity of human and nonhuman animals" (p. 295). Scientific developments coupled with moral advancement are, surely, the basis of biomedical progress; such progress is not in evidence in the further commodification of nonhuman animals that is apparent in the development of transgenic marmosets and in the use of nonhuman animals in biomedical experiments more generally. Progressive biomedical science is that which seeks to achieve human and nonhuman gains without experiments that use nonhuman animals.[8]

ACKNOWLEDGMENTS

I am grateful to the two anonymous referees for the comments on a previous version of this article.

Notes

1. My employment of the word "use" should not be taken to imply that nonhuman animals lack agency; rather, the word "use" is designed to reflect the power wielded by some humans over some nonhuman animals.

2. Not all biomedical research involves nonhuman animal experiments; see, for example, Dr Hadwen Trust (2006).

3. Of course, vast profits are made from nonhuman animal experiments and from the supply of nonhuman animals for use in experiments (Adams, 1995; Greek and Greek, 2002; Peggs, 2010; Rowlands, 2002).

4. Such research is not purely biomedical. For example, Bob Holmes (2010) refers to mice "creations" such as those who do not fear cats and those who can run twice as fast as a usual mouse (p. 33).

5. Nigel Gilbert and Michael Mulkay (1984) identify formal contexts (e.g., academic journals) and informal contexts (e.g., discussions with nonscientists) in which such discourses are used.

6. The transgenic mouse patented as "Oncomouse" has made vast profits for the licensee, Du Pont (Fuller, 2008). Michael Fuller (2008) discusses some of the ethical issues that are associated with such patents and profits, but his focus is on ethics as they relate to human health–related research.

7. However, scientists have published memoirs where they describe their feelings. Irene M. Pepperberg's (2009) book is one example.

8. For example, see research undertaken by Natalia Alexandrov (2009) and the Dr Hadwen Trust (2006).

References

Adams, C. (1995). *Neither man nor beast: Feminism and the defense of animals.* New York, NY: Continuum.

Alexandrov, N. (2009, June 6). Your virtual twin. *New Scientist, 202*(2711), 28.

Augoustinos, M., Russin, A., & LeCouteur, A. (2009). Representations of the stem-cell cloning fraud: From scientific breakthrough to managing the stake and interest of science. *Public Understanding of Science, 18*(6), 687–703.

Beirne, P. (1999). For a nonspeciesist criminology: Animal abuse as an object of study. *Criminology, 37*(1), 117–147.

Birke, L. (2003). Who—or what—is the laboratory rat (or mouse)? *Society and Animals, 11*(3), 207–224.

Birke, L., Arluke, A., & Michael, M. (2007). *The sacrifice: How scientific experiments transform animals and people.* West Lafayette, IN: Purdue University Press.

Birke, L., & Smith, J. (1995). Animals in experimental reports: The rhetoric of science. *Society and Animals, 3*(1), 23–42.

Brown, N., & Michael, M. (2001, Winter). Switching between science and culture in transpecies transplantation. *Science, Technology and Human Values, 1*, 3–22.

Chan, A. W., Chong, K. Y., Martinovich, C., Simerly, C., & Schatten, G. (2001). Transgenic monkeys produced by retroviral gene transfer into mature oocytes. *Science, 291*(5502), 309–312.

Commission of the European Communities. (2008). *Commission staff working paper accompanying the proposal for a directive of the European Parliament and of the Council on the protection of animals used for scientific experiments: Impact assessment* (SEC [2008].2410/2). Brussels, Belgium: Author.

Dr Hadwen Trust. (2006). About us. Retrieved from http://www.drhadwentrust.org /about-us/about-us

Elias, N. (2000). *The civilising process* (rev. ed.). Oxford, England: Blackwell.

Fairclough, N., & Wodak, R. (1997). Critical discourse analysis. In T. van Dijk (Ed.), *Discourse studies: A multidisciplinary introduction* (Vol. 2, pp. 258–284). London, England: SAGE.

Franklin, A. (1999). *Animals and modern culture.* London, England: SAGE.

Franklin, S. (2007). Dolly's body: Gender, genetics and the new genetic capital. In L. Kalof & A. Fitzgerald (Eds.), *The Animals Reader* (pp. 349–361). Oxford, England: Berg.

Frese, K. K., & Tuveson, D. A. (2007). Maximizing mouse cancer models. *National Review of Cancer, 7*(9), 645–658.

Fuller, M. (2008). Twenty years of transgenic animals: Are some inventions so important as to not be entitled to full patent protection? *World Patent Information, 30*(2), 139–143. Retrieved from http://www.sciencedirect.com/science

Garner, R. (2005). *Animal ethics.* Cambridge, England: Polity.

Gilbert, G. N., & Mulkay, M. J. (1984). *Opening Pandora's box: A sociological analysis of scientists' discourse.* Cambridge, England: Cambridge University Press.

GlaxoSmithKline. (2007). *The role of transgenic animals in biomedical research.* Retrieved from http://www.gsk.com/research/about/about_animals_roles.html

Gray, J. (2003). *Straw dogs: Thoughts on humans and other animals.* London, England: Granta.

Greek, C. R., & Greek, J. S. (2002). *Specious science: How genetics and evolution reveal why medical research on animals harms humans.* New York, NY: Continuum.

Greek, J. S., & Greek, C. Ray. (2004). *What will we do if we don't experiment on animals? Medical research for the 21st century.* Victoria, Canada: Trafford.

Halpin, Z. T. (1989). Scientific objectivity and the concept of "the other." *Women's Studies International Forum, 12*(3), 285–294.

Hanahan, D., Wagner, E. F., & Palmiter, R. D. (2007). The origins of oncomice: A history of the first transgenic mice genetically engineered to develop cancer. *Genes & Development, 21,* 2258–2270.

Haraway, D. (1997). *Modest_witness@second_millenium: FemaleMan_meets_Onco-Mouse.* London, England: Routledge.

Henry, B., & Pulcino, R. (2009). Individual difference and study-specific characteristics influencing attitudes about the use of animals in medical research. *Society and Animals, 17*(4), 305–324.

Holmberg, T. (2008). A feeling for the animal: On becoming an experimentalist. *Society and Animals, 16,* 316–335.

Holmes, B. (2010). The mouse that glowed. *New Scientist, 207*(2768), 32–35.

Home Office. (2011). *Statistics of scientific procedures on living animals: Great Britain 2010.* London, England: Stationery Office.

Ingham, R. (2009, May 27). World first: Japanese scientists create transgenic monkeys. *AFP.* Retrieved from http://www.google.com/hostednews/afp/article/ALeqM5Mnh_HguY6DOVeB_xDu4EWa4h23A

Jamieson, D. (2008). *Ethics and the environment: An introduction.* Cambridge, England: Cambridge University Press.

Knight, A. (2008). Systematic reviews of animal experiments demonstrate poor contribution toward human health care. *Reviews on Recent Clinical Trials, 3*(2), 89–96.

Leslie, E. (2007). *Walter Benjamin.* London, England: Reaktion Books.

Linzey, A., & Cohn, P. (2011). Terms of discourse. *Journal of Animal Ethics, 1*(1), vii–ix.

Lynch, M. E. (1988). Sacrifice and the transformation of the animal body into a scientific object: Laboratory culture and ritual practice in the neurosciences. *Social Studies of Science, 18*(2), 265–289.

Lynn, W. (2010). Discourse and wolves: Science, society and ethics. *Society and Animals, 18*(1), 75–82.

Lynn, W. S. (1998). Animals, ethics and geography. In J. Wolch and J. Emel (Eds.), *Animal geographies: Place, politics and identity in the nature-culture borderlands* (pp. 280–297). London, England: Verso.

Macnaghten, P. (2004). Animals in their nature: A case study of public attitudes to animals, genetic modification and "nature." *Sociology, 38*(3), 533–552.

Marks, J. (2011). On due recognition of animals used in research. *Journal of Animal Ethics, 1*(1), 6–8.

Midgley, M. (2004). *The myths we live by.* London, England: Routledge.

Nature. (2010). Getting published in *Nature*: The editorial process. Retrieved from http://www.nature.com/nature/authors/get_published/index.html#a1

Nomura, T. (2008). Goals of CIEA. Kawasaki, Japan: Central Institute for Experimental Animals.

Patent Watch. (2004). OncoMouse patent restricted in Europe again. *Nature Reviews Drug Discovery, 3,* 728. Retrieved from http://www.nature.com/nrd/journal/v3/n9/full/nrd/nrd1509.html

Peggs, K. (2009). A hostile world for nonhuman animals: Human identification and the oppression of nonhuman animals for human good. *Sociology, 43*(1), 85–102.

Peggs, K. (2010). Nonhuman animal experiments in the European community: Human values and rational choice. *Society and Animals, 18*(1), 1–20.

Peggs, K. (2011). Risk, human health and the oppression of nonhuman animals: The development of transgenic nonhuman animals for human use. *Humanimalia: A Journal of Human/Animal Interface Studies, 2*(2), 49–69.

Peggs, K. (2012). *Animals and sociology.* Basingstoke, England: Palgrave Macmillan.

Pepperberg, I. M. (2009). *Alex & me: How a scientist and a parrot discovered a hidden world of animal intelligence—and formed a deep bond in the process.* New York, NY: Harper.

Potter, J., & Wetherell, M. (1987). *Discourse and social psychology: Beyond attitudes and behaviour.* London, England: SAGE.

Rader, K. A. (2004). Making mice: Standardizing animals for American biomedical research, 1900–1955. Princeton, NJ: Princeton University Press.

Regan, T. (2004). *The case for animal rights.* Berkeley: University of California Press. (Original work published 1983)

Research Defence Society. (2007). *Medical advances and animal research. The contribution of animal science to the medical revolution: Some case histories.* London, England: Research Defence Society and Coalition for Medical Progress.

Rowlands, M. (2002). *Animals like us.* London, England: Verso.

Rupke, N. (1987). "Introduction." In N. Rupke (Ed.), *Vivisection in historical perspective* (pp. 1–3). Beckenham, England: Croom Helm.

Sample, I. (2009, May 27). Genetically modified monkeys give birth to designer babies. *Guardian.* Retrieved from http://www.guardian.co.uk/science/2009/may/27/genetically-modified-gm-monkeys-germline

Sasaki, E., Suemizu, H., Shimada, A., Hanazawa, K., Oiwa, R., Kamioka, M., . . . Nomura, T. (2009, May 28). Generation of transgenic non-human primates with germline transmission. *Nature, 459,* 523–527.

Schatten, G., & Mitalipov, S. (2009, May 28). Developmental biology: Transgenic primate offspring. *Nature, 459,* 515–516.

Singer, P. (2002). *Unsanctifying human life* (H. Kuhse, Ed.). Oxford, England: Blackwell.

Tester, K. (1991). *Animals in society: The humanity of animal rights.* London, England: Routledge.

Thacker, E. (2006, November). Cryptobiologies. *Artnodes, 6.* Retrieved from http://www.uoc.edu/artnodes/6/dt/eng/thacker.pdf

van Dijk, T. A. (1993). Principles of critical discourse analysis. *Discourse and Society, 4*(2), 249–283.

Welchman, J. (2003). Xenografting, species loyalty, and human solidarity. *Journal of Social Philosophy, 4*(2), 244–255.

Williams, B. (2006). *Philosophy as a humanistic discipline.* Princeton, NJ: Princeton University Press.

Wolfe, C. (2010). *What is posthumanism?* Minneapolis: University of Minnesota Press.

Wooffitt, R. (2005). *Conversation analysis and discourse analysis: A comparative and critical introduction.* London, England: SAGE.

14 Raising the Bar in the Justification of Animal Research

ELISA GALGUT

Animal ethics committees (AECs) appeal to utilitarian principles in their justification of animal experiments. Although AECs do not grant rights to animals, they do accept that animals have moral standing and should not be unnecessarily harmed. Although many appeal to utilitarian arguments in the justification of animal experiments, I argue that AECs routinely fall short of the requirements needed for such justification in a variety of ways. I argue that taking the moral status of animals seriously—even if this falls short of granting rights to animals—should lead to a thorough revision or complete elimination of many of the current practices in animal experimentation.

KEY WORDS: animal research, animal research ethics, animal welfare, animal rights, 3Rs, animal ethics committee, institutional animal care and use committee

There appears to be something of an impasse in the current climate regarding animal experimentation: Animal researchers claim that experiments on animals are necessary for advancements in the treatment of human illness and disease, while opponents—especially those who believe that animals have intrinsic rights—argue that animal research is morally unjustifiable. In this article, I shall try to avoid the impasse by looking at the ethical justification given by animal researchers and animal ethics committees (AECs) themselves in defense of such experiments. Thus, for the sake of the argument, I shall concede to the researchers and AECs that although animals may have moral *status*—and this is something that AECs do not deny—this moral status falls short of ascribing rights to animals in the sense in which they are ascribed to humans. My aim in this article is to examine the justification for animal research within the current framework outlined by the research community—a framework that guides whether and, if so, how animal

Journal of Animal Ethics 5(1): 41–56

experimental protocols are to be approved by ethics committees—and to argue that, even within this framework, much, if not most, animal experimentation is still unjustified. If my arguments are cogent, they will provide a way of avoiding the existing impasse, which often makes dialogue between animal researchers and those opposed to such research impossible. I aim to show that, if AECs take their own avowed ethical and scientific commitments seriously, then much of the current experimentation on animals should not be taking place.

As noted previously, animal researchers and AECs do not claim that animals have no moral status. AECs acknowledge that animals are deserving of moral consideration and should not be unnecessarily harmed. Nevertheless, experiments on animals are routinely justified on the grounds that the harms inflicted on animals are necessary for advances in the medical sciences, which benefit human health. Indeed, unlike many other practices where animals are exploited for human ends (e.g., eating meat, hunting, entertainment, and testing on cosmetic products, to name a few), if the use of animals in research benefits to a significant degree the health and well-being of humans, this would not be trivial, whether or not one thinks using animals in research is morally defensible. (By this statement, I am not claiming that, since the killing of animals for trivial reasons (i.e., for taste or for sport) is tolerated in society, the use of animals for research purposes is thereby morally justifiable. This is clearly a poor argument.) Many research institutions that use animals state explicitly that research on animals requires ethical justification, evidenced by claims such as these: the University of Michigan (2010), in its policy statement on animal research on its website, claims that it "insists on humane and ethical treatment of any animals used in research, education, and testing"; the Australian National Health and Medical Research Council (NHMRC, 2014) "develops policy and guidelines to ensure that the highest ethical standards apply to NHMRC funded research involving the use of animals"; and the Medical Research Council (MRC) of South Africa (2004) states that "sentient, non-human animals have the capacity to experience a range of physical sensations and emotions and are therefore subjects of moral concern" (p. 2). These, and other, ethics committees adhere to the so-called "3 Rs" of research: Replace animals with nonanimal models if possible, reduce the numbers of animals used in experiments, and refine procedures so as to minimize pain and suffering. Animal researchers are also told to "assume that animals experience [pain and distress] in a manner similar to humans unless there is evidence to the contrary. Decisions regarding the animals' welfare must be based on this assumption" (*NHMRC*, 2004, section 1, p. 7).

If animals do have moral status, how do AECs justify research on animals? These committees appeal roughly to utilitarian considerations in judging experimental protocols. I say "roughly" because the argument for utilitarianism, although often explicitly expressed, is never in itself justified; moreover, the utilitarian principles guiding animal experiments are not usually particularly nuanced, and the arguments do not, for example, refer to any of the philosophical literature on utilitarianism or distinguish between different kinds of utilitarianism. Nevertheless, utilitarianism is the ethical theory that committees appeal to in the justification of animal research; AECs argue that experiments are justified in terms of their consequences, and these consequences are adjudicated in the light of potential benefits (to humans) versus harms done (to animals). This utilitarian calculation is appealed to explicitly in the MRC of South Africa (2004) handbook guidelines:

> The use of laboratory animals as research subjects in biomedical science must be justified by the assurance that the potential benefit to either humans, animals and/or the environment outweighs the potential harm to the animal subjects. Each proposed experiment must therefore be supported by a formal evaluation (an ethical analysis) of harm to animals / benefit to humans, animals or the environment, which will determine that more utility (good) than disutility (harm) will probably result from the proposed experiment—i.e., that the overall likely benefit will outweigh the potential harm to the animals. (p. 2)

The sentiment is also found in Australia's NHMRC handbook (2008):

> Investigators must weigh up whether the potential benefits of the scientific knowledge gained will outweigh harm to the animal. If animals are required for the research, the information in this section must be considered before submitting a proposal to the animal ethics committee (AEC). (p. 17, section 4.1)

Animal experiments are thus justified because the harms caused to the animals are outweighed by the purported good that is produced for humans.[1] I shall put to one side the issue of whether it is even coherent to discuss quantifying and comparing benefits and harms as well as assume—again, for the sake of argument—that such calculations can be carried out, even if imprecisely. I shall also refrain from saying too much about the concern that AECs that evaluate *human* protocols for research do not appeal to a straightforward utilitarian calculation, even though using human subjects in biomedical research makes much more sense from a scientific point of view. I mention this topic because it raises worrying concerns that the appeal to different ethical principles in the justification of research may indicate deeper differences regarding the ways in which animals and humans are regarded, especially with respect to the kinds of harms inflicted on them.[2]

In order to perform a utilitarian calculation, the following conditions must be met: (a) the interests of both parties must be given equal consideration, (b) the consequences must be measurable and predictive, (c) there should be agent neutrality, and (d) criteria that are not morally relevant must not sway the ethical outcome. I shall attempt to show that all of these conditions are routinely breached in the evaluation of animal research protocols.

I: ANIMAL INTERESTS UNDERVALUED

I shall argue that in the evaluation and implementation of research protocols, AEC members routinely undervalue the interests of animals. As my colleague David Benatar (2000) has pointed out, we live in a society where animals are routinely abused in order to satisfy the most trivial needs of humans. The meat, dairy, and poultry industries confine, mutilate, and slaughter billions of animals annually merely to satisfy the human palate; the U.S. Department of Agriculture (USDA) reported that, in the United States alone, 33 million cattle, 113.2 million pigs, 2.18 million sheep and lambs (USDA, 2013a), and more than 8.5 billion chickens were slaughtered for food in 2012 (USDA, 2013b). Given that such widespread exploitation and slaughter is either condoned or tolerated by most humans, it seems extremely unlikely that we are able to give animal interests the consideration that they deserve, since we willingly sacrifice the most important of animal interests for the least important of human needs. It thus seems unlikely that members of AECs who eat meat are able to give animals' interests due consideration. I would argue that this is true even of those members who are at pains to eat only free-range meat, since even in this case the most important interests of an animal (its life) are sacrificed for the sake of lesser human ones. A 2011 study showed that people unconsciously tend to ascribe diminished mental capacities to animals considered appropriate for human consumption and that "meat eaters are motivated to deny minds to animals used for food when they are reminded of the link between meat and suffering" (Bastian, Loughnan, Haslam, & Radke, 2011, p. 247). Researchers showed that this denial of minds to animals used as food is not the *reason* that people feel comfortable eating the meat from certain animals, but is rather the *consequence* of their meat-eating habits. Subjects in the experiment routinely *lowered* their rating of the cognitive and emotional capacities of animals when they were "reminded of the link between meat eating and suffering" (p. 253). This "mind-denial reduces negative emotions aroused by dissonance between our concern for animals and our meat-eating behaviour" (p. 253). In other words, denying mental states to animals considered as "meat animals" is a psychological mechanism designed to make people feel less bad about eating meat. If this is indeed the case, it seems likely that such defensive mechanisms would be transferred to animals used in experiments, such that meat-eating members of AECs would be similarly motivated to deny certain cognitive and emotional capacities to animals considered appropriate for research. Indeed, even AEC members who are vegetarian or vegan are likely to be desensitized to the suffering of animals given the widespread social tolerance of many forms of animal abuse and exploitation. Furthermore, if the phenomenon of mind denial is operative in meat eaters in order to assuage their consciences regarding eating meat, it is likely that those in the business of animal research are similarly motivated to lower the cognitive and emotional capacities of animals used for experiments as a way of psychologically distancing themselves from the animals' suffering.

The interests of animals are undervalued in other ways. For instance, a study by Schuppli and Fraser (2005) showed that, in evaluating harms, many AEC members "focus on harm caused by procedures to the exclusion of housing and husbandry," which are often seen as the responsibility of the animal technicians rather than the researchers. Inadequate housing conditions have significant physiological and psychological effects on animals, including rodents; in a 2006 review article by the ethologist Jonathan Balcombe, he suggested that "substantial changes in housing and husbandry conditions" from current standard practice are required in order to reduce these stresses—standard environmental enrichment to small cages "reduces but does not eliminate" (p. 217) these stressors. Indeed, not only do members of AECs often ignore housing and husbandry, but they rarely consider the stress on animals from routine practices such as daily handling. Balcombe, Barnard, and Sandusky (2004) showed that laboratory routines such as lifting an animal or cleaning its cage can be extremely stressful; they found that "physiological parameters correlated with stress" (p. 42) were associated even with these noninvasive procedures. They argued that, contrary to what might seem like common sense, animals do not readily habituate to these routine procedures. The implication of studies such as these is that AECs are most likely underrating the severity category of protocols by not considering the stress that daily routines inflict upon the animals.

Another way in which the interests of animals are undervalued is that AECs almost never talk about the *loss of pleasure* as a harm. Harms are discussed in terms of feelings of pain or distress that are brought about by the protocol, but depriving animals of pleasures that they might have had is not usually considered. This is so for a few reasons: first, it's only recently that animal pleasure has become a topic for scientific investigation, and second, we humans tend not to be aware of—or even perhaps relate to—the pleasures that animals experience. In his 2011 book on animal pleasure, *The Exultant Ark*, Jonathan Balcombe stated that "rats will enter a deadly cold room and navigate a maze to retrieve highly palatable food" but if they happen to find ordinary rat chow instead, "they quickly return to their cozy nests, where they stay for the remainder of the experiment" (p. 46). Now, if it's true that laboratory animals are deprived of experiencing many pleasures they would ordinarily enjoy, this would increase the harms inflicted on them, which ought to be factored into a utilitarian calculation. By way of analogy, we would not consider the living conditions of human experimental subjects as acceptable if those conditions satisfied only their most basic needs, such as the provision of food and shelter; the privation of basic pleasures—such as reading or even eating a wide range of food options—would very likely, especially over the long term, come to constitute a harm. And similarly, I argue, is the case for animal subjects.

Another way in which the harms suffered by animals used for experiments are undervalued is illustrated by the fact that researchers who violate experimental protocols are not usually seriously reprimanded; there is great reluctance on the part of AECs—on which animal researchers and technicians serve—to take experimenters to task. In an examination of the application of the Animal Welfare Act (AWA) in the regulation of animal experiments in the United States, John Pippin (2013) noted "numerous serious deficiencies" in its enforcement, including the failure by the relevant Animal Care Program, which is charged with oversight of animal experiments, "to aggressively pursue 'enforcement actions against violators of the AWA' despite recommendations from its facility inspectors" (p. 472). The Animal Care Program was also reluctant to "to use enforcement measures" and preferred to fine violators rather than institute other disciplinary proceedings, even when recommended by inspectors. The Animal Care Program typically discounted fines by as much as 75% of the recommended penalty, thereby "creating a climate in which 'violators consider the monetary stipulation as a normal cost of conducting business rather than a deterrent for violating the law'" (p. 473). The unwillingness to take appropriate punitive measures against those who violate experimental protocols involving animals both points to and creates a climate in which the harms done to animals are not taken seriously. In other countries, such as South Africa, AECs are decentralized: "Each institution's AEC operates according to its own policies" (Mohr, 2013, p. 49). There is no external oversight of research institutions that use experimental animals "and there is currently no systematic audit of institutional AECs in South Africa" (p. 50). Although this lack of external oversight is not in itself evidence for lack of enforcement of punitive measures against animal researchers, the lack of institutional accountability to the public at large is itself an issue for concern and adds to the argument that the interests of animals are neglected because they are undervalued.

And finally, surprisingly, death is almost never viewed as a harm in animal experiments! Although *how* an animal dies is always considered, the fact that an animal is killed at the end of an experiment is never taken into account with regard to whether or not the protocol should be approved. This is not only the case for rats and mice but for other animals as well, including dogs and nonhuman primates. It is true that some countries require great apes used in experiments to retire to sanctuaries, but this is not the case everywhere in the world. Even primates who have not been used for research, but who are merely "taking up space," are routinely killed. Now whether or not death is a harm is something that probably requires more discussion than the limits of this article permit; there are certainly cases where death may be less of a harm, such as when it ends the life of someone suffering from a painful terminal illness. Nevertheless—and certainly in the case of other humans—we *do* normally consider that, *ceteris paribus*, death is a harm, even if a person dies peacefully and does not suffer. Even if someone has little sense of his or her own future, such as a child or a cognitively impaired person, the death of that individual is considered a serious harm because that person will no longer be able to pursue his or her interests. Since we do widely acknowledge that causing the untimely death of a person is a great harm to that person, we should, comparably, rate the death of an animal as a harm to *that animal*, as it will now no longer be able to continue to strive for the satisfaction of his or her own desires. The fact that AECs ignore the very possibility that death could be a harm to an animal again raises serious doubts that the interests of experimental animals are given the appropriate weight.

It might be argued that killing an animal at the end of an experiment is better than allowing the animal to languish in misery for the rest of his or her life in a sterile laboratory setting. However, this argument sets up a false dilemma, as it takes the onus off research institutions to care sufficiently for animals that will no longer be used in experiments. If death is indeed a harm, then research institutions are morally obliged to explore ways in which animals used in non-lethal experiments, or "surplus" animals, could be retired and provided with the necessary housing, food, and environmental enrichment necessary for their well-being. That such retirement is almost never considered—except, as noted above, in the case of the great apes—points to a consistent undervaluing of the harms done to animals.

II: HUMAN INTERESTS OVERVALUED

Not only are the interests of animals routinely undervalued by AECs, but the interests of humans are routinely overvalued. Given the harms inflicted on animals, one would expect that the benefits of animal experimentation would alleviate painful, life-threatening, or debilitating conditions or develop cures for fatal diseases. But this is not always the case: Many experiments on animals aim to alleviate discomforting but not life-threatening conditions, such as developing better sleeping pills or alleviating skin conditions. Mimi Brody (1989) reported that the "assistant dean at Tufts School of Veterinary Medicine estimates that toxicity testing of products and development of new drugs together constitute approximately one-half of the total laboratory animal use. . . . Many of these commercial uses are for production of nonessential goods" (p. 425). Animals are used for research in sports medicine (Krueger, Wenke, Masini, and Stinner, 2012) or for elective cosmetic surgery, such as Botox. If animals are routinely used in experiments for nonessential or cosmetic purposes, then the benefits of such experiments are overvalued; if this is the case, then the justification for harming animals for the sake of these benefits is considerably weakened.

Note also that much animal experimentation is involved in *basic* research, which, by definition, is not necessarily intended to lead to applications for humans. The Nuffield Council on Bioethics in the United Kingdom, which is one of the few countries that has national statistics on animals used in experiments, estimated that, of the 2.72 million animals used for research in the United Kingdom in 2003, about one third—more than 900,000 animals—were used in basic research. It is difficult to see how basic research can be justified using the parameters set by the AECs themselves. In order to justify animal experiments on utilitarian grounds, the consequences of these experiments must be measurable and predictive. It's impossible to do a utilitarian calculation if the benefits or outcomes cannot be predicted with a high rate of certainty.[3] This becomes especially important when the harms involved are severe; we might be willing to tolerate unclear outcomes if the costs involved are minimal, but certainly not so for great harms. But if the outcomes of basic research are, by definition, largely unknown, it seems impossible to justify by utilitarian calculation any such research that causes more than negligible harm. A review article by Pound, Ebrahim, Sandercock, Bracken, and Roberts (2004) of the implications of experiments on animals for human health concluded that "Few methods exist for evaluating the clinical relevance or importance of basic animal research, and so its clinical (as distinct from scientific) contribution remains uncertain" (p. 514). This is confirmed by an article by Contopoulos-Ioannidis, Ntzani, and Ioannidis (2003), who "identified 101 articles, published between 1979 and 1983 in six major basic science journals, which clearly stated that the technology studied had novel therapeutic or preventive promises" (p. 477). They concluded that "even the most promising findings of basic research take a long time to translate into clinical experimentation, and adoption in clinical practice is rare" (p. 477). In a follow-up article, Crowley (2003) stated that the authors discovered that

> of the 25,000 articles searched, about 500 (2%) contained some potential claim to future applicability in humans, about 100 (0.4%) resulted in a clinical trial . . . only 1 (0.004%) led to the development of a clinically useful class of drugs . . . in the 30 years following their publication of the basic science finding. (p. 503)

Crowley notes that, although this study did miss some important outcomes of basic research, "even if the authors were to underestimate the frequency of successful translation into clinical use by 10-fold, their findings strongly suggest that, as most observers suspected, the transfer rate of basic research into clinical use is very low" (p. 503). Even if the one article from the 25,000 searched led to the development of clinically useful drugs for serious or life-threatening human illnesses, this would still not justify the use of animals in basic research unless one could predict in advance with a high degree of certainty which of the protocols under review are likely to be successful. If this is impossible, then it raises serious concerns regarding whether AECs can justifiably approve protocols that involve basic research on animals given that the harms to the animals are certain, whereas the benefits of the experiments are statistically extremely low. Animal researchers might object that science is incremental and argue that although basic research on animals may not lead directly to specifiable outcomes, it is necessary in the overall development of cures and treatments. Now whether or not this is the case (see the next section in this article), it cannot justify the use of animals in basic research according to a utilitarian calculation, where outcomes must be predictive in order to perform a cost-benefit analysis. Redefining the notion of a "benefit" in vague and imprecise ways renders the term meaningless. If AECs are indeed justifying research according to a utilitarian calculation, then basic research should be justified rarely, except when the harms to the animals are nonexistent or minimal or when there is a legitimate expectation that the outcomes of the particular experiments are very likely to lead to the alleviation of much suffering. Given that close to a million animals in the United Kingdom alone are used in basic research, upping the justificatory requirement to be in line with what AECs say they require should cut the numbers of animals used in experiments by a significant amount.

III: IS ANIMAL RESEARCH PREDICTIVE?

There is another concern regarding the predictive nature of animal research. Although I don't have the expertise to develop this issue more fully, it is important to mention. There is a growing body of literature that argues that animal models are simply not predictive for humans.[4] One of the people at the forefront of this argument is Ray Greek, a medical doctor who has published extensively on the topic of animal research and its predictive value for humans. Greek argues that animal models—even nonhuman primate models—are simply not predictive for humans and experiments on animals have led to many human deaths. In a 2009 paper, cowritten with Niall Shanks and Jean Greek, they argued that drug testing on animals has as much predictive value as tossing a coin. Citing results from toxicity studies performed in the 1990s, they argued that data revealed that "only 4 of 24 toxicities were found in animal data first" and "in only 6 of 114 cases did clinical toxicities have animal correlates" (p. 6). In a paper on stroke research, Stephen Curry (2003) reported that "fourteen potential neuroprotective agents expected to aid in recovery from stroke, after studies in animal models had predicted that they would be successful" (p. 69) failed to achieve similar success in clinical trials. Wall and Shani (2008) examined the predictive value of animal model studies in preclinical trials and concluded that, "on average, the extrapolated results from studies using tens of millions of animals fail to accurately predict human responses" (p. 2). Tracy Hampton (2006) reported that only 8% of drugs entering phase 1 clinical trials will actually reach the market. If animal models are not predictive, this impacts the justification of animal protocols not only in regard to the harms caused to the animals but also on the possible harms caused to human subjects. In a 2011 letter to *The Lancet*, Kathy Archibald, Robert Coleman and Christopher Foster "on behalf of 19 other signatories" claimed that "adverse drug reactions have reached epidemic proportions and are increasing at twice the rate of prescriptions. The European Commission estimated in 2008 that adverse reactions kill 197,000 EU citizens annually, at a cost of €79 billion" (p. 1915).

The issue of the scientific relevance of animal models to human medicine is a complex one, a full examination of which would take me beyond my area of expertise and the scope of this article. However, if this evidence against the relevance of animal models is cogent, it raises serious doubts concerning the justification of animal experimentation. The scientific evidence against the relevance of animal models is crucial in the evaluation and justification of animal experiments, and the nonpredictive nature of animal models would render almost all human-related animal research irrelevant. Even if it turns out that some animal experiments have, in fact, led to the development of new drugs, this does not obviate the concerns about the nonpredictive nature of animal research for humans. This is so for several reasons: First, cherry-picked examples are not sufficient to show that most animal experiments are necessary for research; this latter claim requires systematic justification. Second, defenders of animal research would also have to show that the animal experiments in question were *necessary* for the development of the drugs and that no nonanimal research could have been conducted instead. Third, the success of the animal model cannot be demonstrated retrospectively, as this would undermine the argument for the predictive nature of animal experimentation. Finally, researchers and AECs would also have to show that no harms were inflicted on humans as a result of failed animal research (see Greek, 2013); any harms suffered by patients would need to be factored into a utilitarian justification of such research. Now whether or not an AEC member agrees with these claims, the person ought to, at the very least (if he or she takes the ethics committee duties seriously), engage with the literature. If it does turn out that animal models are less predictive for humans than is currently supposed, this must impact the justification of animal research. But the scientific literature critical of animal research is generally not compulsory reading for AEC members. If this is so, there is reason to suspect that AECs are derelict in their duties for neglecting to examine more closely the predictive nature of animal models for human health.

Indeed, not only is the scientific literature on the predictive value of animal experiments not compulsory reading for AECs, neither is the literature on *alternatives* to animal research. Although it is stated on most research protocols that animals may not be used if such alternatives are available, the AECs generally do not pressure researchers to look for such alternatives (see Brody, 1989). In their survey of Canadian animal researchers, Fenwick, Danielson, and Griffin (2011) discovered that "researchers currently do not view the goal of replacement as achievable," and that they "prefer to use enough animals to ensure quality data is obtained." On the role of AECs, John Pippin (2013) noted that such committees often failed "to ensure the use of nonanimal methodologies where such research avenues exist" (p. 473). This suggests that the "replacement" leg of the so-called "3 Rs," which are the cornerstone of contemporary animal research, is not pursued with the diligence required of both researchers and AECs.

It seems that once it's accepted that animal experimentation is by and large acceptable, there is great resistance from within both the research community and AECs themselves to find other models. One of the implicit justifications of animal research is that if it seemed to work in the past, why change things? The appeal to tradition is not only a psychological motivation to continue to justify future animal experiments, but it becomes a scientific one as well. Animal models that have become the "standard" model for the studying of certain diseases become the norm against which other research is compared, whether or not that particular model is shown to have predictive value for humans. A recent article in *The New York Times* reported that Ronald W. Davis, professor of biochemistry and genetics at Stanford University, studied the "white blood cells from hundreds of patients with severe burns, trauma or sepsis to see what genes were being used by white blood cells when responding to these danger signals" (quoted in Kolata, 2013). Despite interesting and innovative findings, several journals turned down the paper on the grounds that "the researchers had not shown the same gene response had happened in mice." In this case, data collected from humans was rejected on the grounds that it was not consistent with accepted animal models!

IV: WORRIES ABOUT UTILITARIAN JUSTIFICATION

So far, I have attempted to show that, even if one accepts the current paradigm for animal research, much of the current experimentation fails to conform to the accepted requirements necessary for its justification. This is extremely problematic, and it requires that AECs reevaluate the ways in which they approve protocols. However, the difficulties do not end here: In the remainder of this article, I will examine the use of utilitarianism for the justification of nonhuman primate research, where I will argue that there are worrying moral considerations in addition to the concerns raised already. For the sake of argument, I have by and large accepted the divide between humans and nonhuman animals for the purposes of research, and I have avoided pointing out the inherent contradiction of using utilitarianism to justify research on *nonhuman animals only*, which flouts a central tenet of utilitarianism, namely that of equal consideration of equal interests. Animal researchers may argue that, although it may seem as though speciesist prejudices are inappropriately being used to justify experiments on animals, this is not the case because species is used only as a *marker* for other differences that *are* morally relevant, such as cognitive capacity, self-awareness, and so on. It's morally justifiable to use a mouse for an experiment but not a human, animal researchers argue, because the interests of mice, given their limited capacities, count less than the interests of humans. However, species per se seems to be a "sloppy proxy"[5] for morally relevant characteristics, given that there are many humans who lack the cognitive capacities and self-awareness typical of ordinary adult humans.

However, the current paradigm strains to breaking point when it attempts to justify the use of nonhuman primates in experiments. Here, species is not being used as a *marker* for morally relevant capacities but is used to play a justificatory role in and of itself. Nonhuman primates have been used for research in HIV/AIDS, heart disease, stroke, and head injuries. Because of many shared cognitive capacities with humans, they have also been used in psychiatric and neurological research to study the effects of drugs such as methamphetamine or cocaine and diseases such as Parkinson's and Alzheimer's. Many of these experiments are invasive, causing the nonhuman primate subjects pain and distress, and none of them would be justifiable if performed on human subjects, even if those subjects were of the same cognitive capacities as the relevant nonhuman primate. We would, I take it, consider it morally reprehensible to use small children or people suffering from dementia for such experiments; their cognitive deficiencies, far from justifying their use in experiments, would on the contrary provide *additional reasons* for *not* doing such research—exploiting another person's inability to give consent is morally heinous. But why is it thought that a nonhuman primate's inability to give consent, or his or her alleged lack of cognitive capacities with respect to humans, provides us with *more* justification for such research?[6] It seems irrational to claim that an activity of type X when performed on subject A is so morally reprehensible that it induces widespread moral disgust but when performed on subject B it is morally justifiable—even when the sentience and cognitive capacities of A and B are considered relevantly similar. In allowing such research, AECs find themselves in the following paradoxical situation: They argue that nonhuman primates may be used for neurological or psychiatric diseases, even when such research is stressful or invasive, because nonhuman primates are *cognitively and psychologically* similar to humans. However, because nonhuman primates are of a different *species* from humans, such research is justifiable, even though it would not be similarly justifiable if performed on a human subject with comparable cognitive and psychological capacities. It seems here that species is indeed being used as a justification for research on nonhuman primates. This paradox raises serious concerns about the ways in which utilitarianism is being utilized as the justification for animal research, when the core assumption of AECs runs counter to the very basis of utilitarianism.

A possible reply by a proponent of nonhuman primate research might be the following: Although it may be true that some humans lack many of the capacities that most humans have, this is so in virtue of some *defect* or incapacity. To treat people with cognitive disabilities differently from the way we treat other humans is a disservice to the cognitively disabled; a comparable injustice is not committed with regard to nonhuman primates because they merely lack certain capacities, but they are not, thereby, incapacitated. This is expressed by Cohen (1986) in the following way: those "who are unable, because of some disability, to perform the full moral functions natural to human beings are certainly not for that reason ejected from the moral community. The issue is one of kind" (p. 866). This is a problematic response for several reasons. First, as McMahan (2005) pointed out, the argument seems appealing when it is used to "level up" some humans, such as those with diminished cognitive capacities, to confer upon them the same rights as those we confer upon normal human adults. But, as stated by McMahan, the argument is far less appealing when it is used to "level down." If most humans, except for one special person, were born with the stain of "original sin," we would consider it morally unacceptable for the saintly individual to suffer the same punishments as the rest of us sinners. McMahan wrote: "The nature-of-the-kind argument implies that, if human beings in general deserve to be sent to Hell, she does as well, for it is human nature to have original sin and therefore it is *her* nature to have original sin, though in fact she lacks it" (pp. 358–359). Since we would, I take it, not think that it is morally acceptable to treat a person badly in virtue of her belonging to a group for whom such bad treatment would be appropriate, the converse also must be true: if S and S° are two individuals who share the same cognitive capacities but belong to different groups—S is a human while S° is a nonhuman—it seems equally unacceptable to claim that harming S° but not S is morally justifiable because *other* individuals in S's group possess capacities that the members of the group S° do not.

Another problem, though, with the claim (to refer to the terminology presented previously) that S° may be used in experiments that we would consider morally unjustifiable if performed on S concerns the very question of group membership. Cohen (1986), in the quote above, claimed that there is a difference in *kind* between humans and nonhumans—the former group belongs to the moral community while the latter group does not. This begs the question: In virtue of what does an individual belong to the moral community? This must be so either in terms of some characteristics that the individual possesses, or it must be in terms of some "status-conferring intrinsic property possessed by all human beings but not by any other animals" (McMahan, 2005, p. 359), such as a soul. If membership in the moral community were in virtue of some feature or characteristic, then S and S° should be treated alike, since, *ex hypothesi*, they share the same properties. But it would clearly be irrational to argue that having a soul is what justifies the unequal treatment of S and S°. Moreover, why restrict membership along *species* lines? Why not extend the boundaries and argue that *all* primates share certain intrinsic characteristics that would make it ethically unacceptable to harm S° but not S? To use species membership as grounds for the justification of treating an individual differently is as morally problematic as using race or gender, unless it can be shown that species is somehow morally relevant. This becomes increasingly difficult to do in the case of nonhuman primates, and I argue that the use of nonhuman primates for research requires a radical reassessment. The bar needs to be raised significantly if the use of nonhuman primates in experiments is to be justified.

CONCLUSION

My aim in this article has been to investigate whether animal experimentation is justifiable according to the research community's own avowed criteria. I have argued that the bar for the justification of animal experimentation is too low and that many—if not most—animal experiments fail to meet AECs' own justificatory criteria. Thus, we may not need to resolve the impasse between animal rights and animal welfare in order to reduce substantially the number of animals who are used in experiments. Even within the current paradigm, we have the tools with which to critique seriously the current status quo, and, hopefully, to change it fundamentally from within. Since I have been speaking about utilitarianism, it seems fitting to end with a quote from John Stuart Mill (1863/2004):

> We (the utilitarians) are perfectly willing to stake the whole question on this one issue. Granted that any practice causes more pain to animals than it gives pleasure to man: is that practice moral or immoral. And if, exactly in

proportion as human beings raise their heads out of the slough of selfishness, they do not with one voice answer "immoral," let the principle of utility be forever condemned. (p. 253)

Acknowledgments

I would like to thank Professor David Benatar, Dr. Gregory Fried, Dr. John Oakley, Professor Anne Pope, and the discussants at a seminar held by the Department of Philosophy at the University of the Witwatersrand in Johannesburg for helpful comments on an earlier draft of this article. I would also like to thank the editor and the reviewers of this journal for additional comments and assistance.

Notes

1. It is true that some animal research is also justified on the basis of its benefit for other animals, particularly conspecifics. However, in this article, I shall devote my attention to animal experiments that are carried out for the alleged benefit of humans for two reasons: (a) most animal experiments are carried out for this purpose, and (b) different justificatory criteria may be applicable in the different cases.

2. On this point, it is interesting to note that many respected biomedical journals rarely devote journal space to animal ethics issues; for instance, "the *New England Journal of Medicine*, which regularly publishes papers about ethical issues in medicine, has published, since at least 1966, only three substantial articles about animal experimentation" (Benatar, 2000, p. 834). Of the three articles, two defended the practice.

3. By this I do not mean that research cannot be justified on utilitarian grounds unless the outcomes are certain; utilitarians can appeal to probabilities, but the probabilities must be measurable and predictive.

4. See LaFollette and Shanks (1996); Knight, Bailey, and Balcombe (2006); Hackam (2007); Knight (2007); Perel et al. (2007); Greek and Shanks (2009); Shanks, Greek, and Greek (2009); Akhtar, Pippin, and Sandusky (2009); Pippin (2013).

5. I'd like to thank David Benatar for this phrase.

6. For a fuller discussion, see Walker (2006).

References

Akhtar, A. Z, Pippin, J. J., & Sandusky, C. B. (2009). Animal studies in spinal cord injury: A systematic review of methylprednisolone. *Alternative to Laboratory Animals (ATLA)*, 37, 43–62.

Archibald, K., Coleman, R., & Foster, C. (2011). Open letter to UK Prime Minister David Cameron and Health Secretary Andrew Lansley on safety of medicines. *The Lancet, 377,* 1915.

Balcombe, J. P. (2006). Laboratory environments and rodents' behavioural needs: A review. *Laboratory Animals, 40,* 217–235.

Balcombe, J. P. (2011). *The exultant ark.* Berkeley, CA: University of California Press.

Balcombe, J. P., Barnard, N. D., & Sandusky, C. (2004). Laboratory routines cause animal stress. *Contemporary Topics, 43*(6), 42–52.

Bastian, B., Loughnan, S., Haslam, N., & Radke, H. R. M. (2011). Don't mind meat? The denial of mind to animals used for human consumption. *Personality and Social Psychology Bulletin, 38*(2), 247–256.

Benatar, D. (2000). Duty and the beast. *The Quarterly Journal of Medicine, 93,* 831–835.

Brody, M. (1989). Animal research: A call for legislative reform requiring ethical merit review. *Harvard Environmental Law Review, 13*(423), 423–484.

Cohen, C. (1986). The case for the use of animals in biomedical research. *New England Journal of Medicine, 315,* 865–870.

Contopoulos-Ioannidis D. G., Ntzani, E. E., & Ioannidis, J. P. A. (2003). Translation of highly promising basic science research into clinical applications. *American Journal of Medicine, 114,* 477–484.

Crowley, W. F., Jr. (2003). Translation of basic research into useful treatments: How often does it occur? *American Journal of Medicine, 114*(6), 503–505.

Curry, S. H. (2003). Why have so many drugs with stellar results in laboratory stroke models failed in clinical trials? A theory based on allometric relationships. *Annals of the New York Academy of Sciences, 993,* 69–74.

Fenwick, N., Danielson, P., & Griffin, G. (2011, August 17). Survey of Canadian animal-based researchers' views on the three Rs: Replacement, reduction and refinement. *PLOS One 6*(8). Retrieved from http://www.ncbi.nlm.nih.gov/pmc /articles/PMC3157340/

Greek, C. R., & Shanks, N. (2009). *Animal models in the light of evolution.* Boca Raton, FL: Brown Walker Press.

Greek, R. (2013). *0.004 percent.* Retrieved from http://www.opposingviews.com/i /society/animal-rights/0004-percent

Hackam, D. G. (2007). Translating animal research into clinical benefit. *British Medical Journal, 334*(7586), 163–164.

Hampton, T. (2006). Targeted cancer therapies lagging: Better trial design could boost success rate. *Journal of the American Medical Association, 296,* 1951–1952.

Knight, A. (2007). Systematic reviews of animal experiments demonstrate poor human utility. *Alternatives to Animal Testing and Experimentation (AATEX), 14,* 125–130.

Knight, A., Bailey, J., & Balcombe, J. (2006). Animal carcinogenicity studies: 1. Poor human predictivity. *Alternative to Laboratory Animals (ATLA), 34*(1), 19–27.

Kolata, G. (2013). Mice fall short as test subjects for humans' deadly ills. *The New York Times.* Retrieved from http://www.nytimes.com/2013/02/12/science/testing -of-some-deadly-diseases-on-mice-mislead-report-says.html?pagewanted=all& _r=0

Krueger, C. A., Wenke, J. C., Masini, B. D., & Stinner, D. J. (2012). Characteristics and impact of animal models used for sports medicine research. *Orthopedics*, 35(9), 1410–1415.

LaFollette, H., & Shanks, N. (1996). *Brute science: Dilemmas of animal experimentation*. London, England: Routledge.

McMahan, J. (2005). Our fellow creatures. *The Journal of Ethics*, 9, 354–380.

Medical Research Council of South Africa. 2004. *Guidelines on ethics in the use of animals in research* (Book 3). Retrieved from http://www.kznhealth.gov.za/research/ethics3.pdf

Mill, J. S. (2004). Whewell on moral philosophy. In J. S. Mill, J. Bentham, & A. Ryan (Eds.), *Utilitarianism and other essays* (pp. 228–270). London, England: Penguin Books. (Original work published in 1863)

Mohr, B. (2013). The current status of laboratory animal ethics in South Africa. *Alternative to Laboratory Animals (ATLA)*, 41, 48–51

National Health and Medical Research Council. (2004). *Australian code of practice for the care and use of animals for scientific purposes*. Retrieved from http://www.nhmrc.gov.au/_files_nhmrc/publications/attachments/ea16.pdf

National Health and Medical Research Council. (2008). *Guidelines to promote the wellbeing of animals used for scientific purposes: The assessment and alleviation of pain and distress in research animals*. Retrieved from http://www.nhmrc.gov.au/guidelines/publications/attachments/ea18.pdf

National Health and Medical Research Council. (2014). *Health ethics*. Retrieved from http://www.nhmrc.gov.au/health-ethics

Perel, P., Roberts, I., Sena, E., Wheble, P., Briscoe, C., Sandercock, P., . . . Khan, K. S. (2007). Comparison of treatment effects between animal experiments and clinical trials: Systematic review. *British Medical Journal* 334(197). Retrieved from http://www.bmj.com/highwire/filestream/399261/field_highwire_article_pdf/0/bmj.39048.407928.BE

Pippin, J. J. (2013). Animal research in medical sciences: Seeking a convergence of science, medicine and animal law. *South Texas Law Review*, 54(469), 469–511.

Pound, P., Ebrahim, S., Sandercock, P., Bracken, M. B., & Roberts, I. (2004). Where is the evidence that animal research benefits humans? *British Medical Journal*, 328(7438), 514–517.

Schuppli, C., & Fraser, D. (2005). The interpretation and application of the three Rs by animal ethics committee members. *Alternative to Laboratory Animals (ATLA)*, 33(5), 487–500.

Shanks, N., Greek, R., & Greek, J. (2009). Are animal models predictive for humans? Philosophy, Ethics, and Humanities in Medicine, 4(2). Retrieved from http://www.peh-med.com/content/4/1/2

United States Department of Agriculture. (2013a). *Livestock slaughter 2012 summary*. Retrieved from http://usda01.library.cornell.edu/usda/nass/LiveSlauSu/2010s/2012/LiveSlauSu-04-23-2012.pdf

United States Department of Agriculture. (2013b). *Poultry slaughter 2012 summary*. Retrieved from http://usda01.library.cornell.edu/usda/current/PoulSlauSu /PoulSlauSu-02-25-2013.pdf

University of Michigan. (2010). *Policy statement on animal research*. Retrieved from http://www.vpcomm.umich.edu/pa/key/animal.html

Walker, R. L. (2006). Human and animal subjects of research: The moral significance of respect versus welfare. *Theoretical Medicine and Bioethics, 27*, 305–331.

Wall, R. J., & Shani, M. (2008). Are animal models as good as we think? *Theriogenology, 69* (1), 2–9.

About the Editors and Contributors

JUDITH BENZ-SCHWARZBURG is a university assistant in the Department of Ethics at the Messerli Research Institute of the University of Veterinary Medicine, Vienna, the University of Vienna, and the Medical University of Vienna. Her doctoral dissertation was awarded the Doctorate Prize 2012 of the Faculty of Arts of the University of Tübingen, as well as the German Study Prize 2013. Titled *Verwandte im Geiste—Fremde im Recht*, it was published by Verlag Harald Fischer in 2012.

VANESSA CARLI BONES teaches at the Regional State University of Northwestern Rio Grande do Sul (Unijuí) in the areas of animal physiology and veterinary parasitology, and is linked to the Laboratory Animal Welfare of the Federal University of Paraná, as post-doutoranda. She graduated in veterinary medicine from the Federal University of Santa Maria in 2006, and she received her masters in 2008 and her PhD in 2014, both in veterinary science, from the Federal University of Paraná. She has experience in the fields of veterinary medicine, animal welfare, animal ethics, and alternatives to the use of laboratory animals.

GRACE CLEMENT is a professor of philosophy at Salisbury University in Maryland and a fellow of the Oxford Centre for Animal Ethics. She is author of *Care, Autonomy, and Justice: Feminism and the Ethic of Care* (Westview, 1996), as well as a number of articles on moral relations between humans and other animals. Her current research is primarily in ethics and focuses on questions of moral status, moral boundaries, and moral methods in animal ethics.

SIMON COGHLAN is a philosopher in the Faculty of Theology and Philosophy at the Australian Catholic University. He is also a veterinarian at a companion animal veterinary clinic in Melbourne. He writes on moral philosophy, animal ethics, professional ethics, and environmental philosophy.

PRISCILLA N. COHN is a professor emeritus from Penn State University and is presently an advisor to the Càtedra Ferrater Mora de Pensament Contemporani, University of Girona, and the associate director of the Oxford Centre for Animal Ethics. She is a coeditor of the Palgrave Macmillan Animal Ethics Series and an editor of the *Journal of Animal Ethics*. She has published over fifty chapters and scholarly articles. Included among her seven books are *Etica aplicada: Del aborto a violencia* (Alianza Editorial, first edition, 1981; enlarged edition, 1988; editions del Prado, 1994); *Contraception in Wildlife* (Edwin Mellen Press, 1996); and *Ethics and Wildlife* (Edwin Mellen, 1999).

MARK J. ESTREN is a psychologist, herpetologist, and reptile educator in Fort Myers, Florida. He holds doctorates in psychology and English from the University of Buffalo, and an MS in journalism from Columbia University. He is the author of six books, including *Statins: Miraculous or Misguided?* (Ronin, 2013) and *Healing Hormones: How to Turn On Natural Chemicals to Reduce Stress* (Ronin, 2013), and the editor of and/or contributor to numerous others.

ELISA GALGUT teaches in the Department of Philosophy at the University of Cape Town. She has a PhD in philosophy from Rutgers University and a masters in creative writing from the University of Cape Town. Her poetry has appeared in local literary journals and anthologies.

ELEONORA GULLONE is adjunct associate professor in the Centre for Developmental Psychiatry and Psychology at Monash University, Australia. Her research, writing, and political involvement focus on human–animal interactions, particularly the relationship between animal cruelty and human aggression and violence. She is the author of more than 100 publications, including *Animal Cruelty, Antisocial Behaviour and Aggression: More Than A Link* (Palgrave Macmillan, 2012).

MATTHEW C. HALTEMAN is assistant professor of philosophy at Calvin College in Grand Rapids, Michigan. He holds a PhD in philosophy from the University of Notre Dame, and has published in the fields of 20th century European philosophy and animal ethics. His work has appeared, among other places, in *Continental Philosophy Review*, *Notre Dame Philosophical Reviews*, and *The*

Philosophical Review. He is joint editor of the volume *Philosophy Comes to Dinner: Arguments on the Ethics of Eating* (Routledge, 2015).

ANDREW KNIGHT is professor of animal welfare and ethics, and director of the Centre for Animal Welfare, at the University of Winchester; a European and RCVS veterinary specialist in animal welfare science, ethics and law; an American veterinary specialist in animal welfare; and a senior fellow of the UK Higher Education Academy. His book *The Costs and Benefits of Animal Experiments* was published by Palgrave Macmillan in the Animal Ethics Series in 2011.

DREW LEDER is professor of philosophy at Loyola University, Maryland. In addition to a series of popular books on cross-cultural spirituality, he writes on the phenomenology of embodiment, and its relation to medicine, incarceration, and environmental issues. He is the author of many articles and some six books, including *The Distressed Body* (2016) and *The Absent Body* (1990) both published by the University of Chicago Press, and *The Soul Knows No Bars* (2000) published by Rowman and Littlefield.

ANDREW LINZEY is the director of the Oxford Centre for Animal Ethics, and a member of the Faculty of Theology at the University of Oxford. He is visiting professor of animal theology at the University of Winchester and professor of animal ethics at the Graduate Theological Foundation in Indiana. He is the author or editor of more than twenty books, including *Animal Theology* (SCM Press/University of Illinois Press, 1994); *Why Animal Suffering Matters* (Oxford University Press, 2009); and *The Global Guide to Animal Protection* (University of Illinois Press, 2013).

CLAIR LINZEY is the deputy director of the Oxford Centre for Animal Ethics. She holds an MA in theological studies from the University of St Andrews and an MTS from Harvard Divinity School. She is currently pursuing a doctorate at the University of St Andrews on the ecological theology of Leonardo Boff, with special consideration of the place of animals. She is the associate editor of the *Journal of Animal Ethics* and the associate editor of the Palgrave Macmillan Animal Ethics Series. She is also director of the annual Oxford Animal Ethics Summer School.

KAY PEGGS is honorary professor of sociology at the Kingston University, London; visiting fellow at the University of Portsmouth; and a fellow of the Oxford Centre for Animal Ethics. She is a member of the advisory board of the Palgrave Macmillan Series on Animal Ethics and is a consultant editor of the *Journal of*

Animal Ethics. Her books include *Animals and Sociology* (Palgrave Macmillan, 2012); *Experiments, Animal Bodies and Human Values* (Ashgate, 2015); and the major reference work *Critical Social Research Ethics* with Barry Smart and Joseph Burridge (SAGE, forthcoming). Her research approaches issues associated with discrimination and power from a range of social perspectives. Her current research interests include the human/nonhuman divide, intersectionality and complex inequalities, and social ethics and moral consideration.

MEGAN SCHOMMER is a veterinarian at the Lake Harriet Veterinary Clinic in Minnesota, and a graduate of the University of Minnesota College of Veterinary Medicine. She completed a rotating internship in small animal, emergency, and exotic animal medicine in Tucson, Arizona. Her special interests include surgery, nutrition, behavior, backyard poultry, and exotic companion mammals.

CLIFFORD WARWICK is an independent consultant biologist and medical scientist, whose current main role is as senior scientific advisor to the Emergent Disease Foundation (UK). Among his numerous qualifications, he holds a postgraduate diploma in medical science, a charter award in biology, a charter award in science, and is a registered European professional biologist. Since the early 1980s, he has specialized in reptile biology, welfare, and protection, graduating at the Institute of Biology, London, in 1990. Since 2004, he has also specialized in zoonoses (diseases transmittable from non-human animals to humans), graduating at University Medical School, Leeds. His research interests include reptile behavior, euthanasia, anatomy, physiology, wildlife biology, ecology, and species and environmental conservation.

JAMES YEATES is chief veterinary officer of the RSPCA. He graduated from Bristol University in 2004 as a veterinarian, where he also completed a bioethics degree, RCVS certificate, diploma, and PhD. He is also diplomate of the European College of Animal Welfare and Behavioural Medicine; RCVS registered specialist in animal welfare science, ethics, and law; and a fellow of the Royal College of Veterinary Surgeons. His book *Animal Welfare in Veterinary Practice* was published by Wiley in 2013.

The University of Illinois Press
is a founding member of the
Association of American University Presses.

Composed in 10.25/13.5 New Caledonia LT Std
by Kirsten Dennison
at the University of Illinois Press

University of Illinois Press
1325 South Oak Street
Champaign, IL 61820-6903
www.press.uillinois.edu